THE PRENTICE HALL ENCYCLOPEDIA OF

model business plans

wilbur cross and alice m. richey

Library of Congress Cataloging-in-Publication Data

Cross, Wilbur.
    The Prentice Hall encyclopedia of model business plans   / by Wilbur
Cross & Alice M. Richey.
       p.   cm.
    Includes bibliographical references and index.
    ISBN 0-7352-0024-6 (pbk.)
    1. Business planning.   I. Richey, Alice M.   II. Title.
HD30.28.C76   1998
658.4'012—dc21   98-15279
                                       CIP

Acquisitions Editor: *Tom Power*
Production Editor: *Jacqueline Roulette*
Formatting/Interior Design: *Robyn Beckerman*

Printed in the United States of America

10 9 8 7 6 5 4 3 2

ISBN 0-7352-0024-6

PRENTICE HALL PRESS
Paramus, NJ 07652

On the World Wide Web at http://www.phdirect.com

Contents

Chapter 3

Plans for Small Service Firms   **57**

Chapter 4

Plans for Small Manufacturers   **101**

Chapter 5

Plans for Home-Based Enterprises   **143**

Chapter 6

Plans for Research Organizations **157**

Chapter 7

Plans for Educational Institutions **171**

Chapter 8

Plans for Franchise Coordination **185**

Chapter 9

Plans for Nonprofit Ventures **209**

Chapter 10

Plans for Importers/Exporters   225

Chapter 11

The Wide, Wide World of the Internet   241

Chapter 12

Business Schools as a Small Business Resource   251

Foreword

When entrepreneurs decide they would like to found a new kind of business venture, one of their first priorities is to develop and prepare a business plan. When small business owners and managers want to expand their enterprise significantly, establish a new branch, or merge with another company, they almost invariably have to prepare a formal business plan to propose what changes and additions are desired.

In such situations, where can they turn for information and guidance? One of the best sources is *The Prentice Hall Encyclopedia of Model Business Plans*.

No matter what type of business a reader wants to develop as a new venture, or what aspirations he may have to expand or broaden an existing enterprise, this comprehensive guidebook will substantially improve the chances of success. No other book, in or out of print, contains anything like the dozens of real-life plans that can be reviewed between the covers of this well researched new book. The variety of these examples is such that readers can easily pinpoint the ones whose essentials and requirements simulate just what they are looking for in their own new venture. They can, in fact, copy many of the prerequisites word for word, simply inserting the names and elements that are unique to their own company makeup and organizational structure.

In addition to the basic text and compositions, you will find that *The Prentice Hall Encyclopedia of Model Business Plans* also contains samples of the most acceptable kinds of forms used in proposals and presentations, convenient checklists, and many examples of the phrasing and expressions that give a professional tone to a business plan. All of these elements add up to a quicker and more explicit acceptance by financial executives, bank officers, attorneys, and in some cases federal and local government authorities who may be reviewing specific business plans and proposals.

Equally important, *The Prentice Hall Encyclopedia of Model Business Plans* provides further sources of information for readers to explore, such as small business associations, business schools, reference libraries, the Service Corps of Retired Executives (SCORE), and government agencies. Among the last mentioned, for example, is the Small Business Administration (SBA), which has more than forty programs designed to assist entrepreneurs and small business owners and managers. Since many of these programs can assist readers in preparing business plans, as well as obtaining financing or other assistance, this new Prentice Hall guidebook pinpoints the research facilities they may be looking for and tells them how to use existing studies to best advantage.

This book's value as a time-saving accessory is eclipsed only by its repeated references to strategies and persuasive points that, for readers, can mean the difference between success and failure when they present their working proposal to a target audience in order to launch a new business or enhance an existing one. The value and flexibility of the model plans lie in the fact that they are targeted to cover all kinds of eventualities. Moreover, the business plans depicted can be copied in substance and adapted to the reader's own beneficial use.

The purposes of this book are to help you zero in on your target, set your short- and long-range goals, and determine what financing sources are the most promising for you at the start and as the business grows. The model plans will make it easy for you to line up the facts and elements you can then incorporate into your own plan, as well as to use the kinds of professional terms and phrases that will mark you as a capable and informed manager.

This guidebook is designed to:

- Provide background information about planning

- Suggest helpful and reliable resources

- Show you how to save time, effort, and costs

- Provide working models and examples of all phases of effective business planning

In the long run, though, it is up to you. As has often been repeated, "The business that fails to plan, plans to fail."

About the Authors

WILBUR CROSS is a professional writer of long standing and the author of more than forty books, including many on business subjects. He is an entrepreneur and small business manager in his own right, having founded and directed three small businesses in the fields of publishing, editorial consulting, and writing. He lives and works on Hilton Head Island, South Carolina.

ALICE M. RICHEY is the founder and owner of Computerized Office Services, and has assisted Cross on a number of business book projects. She is also a professional consultant and an instructor in computer operations and programming. She lives and works on Hilton Head Island.

Marketing Sources Used by the Authors

American Business Women's Association (membership 112,000)
Women who own or operate businesses, those in professions, and others who are employed in larger service organizations, education, or companies

American Entrepreneurs Association (80,000)
Persons interested in business opportunities and in managing or starting their own businesses

American Federation of Small Business (25,000)
Largely self-employed professionals and managers of small businesses

International Credit Association (16,000)
Maintains a management service for small-business members who are largely in the credit field

National Association for Business Organizations (50,000)
Includes the Small Business Network, a group of organizations that develop and support small businesses

National Association for the Cottage Industry (30,000)
People who work in, or out of, their homes, producing merchandise or providing services

National Association of Legal Secretaries (20,000)
While not all are in the "small business" category, many are in small firms and might welcome information and creative suggestions about business methods

National Association for the Self-Employed (100,000)
Self-employed and small independent businesspersons; the association acts as a forum for the exchange of ideas

National Association of Women Business Owners (2,700)

Women who own and operate their own businesses

National Federation of Independent Business (508,000)

Independent business and professional people interested in methods and means for improvement

National Small Business United (50,000)

Members in small businesses including retail, wholesale, manufacturing, and services

Network of Small Businesses (not specified)

Separate from the earlier-mentioned Small Business Network, this group is composed of owners and managers of small businesses interested in reaching customers and sources of supply, promotion, and services

Service Corps of Retired Executives Association (12,000)

Retired businesspersons who voluntarily assist small businesses and would recommend effective small-business books

Small Business Service Bureau (6,000)

For businesses employing fewer than one hundred people, the Bureau maintains a Small Business Assistance Center to guide members in all business phases.

Preface

PLANNING A BUSINESS VENTURE

Before you can begin to prepare a business plan, you have to go through the steps of planning your enterprise, whatever it may be, so you have a concise idea of what you need to propose to outsiders. It may come to you in a flash, or you may have been toying for a long time with the prospect of going into business for yourself. But now you have reached a decision. You are convinced that you have an idea that can really take root. You are excited about the market potential and the prospective customers out there who would like your products or services. If you, as the potential founder of this new business, have the experience and knowledge to pursue the venture, you must then determine whether

- Enough capital is available, or can be acquired, to launch the enterprise and maintain momentum

- A suitable location is available

- The population can support this kind of business

- The local economy is healthy enough to assure potential income

- Suitable employees and, if necessary, qualified specialists can be easily recruited

- The business is unlikely to be overly sensitive to economic fluctuations, changing consumer tastes, or political legislation

- There are no legal entanglements or legal risks that could result in setbacks or conflicts of interest

Over and beyond these requirements, you need patience, judging the time needed for the business to take hold and reach a break-even point. This introductory period is the most precarious stage and the one in which most failures occur. Even though you may be steadily adding employees, during the initial stage you must hold a tight rein on the business, controlling all the major management and operational functions. You may be working day and night and on weekends to get the business moving, yet you should not get discouraged if you have little to show for your time and effort.

This starting period can be expected to continue for a year or two, longer in the case of a more complicated enterprise. So you have to ask yourself, long before you actually make the decision to become an entrepreneur:

1. Do I have the self-confidence to undertake the kind of venture I have in mind? Can I get on the phone and make calls to prospective customers, or trudge the streets to conduct personal interviews, without fearing that I can't sell myself or my business idea?

2. Is the timing right for the business I have in mind, both seasonally and from the viewpoint of consumer buying trends? Have I assessed the needs correctly, or would it be better for me to undertake more research or consult with experts in the field of my choice?

3. Are my personal attributes right for the task? Am I self-motivated, a hard worker, comfortable managing other people whom I will need for assistance, and willing to sacrifice my private interests and leisure time in order to devote a full effort to the job?

4. Do I have the competitive spirit required to run a business in the face of stiff, persistent rivalry on the part of other owners and managers who will be aiming at the same clients and/or customers as mine? Do I have both the drive and the imagination to compete in the marketplace?

5. Am I willing to make the necessary financial sacrifices to focus my monetary efforts on this new business, even if it means investing my own money? Or do I have the fortitude and poise to approach banks or other prospective lenders to obtain the necessary financing?

6. Can I survive a situation in which I have no regular, dependable paycheck and sometimes I may even have to hold off some creditors until my business reaches a point where I can pay myself a salary or expenses? Do I know, realistically, how I can cut back on personal financial obligations in order to avoid unmanageable debt?

7. Have I prepared a professional "road map" to guide me in the direction I want the business to take, including the potential areas of growth and development?

8. Do I know how to take advantage of the resources, public and private, that are available to help me chart the best course for my endeavor?

LOCATING BUSINESS INFORMATION RESOURCES

Throughout this book you will find references to resources to which you can turn for help, right from the time you have an idea for an entrepreneurial venture until you have a full-fledged business that has been well established for some time. Yet no single book can provide everything you need to know. Nothing can substitute for on-the-spot personal intelligence gathering—those localized contacts and sources that will bring the picture into sharp focus. Consider exploring the following kinds of sources for the personal and territorial data and leads that can make a substantial difference between success and failure:

1. Your *Chamber of Commerce* (or the one in the area in which you intend to do business), which can give you a concise idea of the local business climate, the number and size of firms that might be competitive, and even the failure rate of small and home-based businesses in the district.

2. *Service Corps of Retired Executives (SCORE)*, which has local offices in cities and towns across the United States. SCORE is a very valuable resource because its members live in the towns where their offices are listed and have an intimate knowledge of the local economy and the pros and cons of starting a new business in any stated field of endeavor. The organization is composed of retired executives, many of whom ran their own businesses, who will sit down with you and honestly evaluate your chances of success. They will guide you to other resources, help you write a business plan, and perform other invaluable services— all without charging any fee.

3. *Your local library*, which is likely to contain two helpful and essential workshop files: back copies of area newspapers, whose business sections can give you specific, homefront accounts of the local business economy; and clipping folders containing news items about specific businesses and regional market conditions.

4. *Fraternal organizations*, like Kiwanis, Elks, and Knights of Columbus, many of whose members own small businesses and are more than willing to share their experiences with you. A little probing and informal discussions can be more rewarding than hiring a professional consultant.

5. *Continuing education courses* in nearby colleges that have business curricula. While a single course, per se, may not offer a great deal of advice for your particular purposes, brushing elbows with business faculty members and other professionals could help you to evaluate the regional business environment. Short of taking courses, you might consult with members of the business faculty to get their estimates of the market and consumer needs.

6. *Your competitors-to-be.* This may sound like trying to bell the cat, but where else could you find a better resource for getting an inside look at the business potential in the field of your choice? Naturally, you have to use tact and a bit of undercover sleuthing to disguise your real purpose and avoid having your intended source clam up. Try using a friend or relative who may be a customer of your future competitor as an "undercover agent" to find out whether business is really booming, holding its own, or slipping in the wrong direction.

STARTING A BUSINESS VENTURE

You've decided on the type of business you want. You've evaluated your talents and judged them to be on target. You've checked out the market potential for the short and long term and are enthused about the prospects. And you're eager to tackle the job, even though it will get you up early and keep you up late.

Now what?

One of your first steps will be to select the legal format of the organization-to-be. Your choices are:

1. *Corporation,* which is a specific legal entity, distinct from the individuals who own or manage it, and generally associated with large or middle-range companies rather than small businesses. However, some small businesses with quick growth possibilities elect to file Articles of Corporation and remain that way as they expand and mature.

2. *S-Corporation,* which can be appropriate for even a one- or two-person company, yet has the advantage of relieving the principal of responsibility in the event of a damaging lawsuit or bankruptcy.

3. *Sole Proprietorship,* the simplest of all legal organization forms, in which the owner is customarily the manager and does not share control of the business with others.

4. *Partnership,* in which two or more people own the business jointly under a mutual agreement, which specifies duties, responsibilities, and accountability, as well as guidelines for administration and management, and even long-range plans for the eventual dissolution of the business.

One of your most essential jobs at this point in the venture's birth is developing a *business plan* (see Chapter 1), which meticulously and accurately defines the business you are starting. Its major components cover the following subject areas:

- *Management*, the names and qualifications of the owner(s) and manager(s) of the new business, their addresses, and other vital statistics.

- *Financial needs*, how much you will require now, and later on, for what purpose, and from what classification of lender. This segment of the business plan also addresses expected income and expenses, sources of additional capital, and the time periods for reducing debt.

- *The market*, as it is today and will be in the future, and the methods you expect to use to attract potential customers, make sales, and provide related services.

- *Competition*, how strong it is and how you expect to survive and prosper despite this commercial rivalry.

- *Duties and responsibilities*, who will do what, and how pertinent functions and operations will be handled on a day-to-day basis.

- *Future prospects*, what they are and why they are realistic to expect; an evaluation of the market area and where the new company fits into it.

As you put all these pieces together, you will also have to do your homework and determine what kinds of *regulations and restrictions* will affect your business. You must find out what you may need in the way of licenses, entitlements, permits, and authorizations in order to conduct business. These may be federal, state, county, or municipal from the standpoint of origin and administration.

At the same time, you will need to obtain the necessary information about *taxes* that will be imposed by each government level so that you can anticipate the short-term and long-range assessments that will affect your earnings and profits. Open a tax account to keep tax collections, such as those relating to sales, Social Security, and income, separate from business revenues and receivables.

If you do not have an accountant as a full- or part-time employee, this is the time to consider the services of an outside professional who can advise you about the types of *record-keeping* available and which one you should use. It is essential that you keep all business transactions separate from personal expenses, that you open a company bank account, and that you pay all expenses by check. If you have a computer, you might want to consider signing up with an online service (see Chapter 11), and acquiring the necessary software so you can keep your records electronically, and even pay bills this way instead of by check.

Decide how often your business will need to prepare *profit-and-loss statements* and *balance sheets*. If you are not sure, find out what the industry practices are for your kind of business. If you are not familiar with profit-and-loss statements and balance sheets, make it a point to orient yourself by reading an accounting and finance reference book or taking a short course in record-keeping. There is more to the procedure than simply keeping tabs on the "bottom line" to see whether your new enterprise is making or losing money.

Finally, if you have employees (even a handful), or if you anticipate hiring people in the future, acquaint yourself with the requirements for effective *personnel administration*. The management of employees, whether full- or part-time, involves a wide range of duties and responsibilities, including recruitment, screening, hiring, compensation, orientation, training, assigning, and discharging. Most personnel activities are affected, at least in part, by government regulations, union demands, and the laws of supply and demand. Most small businesses have problems locating employees who are qualified and efficient, yet whose compensation demands are within the company budget.

MAKING YOUR BUSINESS GROW

How do you know when your business is ready to grow? The growth stage of a small business is characterized by the consolidation and stabilization of the enterprise; progress that is becoming more accelerated, an ascending curve of achievement; steadily increasing numbers of customers, clients, or patrons; a growing number of employees or others necessary to conducting the business; improved capitalization; and evidence of material or substantive acquisitions.

The growth stage is vital to your ambitions and goals because, if you can guide your venture successfully through this critical period, it will achieve maturity, the pinnacle at which the typical small business can be expected to attain its greatest profits or reach its ultimate capabilities. According to the Small Business Administration, one of the most common casualties in the small business world is the company that is on the verge of growth, but then slips into a stagnation from which it never fully recovers.

There are two overall classifications of growth:

1. *Internal*, often associated with a family-owned business, whose stock is sold to friends and relatives, whose partners or principals are acquired on a personal level, and whose profits are plowed back into the venture. This kind of growth can be further enhanced by adding new products, creating new services, or acquiring more capital. Internal growth is generally slower than external growth, but remains under more rigorous control.

2. *External*, which might be accomplished by a number of means, such as going public and issuing common stock, becoming a franchise, acquiring a new division, or merging with another company. External growth tends to be faster than internal because it is based on the acquisition of blocks of capital or tangible facilities, rather than steady evolution. In the case of mergers and acquisi-

tions, for example, there are immediate and measurable additions in the form of personnel, real estate, or other substantial augmentations.

Mergers and acquisitions also fall into two categories:

1. *Vertical,* in which the participants are in the same field but in different operational modes, such as a manufacturer joining forces with a distributor of the company's products.

2. *Horizontal,* in which similar business operations are combined to increase or improve the available service, such as a merger of two hotels, retail stores, or professional services.

Another factor that enters frequently into a small-business pattern of growth is diversification. Customarily, small businesses diversify into operational functions that bear close resemblance to the original venture, such as adding new product lines to a retail store or expanding a "fixit" service to include other types of repair facilities. Unfortunately, diversification is not a ready answer for the growth-minded owner, and is actually classified by business associations as a real risk. Fewer than 20 percent of the small businesses in the United States have been successful when they attempted to diversify, and that statistic includes only those enterprises that were successful prior to diversification.

Preparing for Growth

"Before you can get your company ready for more growth," advises *Kiplinger's Guide to Small Business Growth,* "you need to know its strengths and weaknesses. Looking for what's working well serves to concentrate your efforts where you have the best chance for success. And by looking for strengths, you'll also spot the weaknesses."

Start with these areas:

COSTS AND REVENUES Examine them for every part of your business. Are revenues rising or falling? How about profit margins? Which divisions or departments stand out? Why?

PERSONNEL Do certain employees show exceptional skills or produce outstanding results? Where in the company is the strongest management, organization, and planning? Do you have the talent on staff to handle anticipated growth, or would you have to hire someone new?

OPERATIONS   Are there areas that seem to be trouble-free, functioning with little supervision but always delivering results? How do the managers in those areas achieve such consistent results?

MISSION   Do you have a written statement describing your company's philosophy or mission? Does it define the essence of your business exactly so that you know which kinds of activities fit your goals and which do not? Are you diluting your resources by engaging in any activities outside your mission?

MARKET   Is your market share—your company's percentage of estimated total business available—increasing or decreasing? Is your marketing strategy based on careful research or on instinct and hunches? Is your customer or client base shrinking?

COMPETITION   Do you know exactly who your competitors are and where they pose the largest threat? Which part of your business is most vulnerable to competition and which part is strongest? Are some parts of your market becoming crowded with competitors?

ECONOMIC CLIMATE   Are changes in economic conditions, such as interest rates, inflation, housing starts, and industry earnings, likely to affect your company? Do you try to stay on top of things so that you can anticipate changes in the marketplace, or are you often surprised by developments that affect your company?

Your answers to these questions will give you an idea of where your company is strong and where it needs to improve. They will also guide you in the preparation of a business plan, whether for a company not yet born or one that has been in operation for years but needs a facelift.

Are You In a Growth Industry?

The answer to this not only will help you determine whether to continue in the same business, but may well be the secret to whether your business plan succeeds or fails in convincing outside firms and individuals to approve your proposals and requests. Parts of your business may be operating in shrinking markets while others enjoy expanding markets. But which is which? The following signs will help to guide you:

A growing market

- The number of competitors is increasing
- Someone is franchising a similar business

- You get offers to buy your company
- People are more and more eager to work for you

A shrinking market

- Companies like yours are failing
- Business cycles are getting longer and weaker
- You have a hard time keeping good employees
- Your gross profit margin has a shrinking trend

Once you have evaluated all of these growth factors, you may have to review your business plan and rewrite it to fit the business as it has now become in this period of growth.

COPING WITH PROBLEMS THAT THREATEN YOUR BUSINESS

Is your business growing obsolescent to the extent that a business plan might have to scrap most of the fundamental descriptions of company units and create new ones? When the growth stage of a small enterprise starts to level off, the business reaches maturity, the point at which it is realizing its top potential and is achieving its peak earnings. Now, one of two things will happen: The business will evidence signs of going downhill, leaving the owner skeptical about the future and inclined to consider selling out; or it will continue on a fairly level course for an indefinite period. According to the Center for Entrepreneurial Management, many owners are not content to see their brainchild—on which they have nurtured so much time and care—simply coast along. Even those managers who were once very competitive become downhearted and passive. Or, if they still have the old entrepreneurial spark, they start looking around for other ventures to which they can devote their energy and imagination anew.

A limited-growth condition can dominate the workplace for years, persuading some owners that they have been fortunate because the business is now so stabilized they can turn the management over to an associate or an outsider and enjoy holidays and vacations. However, signs of an imminent decline can arise as quickly as a summer squall. The signs are many, including the realization that profits are harder to come by, recruiting becomes difficult, employees start drifting away, advertising fails to stimulate sales, and maintenance expenses and upkeep get out of hand. It is at this point that owners panic, realizing that they might have sold the business for a tidy sum ten months ago when it was still in maturity, but now may have to put on a sacrifice price tag to make a sale before the business declines still further.

CAUSES OF FAILURE

Failure is nothing new to the small business world. One statistic claims that "four out of five businesses fail during their first five years." While some economists dispute this high depletion rate, the fact is that the life expectancy rate of these modest enterprises has discouraged many would-be entrepreneurs from getting involved. Data from the Administrative Office of the U.S. Courts documents the fact that more than 95 percent of businesses filing for bankruptcy in the 1990s were classified as "small." The basic reasons for failure included the following, among others (not necessarily in order of impact or degree):

- The inability of owners to make clear decisions
- Failure to anticipate market trends
- Insufficient capital
- Overextension of credit to customers
- Poor communications and relations with suppliers
- Sloppy inventory control
- Lack of basic training
- Reluctance to seek professional counsel and help
- Insufficient knowledge of merchandise or equipment
- Inadequate record-keeping
- Disregard of competition

Chapter 1

The Basic Business Plan

The business plan is to a for-profit venture what a marine chart is to a vessel leaving its home port for an extended cruise in unfamiliar waters. Not only is it indispensable to the development and direction of your business, but it may be indispensable to you when you need financing to get started in the first place, or to underwrite the cost of adding structures or facilities, starting a new division, or purchasing an affiliate.

The business plan is also part of an overall evaluation process whereby you can determine whether your venture is succeeding or failing, as you try to attract customers or clients and eventually turn a profit. It does not matter whether the nature of your business is in the realm of product retailing, home and residential services, education, research, manufacturing, mail order, transportation, or any other field.

WHAT IS A BUSINESS PLAN?

As an entity, rather than a procedure, a *business plan* is a formal statement that describes in great detail an enterprise that is about to be launched, substantially reorganized, or expanded, and is most commonly prepared and presented in order to obtain financing and secure necessary permits and approvals for legalizing the venture. It is also useful for such secondary purposes as recruiting managers, partners, employees, suppliers, and others who might be essential to the successful operation of the business. As has been emphasized by the experts and professionals, most business beginners seriously underestimate both the importance of planning and the time it takes to research and prepare a competent plan and well-documented presentation. A sound business plan contains the following basic components, among other essential ingredients: description of the venture, nature of products and/or services, the market (both geographical and consumer), competition, location, management, personnel, current financial condition, and financing needed, both short-term and long-term.

The importance of planning cannot be overlooked, and must be carried out in an objective manner, realistically, and with attention to the weaknesses, as well as strengths, of the organization. A sound business plan for an untried venture can not only prepare for the future, but help to avoid even starting an enterprise that is doomed to failure. If the proposed venture is marginal, a business plan can indicate why this is so, and may help the proposers to avoid the expense and frustrations of learning about business failure. As has been pointed out by the experts, it is far less traumatic to scrap plans for an ill-fated business than to take the hard knocks of learning by experience how a sensible business plan could have saved all that grief at the cost of nothing more than a couple of days or so of concentrated planning and evaluation. See *management, business administration,* in Glossary.

outline of a business plan

A business plan is designed to provide information and statistics required by others who are evaluating a proposed venture, most often to determine its potential for financing and support. A well-structured, thoroughly documented business plan can serve not only as a guide to a company's future development, but as a financing proposal that will satisfy the criteria and conditions of banks and other lending institutions. The following components are requisites of an effective business plan:

Section 1: Basic Data

- Cover sheet, with the proposed name of the business, names of principals, addresses, and phone numbers
- Statement of purpose
- Table of contents
- Illustrations and graphics, if any

Section 2: The Business

- Description of the venture and related operations
- Classification of the business
- Products and/or services involved
- Location(s) of the business
- Economic environment
- The market for products and services
- Description of the management
- Personnel, on hand or to be recruited
- Nature, strength, and extent of the competition
- Application for loan, or alternate types of financing, if applicable

Section 3: Financial Data

- Source(s) of financial support
- List of capital equipment
- Existing inventory(ies), if any
- Balance sheet
- Evaluation of break-even figures
- Income projections for profits and losses
  - Monthly projections for first year
  - Details, by quarter or month, for second year
  - Three- to five-year summary
- Cash flow projection
  - Figures by month for first year
  - Projections by quarter for next two years

Section 4: Financial Reports for Existing Business

- Balance sheets for past two to five years
- Income statements for the same period

Section 5: Supporting Documents

- Tax returns for the previous two years
- Management resumes
- Credit reports or other financial backup
- Leases, contracts, and other legal documents
- Newspaper and trade clippings about the business and/or managers and personnel
- Letters of reference

For small firms operating in a limited area and in a stable economic environment, the business plan need be nothing more than an informal review of certain key functions by the owners. If the firm is large and has interrelated departments and subdivisions, a more formal plan is required to present a complex overview.

Large versus Small

A common example of formal versus informal business plans can be seen in a comparison between a chain of department stores, like Wal-Mart, and a local variety store that is independently owned and serves mainly as a convenience outlet in a limited area. The neighborhood store may have a considerable variety of products, but maintains inventory levels that are small enough to be listed in an old-fashioned ledger. Cash flow can be managed with relative ease, and usually on a week-to-week basis, rather than being complicated by annual projections.

By contrast, the chain has to carry separate books for each line of products, and generally for different locations as well. Unlike the small store, it may be concerned with related functions and operations, such as the supply of raw materials, manufacturing processes, long-range delivery, mail order, interstate regulations, research and development, training thousands of employees, and managing complex benefit and insurance plans. The planning time frame for a small firm is likely to be confined to one or two years, rather than a decade or so for a larger corporation.

The Essential Elements

Refer back to the list under the heading 'What Is a Business Plan?' Jot down the elements that apply to your organization, such as minutes of meetings, tape recordings, and charts, and keep them handy for incorporation into the written plan you are undertaking. You will find that you already have more plan-oriented information at your fingertips than you may have realized. You also have an advantage over large organizations in that you can obtain missing data more quickly and easily—usually from local sources, such as the Chamber of Commerce, a county branch of the Small Business Administration, commercial associations, and city hall. You don't have to search nationwide for facts or figures, or undertake expensive statistical research to obtain what you need for your planning. Furthermore, when circumstances change, the implications are likely to be more readily apparent than in a large corporation where there are more numerous, and far more complex, factors that have to be studied before the changes can be properly evaluated.

A Basic Step: Describe Your Business

If you were asked by the business editor of the local newspaper to describe your operations in 200 words or less, what would you reply? It's as simple as that—no need for formal terminology, legal language, or shop talk. Just tell it the way it is, in your own words.

Where are you located? What are you selling? How do your sales operations resemble, or differ from, those of your closest competitors? Who are your customers? What are your best selling seasons? How much have you grown since you started?

Once you have drafted a brief description, sort out the details for the next portion of your written plan. Here are the kinds of information you should outline:

- Description of typical customers or clients, past and present, from the standpoint of age, sex, income, place of residence, and other reference points
- Changes anticipated to take place in the makeup of these customers during the next year or so
- Merchandise being sold, or to be added to stock later
- Sources of merchandise from wholesalers and other suppliers
- Nature and locations of competitors
- Advantages and weaknesses of your business in comparison with the competition
- Description of present retail facilities or other facilities
- Expected changes in these facilities in the near future
- Company image in the community, and steps needed to improve it
- Number of permanent managers and employees now active
- Business hours and calendar of days open during the year
- Salary and wage scales, and comparisons with similar businesses in the area

Motivation: Your Marketing Plan

Although your business may be one of the best organized in town, offering products and services that are in demand, and at costs that are competitive, your business cannot succeed without a realistic, continuing marketing program. This area of activity should be a focal point in your small business plan. Marketing includes (or is directly associated with) each of the following essentials:

- Sources of supply
- Sales programs
- Special projects

- Pricing
- Advertising
- Promotion
- Publicity
- Public relations

Your marketing plan establishes, first, the reasons why your business should be successful, and second, what actions you have to take to make success a reality. Look at the list suggested in the previous section, 'A Basic Step,' and ask yourself what actions you plan to take to produce positive results in each category. Some examples:

What can be done to reach the types of customers you listed who would be interested in your products and services?

What kind of marketing do you need to activate to win an advantage over your competition?

How can you improve your present facilities at reasonable cost?

How can you quicken or upgrade your service to customers?

What flaws in your firm's image could you overcome through better communication?

Are your sales people and other employees aware of your marketing plans, both current and for the immediate future?

Do you communicate with customers and prospects to determine what they need that you have not been providing sufficiently?

Could you profit by expanding your line(s) of goods and merchandising them more aggressively?

Would it pay to expand your physical facilities to extend your market?

Is your advertising budget rich enough?

The Work Force: Your Personnel Plan

If you have nothing more than a list of employees and their qualifications and salaries, you already have a basic *personnel plan*. But the chances are that it is too incomplete to be of much use as part of your overall small business plan. You need to establish goals, in part to counter the most common and frustrating complaint by business owners, "We just can't find enough reliable and experienced help anymore." But that situation has existed ever since our forebears first set up shops in the new world. It may fluctuate for better or worse from season to season or year to year, but you *can* take steps to improve the situation if you build a personnel training program into your business plan. Here are some essential elements to review:

- The number of reliable employees you have versus the number you would like to have

- Salaries, wages, and pay scales for permanent and part-time employees

- Other incentives that attract good employees, such as bonuses, commissions, and benefits

- The working environment

- Hours of employment, as well as calendar days

- Managers and supervisors, and their proportion to sales and service personnel

- In-house training programs, to improve personnel efficiency

- Outside seminars or courses that could benefit employees and improve your business

- Orientation by suppliers, especially during the introduction of new products, materials, or equipment

- Effectiveness of your personal communications to employees

Motivation and Goals

No venture can succeed without realistic goals and the motivation to attain them. Before you can activate those who are working with, or for, you in your business, you have to define the objectives that you believe in. What do you desire most?

Profits?

Stature?

Satisfaction?

Security?

Providing a community service?

Something to keep mind and body active?

A legacy for your children?

The chances are that you are motivated by a combination of these desires, and probably others as well. Some can be exploited as motivational forces for people you want to hire, such as offering a share of profits in the form of bonuses, commissions, or stock in the company. Some are intangible and difficult to promote, such as improving one's stature and image in the public mind. Some may even scare off prospective employees, as might be the case if your main interest was to pass along a business to your children.

Take stock of your personal goals to make sure they do not conflict with the goals the business needs in order to grow and prosper. Too many entrepreneurs set their own desires ahead of fundamental business objectives.

Risk Management

Your business plan will not be complete without an evaluation of the risks involved. There is not an enterprise in the world that does not have to face up to the risks entailed in its planning, implementation, and operation. They may be physical, legal, ethical, competitive, medical, environmental, financial, or otherwise. Here are examples of common risks that plague small businesses:

Financial flaws. Obtaining enough money to launch a venture is only the first risk. Keeping the cash flowing and the profits coming in, staying solvent, and trying to avoid bankruptcy are never-ending efforts on the part of the owners. One of the underlying risks is that entrepreneurs tend to indulge in wishful thinking, and overlook functions and circumstances that result in financial losses.

Aggressive competition. After you have listed your direct competitors, go back and classify some of your indirect competitors. In the retail field, for example, these are sellers of large-ticket items who are in a completely different sales category, but who can sidetrack a customer's available cash. A hustling car dealer can be a competitor to an appliance dealer when he can talk a man into buying a car, leaving no money in the budget for the new refrigerator his wife had hoped they could afford.

Seasonal vacillations. For company owners who have not anticipated changes in consumer demand from month to month, it comes as a shock when business slacks off. Even more traumatic are the occasions when they are deluged with would-be customers at certain times of the year and have run out of stock or do not have enough employees to handle service requests.

Consumer fickleness. If the kinds of products and services you are selling depend on customer loyalty, it is mandatory that you communicate closely and effectively with these customers, as well as with new prospects. This area of activity should therefore be incorporated into your business plan. To avoid losing customers whose demands and tastes are changing constantly you need to know what is 'in' and what is going 'out.'

Underinsurance. With insurance rates soaring, it is tempting for company management to look for bargain policies, cut corners, or hope they will be fortunate enough to get away with partial insurance coverage. But this is a dangerous practice, with natural disasters, fires, burglaries, vandalism, equal employment opportunity and sexual harassment lawsuits, and other legal and casualty onslaughts now commonplace.

Labor disputes. You may find it difficult to evaluate the risks from strikes, walkouts, and other employee-related controversies. Nevertheless, this is an area that can be a high risk in a business that is labor-intensive.

In your business plan, the risks should be listed in order of (1) probability of occurrence, (2) amount of potential disruption possible, and (3) the degree to which you can offset the consequences. Weighing these three factors will help you determine which risks require more planning and attention to avoid or alleviate them.

The Small Business Plan as an Instrument for Financing

As stated earlier, the first reason for committing your plan to paper is to clarify the business in your own mind and make certain you have covered all the essentials. For this purpose, the presentation need not be neat or formal, so long as it covers the bases. But another reason for putting your comments on paper is to compose a document that can be used to apply for a business loan or other financing. In this case, the writing must be grammatical, explicit, and professional, and the instrument must be readable and visually neat if you expect to convince a lending institution that your business has real potential.

This kind of document should be concise, to the point, and accurate, and should contain the following elements:

- An introduction that sums up the situation well enough to persuade most lenders on the spot that you are a good financial risk.

- Supporting texts to emphasize key points in the introduction, for all who care to read further. These should be clearly itemized so a reader interested in, say, production facilities does not have to shuffle through paragraphs on personnel or research in order to reach that topic.

- Statistics or charts, preferably simplified, if they are essential to technical references in the text. Such attachments or enclosures are seldom read, but their very presence can be influential.

Using Judgment in Selecting Enclosures

Avoid the temptation to include nonessential materials in an effort to make a good impression. Here are some do's and don'ts listed by one experienced loan officer who reviews many small business applications:

Do include condensed technical data to confirm facts that might be unfamiliar to laypersons.

Don't include press releases or flattering clips from your local newspaper.

Do cite sources for opinions and quotes about the future of your type of business.

Don't quote relatives and friends, no matter how noted they may be.

Do attach pictures or diagrams if they will help to avoid wordy descriptions.

Don't enclose personal snapshots of facilities, unless you are an accomplished photographer.

Do enclose copies of bids (or extracts) for any construction work to be covered by the proposed financing.

Don't attach lengthy leases and legal documents that can be cited convincingly, or referred to, in less than 100 words.

Profile of the Small Business Plan Financial Package

The size and scope of your presentation depends on (1) the size and scope of your business, (2) the magnitude of the financing you are seeking, and (3) the nature of the underwriting being requested. An application for a conventional loan to buy an employee shuttle van, for example, would differ considerably from a proposal for financing the construction and furnishing of a new office wing for a research center.

A typical business plan and loan proposal for a retail operation might contain the following components:

Title page: a clean, simple sheet with the name of your company, title of the business plan, significant dates, and purpose of the presentation

Introduction: preferably not longer than one page, defining the business (as described earlier)

Table of contents: in order of appearance, a list of the points covered, with a thumbnail description of each topic

Marketing plan: essential only if sales and merchandising operations will influence the application for financing

Risk analysis: a realistic evaluation of all the risks you envision in your business. To avoid the acknowledgment of risks could be more detrimental to your objective than tackling them head on

Personnel review: a brief list (by title) of employees, supervisors, and managers, current or projected, and what they will do to assure business success

Financial statistics: these might include profit and loss (P & L) projections, a cash flow forecast, and a capital spending proposal, if this is an element in your business plan.

Coordination and Review

"For maximum sustained results," advises the Office of Business Development of the Small Business Administration, "an overall coordinator for the *business plan* must be appointed. That person should be responsible for bringing together the various pieces of the plan into one comprehensive plan, and for monitoring the continuing process of following the plan."

Michael McKeever, a business school professor and lecturer, says "It is often wise to have your plan reviewed by an experienced business consultant after you think it is in good shape. For a modest fee, a good small business consultant or C.P.A. who specializes in this area may either be able to save you from a costly mistake or point out additional profit opportunities."

What kind of consultant will serve your objectives best? Look for these qualities in the person you select:

- Substantial experience in managing a small business personally, or at least being directly involved in consultation services for small businesses

- An understanding of the kind of business you own and familiarity with the fields in which you are active

- Residing in, or doing business in, the marketing region in which your business has, or will have, its operations

- A sound professional reputation in that same region

- A personality and method of conducting business that is compatible with your own nature

- A willingness to discuss your needs and propose a program and payment range before charging any fee.

If you need assistance locating the proper consultant for this kind of an assignment, ask for suggestions from such sources as an officer you know at a bank, an attorney who has small business clients, your C.P.A., the Chamber of

Commerce, or the Service Corps of Retired Executives (SCORE), which may even provide substantial guidance itself at no cost.

Why Some Small Business Plans Fail

If you follow the suggestions made in this chapter and those to come, you have every right to expect you will evolve a plan that is feasible, sensible, and just right for your kind of company and its operations. Yet, reports the SBA, some plans have so many shortcomings that they sabotage the profile of the very company they are trying to present in a glowing light. According to the Office of Business Development, the major reasons for failure are these:

1. The plan is constructed around strategies that are inaccurately defined.

2. The plan is substantial enough, but cannot be clearly and properly described by management.

3. The plan lacks detailed information about job descriptions, responsibilities, and operating schedules.

4. The plan does not state goals and objectives clearly and in professional terms.

5. The plan fails to specify how all principals in the venture can share a common view of the organization's future.

6. The plan is incomplete, overlooking or ignoring functional parts that are important to the whole.

Keeping Your Plan Up to Date

The best possible plan you can draw up may get your business launched and be useful later in applying for financing capital improvements, but it will eventually fail if it becomes outdated. Management must continually review it and modify it as needed to keep objectives realistic and current. The kinds of changes to anticipate may be (a) internal, relating only to your organization; (b) external, relating to your industry; (c) regional, relating to the area(s) in which you operate; (d) demographic, relating to the needs and desires of the population within your marketing boundaries; (e) economic, relating to fluctuations in the national or local economy, or (f) complex, a combination of the above.

Whatever the changes and their causes, you must adjust your plan accordingly. Changes that affect your planning strategy can be as broad as a nationwide financial recession or as narrow as the resignation of one of your partners. In any case, you have a triple obligation:

1. To be alert to changes that occur in your company, your field, your market, and your region

2. To identify these changes with those facets of your business plan that are affected

3. To determine what revisions are necessary

If your business is relatively large and extensive, or segmented into numerous divisions and departments, consider delegating the reporting responsibilities to others who are closer to day-to-day operations than you can be. A moderate-size retail organization, for example, might delegate an experienced buyer to monitor changes in sources of supply, a sales manager to keep an eye on fads and fashions that affect consumer demand, a C.P.A. to review competitive pricing and inflationary trends, and a transportation manager to anticipate increases in freight rates and warehousing costs.

Once you have established a sound, realistic business plan, it is relatively simple for you and your associates to devise sound contingency plans for all operations and circumstances. An alternate plan, for example, might provide guidance if your income fell 20 percent below expectations, your operating costs were 15 percent higher than last year, or a new competitor moved into town and threatened to siphon off some of your business.

In business planning, *anticipation* is the key word.

---

how to use this book's format

The rest of this chapter contains supplementary information that will help you in your overview of the subject at hand:

- Summation: Outline for a Business Plan
- Creating a Start-Up Business Plan
- Loans: How to Qualify for Small Business Help
- Working a Grant Request into Your Business Plan
- Work People into Your Business Plan

In the chapters that follow, you will find three different formats to study:

1. A few detailed business plans, to show you the length, language, and components you will need in a business plan that is complete, well structured, and ready to present to the kinds of individuals and organizations to whom you might be turning for help and financing.

how to use this book's format, *cont'd.*

2. Short plans that focus on the essentials, to give you a better idea of the kinds of situations that call for business plans in the major categories into which small enterprises fit, such as retailing, servicing, manufacturing, and franchising.

3. Thumbnail descriptions of the kinds of entrepreneurial endeavors that call for business plans, to give you an overview of the wide variety of types and sizes of businesses that have been successful in attaining their goals.

SUMMATION: OUTLINE FOR A BUSINESS PLAN

Components necessary to a small business plan

INFORMATION ABOUT THE BUSINESS

1. Describe your business. What is its purpose? What does it do?

2. How do you plan to market your business?

3. Describe the competition. What kinds of other businesses will compete with your company?

4. Describe your operating procedures. How do you plan to organize and run your business? How many people will you employ? What kind(s) of inventory/supplies will you need and use?

FINANCIAL INFORMATION

1. Give an estimated breakdown of the expenses the business will have, such as equipment, supplies, rent, communications, transportation, training, research and development, and vehicle and equipment maintenance.

2. Include a cash flow projection or analysis sheet. How much money does your business need to operate?

3. Include your break-even analysis or plan. How much revenue do you need to take in before your business can make a profit? Can you make more revenue? What is the limit of your company's revenue?

4. Include, if germane, an application for a prospective loan from a bank or other lender, or a possible loan or grant from the Small Business Administration (SBA).

SUPPORTING DOCUMENTATION

Include the following:

1. A personal financial statement, which might also include your individual income tax returns for the past two or three years. Your personal reputation can help mold your company's image.

2. A listing of your education, professional experience, and other qualifications that relate to your field of business. Reliable references can also aid you in setting up a new business.

3. Copies of leases, commercial licenses, and any other relevant legal documents.

4. Contracts and letters of intent from all supporting parties, such as vendors, independent contractors, and negotiators. These can be helpful at tax time, as well as with state and federal licensing.

5. Insurance documentation. What is your personal and/or professional liability in your business? Do you need to be bonded? How much vehicular insurance do you need? Does your liability extend to your employees and coworkers?

LOANS: HOW TO QUALIFY FOR SMALL BUSINESS HELP

When you are preparing a small business plan, funding is usually an essential element. You may be looking generally to local banks or other financial institutions for help. But bear in mind that for the small-business owner seeking a loan, the Small Business Administration is often the best resource to turn to, if not for the loan itself, at least for information and counsel. The criteria for SBA loans can be an excellent yardstick for outlining the steps you must take and the requirements you must meet to obtain financial aid.

The procedure for an SBA loan begins with a loan application to a lender for initial review. If the lender finds the application acceptable, it forwards the application and its credit analysis to the nearest SBA office. After SBA approval, the lending institution closes the loan and disburses the funds. The borrower then makes loan payments to the lender under the latter's terms, the length of time for repayment depending on the use of the proceeds and the ability of the business to repay. SBA standards call for an interest rate that cannot exceed 2.75 percent over the prime rate.

As a loan applicant, you must:

- Be of good character and reputation in your community;

- Demonstrate sufficient management experience and responsibility to be successful in your business;

- Have enough funds in the company, plus personal moneys, to operate the business on a sound financial basis;

- If you are a new business, show sufficient resources to fund start-up expenses and the initial operating phase when losses are likely to occur;

- Prove that the past earnings record and estimated future earnings will be, realistically, sufficient to repay the loan in a timely fashion;

- Pledge specific, identifiable assets to secure the loan adequately;

- Be willing and able to provide personal guarantees, not only from yourself, but from any associates who are principals in your business;

- Submit a current personal financial statement of all principals and stockholders;

- Prepare a current balance sheet listing all assets, liabilities, and net worth.

To be eligible under SBA standards, a company must be operated for profit, meet "small business" size and earnings standards, and not be engaged in speculation or investment in rental real estate. Eligibility of a company varies with its industry category. For example:

Manufacturing: the maximum number of employees may range from 500 to 1,500 depending on the type of product manufactured.

Retailing: the average annual receipts may not exceed $5 million to $21 million, depending on the industry.

Wholesaling: the maximum number of employees may not exceed 100.

Service firms: the average annual receipts may not exceed $2.5 million to $14.5 million, depending on the business.

Construction: the average annual receipts may not exceed $17 million.

Agriculture: the average annual receipts can range from $500,000 to $7 million, depending on the products and services.

WORKING A GRANT REQUEST
INTO YOUR BUSINESS PLAN

A grant, as distinguished from a loan, is a sum that is awarded to a small business that does not have to be repaid in cash. The SBA, which can provide you with sources of information on grants, particularly through SCORE, narrows the term to mean "money that you are given to pursue a project and produce something that is beneficial for the greater good of society."

While there are more than 1,000 federal assistance programs alone, not to mention hundreds of others administered by state and regional agencies, a business cannot qualify for a grant without documenting and proving a need that will benefit the public as well as the recipient.

If you feel that your company might qualify for this kind of nonrefundable financial award, your primary responsibility is to determine whether you can satisfy, realistically, the required criteria. Once you have done so, of course, you have to explain your rationalizations clearly and concisely in your business plan. Here are some examples of grants made to small businesses, as a result of the successful presentations they made for their plans:

1. A local forest products company, which learned that the bark of certain trees in its woodlands contained valuable elements for medicinal applications, was awarded $200,000 to determine how to process the bark—then being dumped as a waste—to make it marketable to pharmaceutical manufacturers.

2. After the owner of two printing firms, in New Mexico and the coast of South Carolina, had made numerous complaints that the paper company supplying both plants was shipping an inferior product to the southern plant, it was proved in the laboratory beyond all doubt that the quality of the paper was exactly the same. When the owner then suspected that salt air and humidity were the culprits affecting paper temporarily held in stock, he prepared a business plan and applied for a research grant to (1) reduce in-plant humidity, and (2) test other types of mold-resistant paper available at no increase in cost. The grant was given on the hypothesis that other printing firms and the paper industry would benefit from the research findings.

3. Plagued by complaints from customers that their vehicles were being sloppily serviced and often had dangerous defects, a truck-leasing dealer in the midwest traced the problem to a frustrating regional situation where it was almost impossible to find and hire properly trained mechanics. He solved the problem by preparing a plan of action and convincing the state department of motor vehicles that a grant should be allocated to his county's technical trade school to add a mechanic's curriculum, to which he could send his mechanics at very little cost. Although the grant did not go to the dealer, it greatly alleviated his problems and improved his customer relations.

What are your chances of obtaining a grant? A study cited by the SBA reported that "more than 15 percent of those businesses who applied for business research grants were approved." Not a very high figure, especially by comparison with a success rate of about 70 percent for business loans. But bear in mind that almost half of all grant applications are rejected at the start because of sloppy or inadequate business plan proposals, and that many are motivated by a company's highly inflated concept of what it can do to improve and upgrade business or society. The key is to prepare a grant proposal document that is realistic to begin with, presents your company's case in a positive manner, and itemizes the benefits that will be derived from the grant and would be impossible without it.

Some tips:

- Make sure at the start that you are aiming your request for a grant at the right agency or committee.

- Ask for assistance in a positive way, not looking at such funding as charity or a handout.

- Use an enthusiastic sales approach and be assertive (not aggressive) in presenting your cause.

- Enumerate the benefits to the business world and/or community that would follow the work made possible by the grant. Be specific, bearing in mind that this need not be totally altruistic. You might, for example, emphasize that by helping your company to improve a business situation, the grant would open up new jobs in the community and offer wider employment.

- Picture the recipients of your grant proposal and how you would react to your reasoning if you were in their shoes.

- Before even attempting to draft anything on paper, request from the grant committee (or similar body) a written description of its criteria for proposals.

- Fine-tune the technical details of your proposal, following instructions from the grant committee, and make sure your facts are accurate and to the point.

- Employ a respectful tone and dignified style in your presentation. If you are uneasy about your writing skills, seek professional help. (Here again, SCORE can provide excellent advice, and at no fee.)

- If at first you don't succeed, try again.

WORK PEOPLE INTO YOUR BUSINESS PLANS

When you prepare a business plan, bear in mind that your review of human resources might well be the most important single ingredient in your presentation. According to the Small Business Administration, the number of small businesses in the United States increased almost 50 percent in the decade just prior to 1995. By the mid-90s, there were approximately 21.5 million nonfarm businesses, of which 99 percent were small by the size standards category established by the SBA. These include sole proprietorships, corporations, S-corporations, and partnerships, about two-thirds of which operate full time.

In all of these, people are more important to the success-or-failure rate than funding, equipment, marketing, or other key functions. So the way you interpret and define your business in terms of personnel and human resources is vital.

Under a broad definition, which includes not only persons running a business full-time but also those doing so part-time, about 15 million American sole proprietors are engaged in some entrepreneurial activity. These 15 million entrepreneurs represent about 13 percent of all nonagricultural workers in the United States.

The number of new small businesses has increased steadily during the past thirty years. In 1993, new business corporations reached a record 706,540, or 18 percent more than had been recorded a decade earlier. In addition, part-time entrepreneurs have increased fivefold in recent years. The most recent statistics indicate financial gains for most small businesses. For example, the earnings of sole proprietors and partners increased 7.2 percent, well above the 3.6 percent increase in big-business wage-and-salary earnings during the same period.

Small businesses employ 54 percent of the private work force, contribute 52 percent of all sales in the country, and are responsible for 50 percent of the private gross domestic product. In addition, they produce more than 70 percent of the new jobs that are created.

Data on women- and minority-owned businesses at the start of the 1990s reveal that these businesses fared well and that the number of women-owned businesses rose about 58 percent in a single decade. The total receipts of women-owned businesses—some $5.5 billion—nearly tripled during this time period, and the number of black-owned small businesses rose by 38 percent while their receipts more than doubled. In terms of numbers of businesses, Hispanic-owned businesses have proved to be one of the fastest-growing segments of the U.S. business population, with a steady annual growth record of almost 10 percent. Similar increases in numbers and earnings were documented for other small-business minority groups.

Chapter 2

Plans for Retailers

This chapter introduces you to samples of the leading descriptions and proposals of some business plans in the most common industry: retailing. As will be true throughout the book, names and data have been changed in most cases to protect the privacy and anonymity of the owners or any trade secrets that might apply to their businesses. The plans that follow are presentations or proposals to a wide variety of financial institutions and professional lenders in the business world.

Omitted from the sample plans are the statistical records and dollars-and-cents figures that are generally basic elements in a business plan, because these are not only too complex and specialized to be helpful to readers, but would be meaningless for the most part. You will find ample models of financial forms and documentations in the back of this book—samples that will help you to organize your own calculations on paper.

As you will note, the first sample plan is for a well-organized consortium of retailers in South Carolina, and is addressed to an area bank as a request for financing to help develop the company. The group's accounting firm has helped to prepare the document, which follows the kinds of suggestions that make up the first chapter of this book. The essentials of the plan are seen in the elements that are highlighted:

1. Title cover, which is kept simple and in outline form

2. Agenda, a list of the contents

3. Organizational summary, describing the company

4. Collaborative growth, explaining how the consortium originated and grew

5. Corporate strategy, where and how the business will go in the days ahead and in the long term

6. Competition, what the business has to evaluate, realistically, as its chief competitors

7. Marketing and sales, the marketing, merchandising, and promotional plan

8. Activation, the positive actions that will be taken

9. Operations, what the business does, is, and is not

10. Financial analysis, the amount of financing needed and how it will be applied to the business

11. Timetable, when the actions will be taken

12. Risks, what the lender should know about any financial risks inherent in the proposed loan

13. Appendices, data sheets that were attached to the original business plan proposal

This plan was selected for the lead, since it presents a number of illustrative and creative approaches to the subject. The others that follow in this chapter will provide different outlooks and reasons for developing a business plan. Use them as idea stimulators and feel free to incorporate any of the ideas you like in a future presentation, as well as the language and format of the model plans.

RETAILING: DOES YOUR BUSINESS PLAN STAND A CHANCE?

If you are thinking of starting a retail business, says the National Retail Federation, the success of your business plan will depend a great deal on a number of key factors, including the following (not necessarily in order of priority):

- The nature of the competition
- The demography of the local population
- Proximity to a place of ongoing public interest
- Parking facilities
- Safety and security of the area
- The volume of traffic
- The availability of public transportation
- The compatibility of neighboring shops and services
- The attractiveness of the architecture and environment
- The storefront and layout of the building
- Ample merchandise display space
- Sufficient space for storage and work rooms
- Inventory and quick availability of back-order goods
- The courtesy, knowledge, and training of the clerks
- A location where the economy is on the ascendancy

You have many factors to consider. As you start drawing up a business plan, only you can decide which elements take priority and which drawbacks are outweighed by advantages.

A Comprehensive Business Plan for the Financial Development of

Coastline Pool Consortium

as presented to

The Anchor Bank
West Charleston, South Carolina
By The Consortium

WHITECAP POOLS
THE BEACH & POOL SHOP
ST. HELENA SWIMMING ASSOCIATION
THE HARBOURMASTER'S CLUB
WATERWAY ACCESSORIES
AQUATIC BODY BUILDERS

presented by

THOMPSON & SWIFT,
CERTIFIED PUBLIC ACCOUNTANTS
26 Bay Street, East
Beaufort, SC 29902

■ AGENDA
Organizational Summary
Collaborative Effort
Corporate Strategy
Competition
Marketing and Sales
Activation
Operations
Financial Analysis
Timetable
Risks
Appendices

ORGANIZATIONAL SUMMARY

Coastline Pool Consortium is a closely knit organization composed of six product/service businesses that have a basic interest in developing the installation and use of swimming pools of all sizes and types, private and public alike. The activities of these subsidiaries of the consortium include the sale and distribution of pool- and swimming-related products and materials, instruction in swimming and events related to natatorial activities and recreation, the use of pools and related facilities for body building and health improvement, the promotion of contained swimming facilities as a vital part of social club advantages, the merchandising of swimming and pool attire, and many other related functions.

The major difference between the consortium and, say, an association is that the former is an active marketing organization and merchandiser, rather than a confederation of businesses with similar interests who benefit from group knowledge and services, but function independently in the marketplace. Coastline Pool Consortium is directly involved with the joint sale of products, services, materials, and consultation by its members, as well as with collective advertising, promotion, accounting, and public relations. It was founded with the conviction that a mutual commercial enterprise would be far more valuable and would be more profitable for individual members than each one could possibly hope for on its own.

COLLABORATIVE GROWTH

Coastline Pool Consortium originated in 1984 when two of the present members, Whitecap Pools and Waterway Accessories, joined forces in an advertising campaign to promote the installation and use of pools and related products. As the president of Whitecap Pools commented later, "We discovered that we could stretch the advertising dollar almost twice as far and yet each could double the consumer response to individual ads and commercials. We also found that we could slice administrative and staff costs through this kind of cooperative effort, and in many cases receive from each other sound sales and marketing advice that we might not have thought of on our own."

The collaboration was so successful that a third partner, St. Helena Swimming Association, was added in 1986 and the idea of a consortium began to grow. SHSA was a natural because it was a teaching organization. It benefited by being able to use pools in many more locations for instruction; in turn it was a great promoter because Whitecap and Waterway could then schedule introductory free swimming lessons.

The Harbourmaster's Club and Aquatic Body Builders were the next to join, in 1989, the former offering the facilities and activities of a large indoor/outdoor resort pool complex, and the latter making available water-related health and body-building courses and programs. The group was rounded out with the addition of the Beach and Pool Shop the following year, offering a wide range of products, equipment, and clothing.

CORPORATE STRATEGY

Where will this business be going in the long term? This question was asked repeatedly in the founding years and again each time a new arm of business was added to the consortium. The answer, spelled out in annual reports, made it possible for the owners and managers, individually and collectively, to have an overview of the entrepreneurial vision of the business and understand the benefits, impacts, and challenges of their respective business operations and responsibilities. Some of the key questions discussed and answered were these:

> What is the potential economic boom down the road?
>
> What is the potential strategic impact?
>
> What products and materials are offered to consumers, other customers, or clients?
>
> What services are offered?
>
> What new or additional products and services will be offered in the future?
>
> What organizations outside the perimeter of the consortium are contributing to the organization's growth and profitability?

The answers to these questions—positive and relevant—will all be found in the annual report of the consortium.

COMPETITION

There is no direct competition to Coastline Pool Consortium for the simple reason that there is no single organization in the company's marketing region that offers this kind of six-part mix of products, materials, services, and consultation. It could be said that there are competitors to the various *segments* of the consortium, specifically as follows:

1. Pool installers
2. Pool service firms

3. Beachwear and accessories

4. Health and fitness clubs

5. Pool and swimming accessories

6. Swimming instruction and competition

7. Recreational consultants

Market research by the advertising agency for Coastline Pool Consortium reveals no evidence that any similar company is being organized or even contemplated.

MARKETING AND SALES

The marketing region for Coastline Pool Consortium has been designated by the company's managers as the South Carolina counties of Beaufort, Jasper, Colleton, and Dorchester, all situated in the southwestern tip of the state. Corporate plans call for this region to be extended to include Chatham County, Georgia, to the south and Berkeley County, South Carolina, to the north.

Evaluating the markets, both current and extended, the managers of the consortium engaged in studies toward answering the following questions (which are similarly covered in the annual report):

What are the (a) target markets and (b) secondary markets for products, materials, and services?

How many potential customers and clients are there in each of these market categories?

Are there distinct subsegments of these markets that would be more likely to turn to the consortium for goods and services?

What reasons would potential customers and clients have for turning to the consortium for multiple selections, rather than to competitors offering a lesser choice of goods and/or services?

Looking at it from the purchaser's point of view, exactly how will customers save money or get a competitive advantage by dealing with the consortium rather than another supplier?

When we are dealing with other companies or groups, instead of individual consumers, who are the persons who make purchasing decisions?

The objectives of our sales evaluations and marketing analyses are to create a clearer picture of the customers who stimulate the bulk of our business. Such perspectives make for two accomplishments: (a) avoiding an inordinate amount of time and money chasing down leads that do not turn into sales, and (b) selecting product lines and tailoring services to meet the realistic needs of customers, rather than what we may think their needs are.

Activation

The marketing plan specifies the attitudes that must be held and the actions that must be taken to stimulate sales. Our focus for this purpose is on the following, at the minimum:

- Advertising, both print and broadcasting
- Printed communications in the form of brochures, on-site literature, and mailings
- Videotapes, audiocassettes, and educational media
- Article placements, press releases, and other public relations functions
- Participation in seminars, Chamber of Commerce programs, adult education curricula, and other community events
- Participation in programs that render a public service to the residents of the region

OPERATIONS

Coastline Pool Consortium has no manufacturing facilities and is not a *producer* of product or materials in industrial/commercial connotations. However, it does exert substantial influence over its suppliers and can demand exacting specifications in the matter of product design, cost (pricing), characteristics of performance, and compliance with environmental compatibility. In the supervisory sense, it can thus be said to be a "producer."

Equally true, the consortium is not a *distributor*, but it can wield strong influence in determining how products, supplies, and materials are packaged, transported, and distributed. Management can decide whether to opt for multiple channels, single channels, or even for an internal distribution system.

Likewise, the consortium is not a *repair* facility, but it does make it a point to be responsible for product quality and extend guarantees as far as reasonable.

The administration's theory is that customers in today's world are very leery about product reliability and will flock to suppliers who stand behind their products and never try to weasel out of responsibilities to the customer. Hence, it has long been the policy of the company to bend over backward and take the stand that "the customer is always right" when it comes to repairing, replacing, or otherwise handling a purchaser's complaint.

In accordance with the above standards, policies, and concepts of doing business, the consortium continuously maintains a staff that is large enough and skilled enough for the job.

FINANCIAL ANALYSIS

Coastline Pool Consortium interprets the financial as the scorecard by which the potential of the entire venture is judged, the performance of the venture is measured, and the success or failure of the venture is seen in the public eye.

Because the venture is a business undertaking, in the final analysis the financials really are the venture. They do not create, drive, or guide the venture-they describe and, in the end, are it.

With this management philosophy in the forefront, Coastline Pool Consortium hereby proposes that the Investment Trust Department of Anchor Bank back a proposed securities option plan in which participants in the trust can obtain stock in the consortium for a ten percent (10%) interest in the company's net proceeds for each calendar year for the next three years. It is also hereby proposed that the total amount of the investment be $2,400,000, which sum would be used for the company's development during the period in question. The financial maturation would include the following, among other motions:

1. Assignment of a financial adviser to fine-tune the company's accounting and reporting system and pinpoint areas that should be rendered more efficient

2. Planned expansion of the consortium's headquarters and administrative offices

3. Addition of three experienced managers to the company, respectively in marketing, finance, and distribution

4. Reorganization of the inventory control system, procedures, and applications

5. Development of a new line of portable spas for both recreational and therapeutic uses

6. Design and issuance of a consortium credit card for regular customers

Timetable

The proposed developments will take place in the order listed previously, at intervals of approximately two months for the starting times, but will in some cases overlap. Nothing would be initiated, however, without the full concurrence of Anchor's Trust Department and all bank officers involved in the decision-making process.

Risks

According to a preliminary evaluation by Anchor representatives, the financial risks to the bank, Trust Department, or private investors are negligible. The fact of participation alone assures participants that they would have sufficient ownership in the consortium to be the first to recoup their initial investment should the company fail or seek protection through Chapter 11 of the federal Bankruptcy Act.

APPENDICES

Although not incorporated into this financial presentation and proposal, backup data are available to support the body of this business plan and will be provided upon request. These documents include:

- Resumes of the officers of the consortium
- Resumes of the principals of the member organizations, citing their qualifications and experience
- Detailed descriptions of all products distributed by the company, with quality ratings and current prices
- Lists of materials and supplies available, with current prices
- Description of services available through the consortium, in categorical sequence
- Documented market research data
- Demographics of consumers in the counties that comprise the geographical market area
- Map of the marketing area and the locations of Consortium facilities and members' headquarters
- Delineation of the methodology used to make financial projections and the evaluation of revenues

New Business Expansion Plan
for an Historic Village Institution

Grandma's Closet
Chestnut Hill, Pennsylvania

presented to

The Wallstreeters
A New York State Venture Capital Group

presented by the owners

LINDA MAY BERQUIST
AND
HELEN TROTTER TRUSLOW

A MINI-HISTORY

Grandma's Closet may well be one of the oldest businesses in the historic village of Chestnut Hill, north of Philadelphia. It started more than 150 years ago as a community bartering place, converted from two horse stalls and a grain bin. It is now owned by two descendants of the founder, who are assertive in stating that the purpose and character of the establishment has been retained all these years, with the exception of two short periods, during World Wars I and II, when it was temporarily given over to the Red Cross for programs of wrapping and shipping clothing for servicemen overseas.

In 1946, the "Closet," as it is called by local residents, featured second-hand—or, as the owners liked to say, "previously owned"—clothing mainly coats, jackets, sweaters, and other outerwear. Sales were brisk, since the nation was then recovering from a wartime economy during which many garment manufacturers had retooled their assembly lines to produce uniforms and other clothing for the military, and there was a shortage of civilian garb of all kinds. By the 1960s, Grandma's Closet was carrying a broad assortment of resale items, including not only clothing for both sexes and all ages, but also household goods, furniture, garden supplies, fine art, toys, wall hangings, silverware, and jewelry. The store thrived on the fact that its marketing strategy was to offer something for everyone and meet a wide variety of needs. As a local newspaper reported, "You can't beat a business that has had more than a century of experience."

OUR BUSINESS PLAN

Grandma's Closet over the years has added only those kinds of merchandise for which there is a local demand. Whenever a category of products has been introduced that failed to sell well, it was discontinued. But even so, the emporium is bursting at the seams, so loaded with inventory that customers often have to squeeze between objects to look at items that have caught their fancy. Some items have to be placed on shelves too high for selection.

There has never been any problem with supply, as residents of the village arrive day in and day out to offer goods they would like to have placed on consignment. Many promising items have had to be rejected or in some cases placed temporarily in the garages of the owners until in-store space was available.

Because of this congestion, Grandma's Closet herewith offers a share of the business in return for a private venture-capital investment in the range of $20-$28,000. This sum will be used for a 1,600-square-foot addition to the existing building and will contain a display room for larger resale items (such as furniture), a small office, and a temporary "holding" room for items that are being cleaned, restored, and marked for sale. The terms are open to negotiation with prospective investors.

At the present time, the business is grossing more than $12,000 a month, after payments averaging 50% of each sale to the persons who placed goods on consignment.

MARKETING AND MERCHANDISING PLANS

At the time that new capitalization is received and the intended expansions are underway, the shop will be closed for one month, probably during midsummer when many village residents are away and sales are customarily at their lowest. During this shutdown time, the owners intend to devote their time to five phases of business:

1. Reclassifying the different categories of merchandise

2. Repositioning the location of these groupings in the shop

3. Improving displays of major items—the ones that are most profitable in proportion to space occupied, such as jewelry and silver

4. Preparing brochures and print advertising to promote the new look, enlarged selections, and special bargains that prospective customers can see when they attend Grandma's Closet Open House

5. Soliciting a higher quality of merchandise from regular on-consignment donors, and evaluating new categories of commodities that appear to be likely to sell well

Presentation of a Coordinated Business Plan for

Horizon Galleries
of Tulsa, Oklahoma

presented to

Oil State Investors, Inc.
Oklahoma City, Oklahoma

presented by

ALISON SLATER MCBAIN
CHESTER W. MCBAIN
JENNIFER ANN MCBAIN
323 The Byway
Ponca City, OK 74601

DESCRIPTION OF THE BUSINESS

Horizon Galleries has experienced rapid growth in sales over the past four years, following a period when sales were slow and growth was at a standstill. As a result, however, this new vitality has generated an increasing need for information and data processing and it has become evident that a computerized system is needed as a tool for helping to evaluate the market, maintain the best possible inventories, and make vital business decisions. The three owners of the galleries have tried to cope with financial analysis and marketing strategies, and have assigned an outside consultant to assist them. Among their joint actions have been:

- Financial analyses
- Attempts to identify and revise prices for slower-moving inventory items
- Supplementing more detailed information on inventory tags
- Changing the product mix (varieties of gallery objects) to maximize sales and profits

It was eventually decided that computerized accounting and inventory systems were mandatory if the business was to continue in a highly competitive marketplace, one in which major chains were squeezing many smaller stores out of business.

STATEMENT OF PURPOSE

Horizon Galleries is in need of equity financing or a commercial loan in the amount of $10,000 for the purpose of establishing a comprehensive computerized system to improve its accounting and inventory control and to enhance its marketing programs. The owners have researched available hardware and software computer configurations designed to aid businesses in financial recordkeeping and inventory analyses, and have narrowed the choices to two moderately priced systems. Our electronics consultant has recommended an IBM-compatible system that would provide a broad choice of pertinent software programs, with a 386 chip that would support the user-friendly Windows operating program.

The requested financing would also underwrite the initial cost of a computer-generated mailing and promotional program to publicize Horizon Galleries, inform prospective purchasers about the range of products and materials in stock, and establish valuable consumer contacts.

OFFERINGS AT THE GALLERIES

This business was started by the mother of one of the owners as a kind of hobby, to sell and exchange Ponca Indian arts and crafts objects she had on display and had been collecting almost since childhood. When she discovered that many other people—both local residents and visitors—were interested in these creative items, she began buying, collecting, and adding works from other Indian tribes in Oklahoma and parts of the southwest. What was originally known as Maggie McBain's Trading Center assumed the more cultural name of Horizon Galleries at about the time that Mrs. McBain retired and her son and daughter-in-law took over the growing business.

Today, Horizon Galleries deals in a wide range of creations, from simple arts and crafts to painting and sculptures by nationally recognized artists. Among the items on sale in the 3,000-square-foot adobe gallery are oil paintings, watercolors, bronzes, decorative pottery, fine jewelry, studio glass, limited edition prints, kaleidoscopes, wood carvings, tapestries, quilts, wearable art, costume jewelry, metal castings, collectibles, prehistoric reproductions, crystal, and religious icons.

Although many visitors to the region are interested in buying inexpensive souvenirs, the owners have intentionally avoided being classified as a "tourist" or "gift" shop and have therefore continually upgraded the quality of the merchandise they select for presentation and sale. To further this endeavor, they have toured almost every corner of the southwest and sought out objects that were authentic, attractive, and unique.

MARKETING STRATEGIES

The owners of the galleries conducted a marketing survey, using the incentive of chances on a $50 gift certificate, which disclosed that Horizon has been successful in attracting new customers and retaining existing ones—largely because of the continual introduction of new and exciting "finds." While the survey revealed some aspects of consumer product preferences, the most important findings related to promotional campaigns that could be effective in building sales and eventual profits. Specifically, for example, it was pointed out that regular customers (those who had made five or more purchases in the course of a year) would welcome some kind of recognition in the form of credits or "points" toward discounts on future purchases.

Another revelation, which was unexpected, was that more customers had heard of the galleries by word of mouth than through advertising—suggesting that previous ad campaigns had been ineffective and should be discontinued or revised.

Other data compiled indicated that the galleries were patronized by upscale customers who were more likely to be found in a mall adjacent to the one in which Horizon has been located for the last five years. The implication was clear: the owners should consider *relocation* in their plans for the future. This option, however, is not part of the business plan presented herewith, and would have to be covered by a new plan and an evaluation of the financing required to make such a move.

COMPETITION

Horizon Galleries has only one competitor in its direct marketing area that carries similar merchandise and appeals to comparable categories of customers: The Barn Owl, located closer to a main residential area of Tulsa, a long-established emporium that is almost an institution in its own right, located in a mid-nineteenth-century schoolhouse with an historic background. The "Owl," as it is popularly called, also carries antique furniture.

Several other shops, however, can be classified as competitive, since they specialize in items of the type sold at Horizon Galleries—though without the range of choices—and tend to offer more discounts. These carry only merchandise rated high on the list of consumer preferences, such as decorative pottery, costume jewelry, and carved wooden household products.

Business Plan for

Family Eye Care

submitted to

The Bank of New London
New London, NH
and
The New Hampshire State
Small Business Administration

submitted by

JOHN T. PETERS, JR. AOA
ANNA STURGIS MEANS, RN
57 Rocky Creek Drive
South New London, NH 03257

STATEMENT OF OBJECTIVES

Family Eye Care has been in operation in the Lakes region of New Hampshire as a family business since the end of World War II, when it was established by the father of the present principals, John T. Peters, Sr., an experienced optometrist. Since that time, it has served a growing list of patrons of all ages. Facing an increasing need to upgrade its examination facilities and provide more comprehensive optical needs, FEC is seeking a long-term investment of $45,000 and a short-term loan of $18,000 for the following improvements:

- A wider selection of fashion frames for all budgets

- Expansion of building facilities for a full-service optical lab

- Orientation programs for the principals in the field of low-vision improvement

- Development of a specialized, selective program of eye care for senior citizens

- State-of-the-art testing equipment for the servicing and care of contact lenses
- A new counter for the sale of nonprescription sun and sport glasses.

DESCRIPTION OF PROFESSIONAL SERVICES

Family Eye Care is a professional community business devoted to the needs of individuals, families, and groups to provide accurate and reliable optical information about eyesight and eye care, examine the eyes of persons with sight problems or injuries, recommend suitable corrective lenses, maintain eyesight standards, and particularly assist those with low-vision problems, aging deterioration, and special needs.

The patients and patrons using FEC services are largely members of families in the New London area, as well as a growing influx of visitors and vacationers who come to the Lakes region during all four seasons of the year for recreation and often recuperation. The business has gradually been extended to serve students at nearby Colby College and Andover Academy, and has volunteered, at no cost to the public, to institute a comprehensive eye-care program for pupils in Merrimack County's secondary education system.

Family Eye Care maintains a close liaison with two area hospitals, Concord General and New London Hospital, and calls on staff members for consultation and treatment in all cases where services or care are required beyond the capabilities of the firm. It also receives regular bulletins from the Dartmouth Medical Research Center in Hanover, covering new developments in eye care and the treatment of eye diseases.

MARKETING AND PROMOTION

Utilizing the requested investment monies and loans, the firm intends to enhance its promotional and orientation capabilities to accomplish the following:

Be more competitive in the regional Merrimack County market, particularly to attract prospective patrons who now go to Concord, Lebanon, or even Boston (two hours away) for eye care.

Gain the confidence of people with eye and optical problems who are currently getting little, or improper, care.

Establish an extended-payment plan for patrons who are elderly, unemployed, or otherwise limited in their budgets.

Increase the educational opportunities of the principals to stay abreast of the latest research and developments in the field of eye care and optical facilities.

COMPETITION

There are three competitors in the immediate marketing region of the firm, all of which are owned and operated by experienced, reliable opticians: Lakeside Opticians, two miles outside of the town of New London, also a long-standing family business; Eyes, Inc., a subsidiary of Major Department Stores in White River Junction, Vermont, with an office in Newbury, New Hampshire; and The Eye Clinic at Sugar River Hospital, ten miles distant.

It is not expected that the developments desired and outlined above will adversely affect such competition. Rather, the results will see an increasingly greater penetration of the market of people who do not have proper eye care or implementation and who will benefit by using the improved facilities and services.

Business Development Plan for

Sebasco Dockage & Marina
Sebasco, Maine,
on Casco Bay

submitted by

MIKE AND GERMAINE FUSCO
Parker Head, Maine

submitted to

The Pine Tree State Bank
Pine Tree Building
Portland, Maine

With the Prior Approval of
Maine State Department of Docks
Brunswick, Maine

DESCRIPTION OF FACILITIES

Sebasco Dockage & Marina began in 1953 as a private boat dock and landing, mainly used by people living on outlying Casco Bay islands who needed space for securing their boats while shopping or picking up mail. It was founded by relatives of the present owners. By 1960, it had expanded into a complex of two landing and temporary parking docks, and three docks with permanent slips for rental boats. In 1969, a small marina, storage shed, and boat ramp were added. And in 1987, following the enlargement of the marina and reconstruction of the docks, a small dockside cafe was built, mainly for the convenience of customers.

While the last-mentioned business was successful, largely because of home-made seafood entrees and soups, and was enlarged three times, a firm decision has been made by the owners. We are *not* in the restaurant business, and never really intended to be. The fact of the matter is that food service is too time-consuming and distracts the owners and staff from their primary business: small-boat dockage, service, and storage. With this in mind, we intend to convert the restaurant into a marine shop, for which purpose we require financing in the amount of $27,550.

SALES POTENTIAL

Our customers will be more of those we served prior to our unintended entry into the food business. These are the people who live on outlying islands from the vicinity of Yarmouth to the west to Pemaquid Point to the east. Others live on isolated portions of the mainland that are generally easier to reach by boat than by car. We estimate that there are at least 4,000 such prospective customers and that, over the years, we have established long-standing service arrangements with about 700 on either an annual or seasonal basis. A preliminary survey, undertaken for us by the marketing firm of Sharon and Roe in Bath, foresees an increase of 25 percent to 35 percent in business when our reorganization plan has gone into effect. This estimate is based on our ability to offer high-tech repair and rebuilding facilities and skilled labor for boat engines and instrumentation when SD&M's renovation program is completed.

NOTE: See the Income Projection Statement attached to this business plan.

MARKETING PLAN

Sebasco Docking & Marina will extend its present market almost entirely in the direction of the historical market for the company, basing its promotions on the ability to reach a known group of potential customers. About 75 percent of these prospects are listed on the government-supported island survey, which is updated every three years. This is a complete listing of the owners of island properties, which is recorded by the coastal counties of Cumberland, Sagadahoc, and Lincoln, mainly as a census taking to safeguard citizens in the event of hurricanes or other violent storms that might threaten those living in offshore areas. This list of prospects will be supplemented by names and addresses of boat owners whose homes lie in the remoter onshore areas where roads are difficult to traverse and may even be inaccessible following storms, flooding, or extremely high tides.

SD&M's marketing plan has four stages: (1) reaching a high percentage of boat owners who are prospective customers; (2) making them aware of the company's new capabilities and expertise; (3) gaining their confidence by reminding them of SD&M's heritage of more than forty years of reliable service to them, their parents, or their neighbors; and (4) offering a special discount to customers who make referrals to other prospective customers.

COMPETITION

Our major competitors in this specialized field of small-boat docking and servicing are Bristol Boat Works, which overlaps in a narrow region of customer locations, but in general services sections of the coast much farther to the east of SD&M's marketing map; West Bath Technologies, which offers some competition in the field of high-tech engine service, but almost none in the fields of docking or marina facilities; and Yarmouth Landing, a facility that is used by some islanders for docking and service, but almost exclusively by those with vessels too large for SD&M to handle anyway.

OWNERS AND STAFF

The owners and managers of Sebasco Dockage & Marina are:

Michael ("Mike") Fusco, a former lobsterman with a certificate in marine mechanics and navigation from the Bowdoin Department of Adult Education, and a small-craft master's license from the U.S. Coast Guard;

Germaine ("Gerry") Fusco, whose parents were the founders of the business and who is one of the few women holding a state certificate in marine engine maintenance and repair;

Arnold ("Arnie") Custer, originally a shipbuilder's carpenter, and more recently an engine mechanic specializing in electronics and control;

Sanford ("Sandy") Harpswell, manager of yard and storage; and

Mary Jane ("MJ") Fusco, daughter of the owners and marketing manager.

Business Plan for

The Whole Enchilada Mexican Restaurant
(a franchise operation)

submitted to

West Sun Bank of Austin, Texas
and
The Small Business Administration
Austin, Texas Office

submitted by

Madeline Tierney
Walter Tierney
3342 Cactus Grove Way
Austin, Texas 30045
(512) 435-0909

STATEMENT OF PURPOSE

The Whole Enchilada Mexican Restaurant is seeking a loan of $325,000 to refurbish and upgrade an existing building in Austin, Texas for the purpose of bringing a national and well-known chain restaurant to the area. The franchise will be operated by local parties with the assistance of the parent franchise firm, National Restaurants, Inc. An insurance policy will also be written to cover any liability on the part of the franchisee to the franchisor not only in regard to servicing the debt but also in regard to personal liability.

DESCRIPTION OF BUSINESS

The Whole Enchilada Mexican Restaurant is part of a national restaurant chain that prepares Texas-style and authentic Mexican-style food in a medium-to-higher-priced food market. The restaurant will have a 325-seat capacity and will be open seven days a week. The owners/franchisers will be Madeline and Walter Tierny, who will manage the restaurant. The restaurant staff will be comprised of four cooks, five busboys, three hostesses, and twenty-five servers. Due to the restaurant's prime location in the shopping mall district of Austin, the demand and activity should be constant. It is also the only Mexican-style restaurant in an eight-mile area.

LOCATION AND ENVIRONMENT

The restaurant will be located in the shopping mall district or "Cactus Drive" area of Austin. The building will cover 3,000 square feet of floor space and will have two separate exits. The outside decor will be in a "Southwestern motif" with landscaping to match the building style. The roof will be clay tile and the building will be brushed with stucco facing. The parking lot is in the front of the building with extra spacing on both sides of the property.

The atmosphere will be light and cheery with lots of window space and plants and baskets to brighten up the surroundings. The floor plan consists of two main dining rooms, two bathrooms, an office, bar, and the kitchen area, which is unusually large and spacious.

COMPETITION

There are four other primary restaurant competitors in the area:

1. Bronco's Steakhouse, Inc., a steak and beef restaurant that seats only 150 customers at a time, but has been in the area for the last ten years and is extremely popular with the community.

2. Bradley's Pancake and Breakfast House, Inc., a breakfast restaurant that serves breakfast all day long, and seats about 235 customers at a time. It has about the same amount of building space as The Whole Enchilada, but serves a different kind of cuisine to the same clientele.

3. Garino's Italian Restaurant, Inc., fine southern Italian cuisine, open only for lunch and dinner, six nights a week. A family-owned business that has been in operation since 1973, Garino's has a strong, loyal customer base and an extensive menu with daily specials. The floor space for the building is small and the seating capacity is only 112 persons.

4. Hoffman's House of German, Inc., serving tasteful Bavarian cuisine and open for lunch and dinner, seven days a week. A locally owned business that has been in operation for the past two years, it shows strong customer loyalty and is well accepted by the tourist trade. Seating capacity is 120 persons.

MARKETING PLAN

The restaurant will focus its marketing strategy on local coverage through the newspapers, television, and radio stations as well as through the national/statewide promotions of its parent company and other franchised Whole Enchilada restaurants.

The restaurant, because it is a franchise, will rely on the marketing talents of the parent company, National Restaurants, Inc., to organize and finance 80 percent of the advertising and marketing.

Other enclosed documents are:

1. A lease agreement for the building
2. Architectural renderings of how the restaurant will look after improvements have been made
3 A resume of the owners
4. Any insurance documentation
5. A copy of the franchise agreement
6. Personal financial statements of the owners
7. A resume of the building contractor
8. A business license application
9. Any zoning variances regarding the restaurant's sign
10. A description of the parent company, National Restaurants, Inc.

Business Plan for

The Westmoreland Art Gallery

submitted to

The First National Bank of Scottsdale
Scottsdale, Arizona

submitted by

MRS. GEORGE H. WESTMORELAND
MR. DAVID BOSEMAN
*2270 Ventura Avenue, West
Scottsdale, Arizona 70051
(419) 737-2001*

STATEMENT OF PURPOSE

The owners of The Westmoreland Gallery, Mrs. George H. Westmoreland and David Boseman, curator, being equal owners in the gallery (50 percent each), are seeking a refinancing loan of $425,000 for the purpose of refurbishing and expanding the present gallery building. The building, located at 2270 Ventura Avenue, West (located in downtown Scottsdale), is also owned by The Westmoreland Gallery. There is at present a small mortgage on the property that is due to be paid off at the end of the current fiscal year by the gallery.

Mrs. Westmoreland and Mr. Boseman wish to expand the exhibition ability of the gallery and therefore need more space (three new large rooms—see enclosed architectural drawings) and new and modern lighting in order to "showcase" effectively the artwork for sale or on exhibition.

DESCRIPTION OF THE BUSINESS

The Westmoreland Gallery was founded in 1985 by the late George H. Westmoreland, a renowned southwestern painter and sculptor, to showcase his works and those of his artistic peers. The Westmoreland Gallery since its beginning has done very well financially for an art gallery, primarily because of the ability of his wife, Mrs. Judith Westmoreland to select saleable and profitable art for the gallery at the correct time. Mrs. Westmoreland's ability to find and move saleable art has been phenomenal and has been a primary reason for the gallery's success.

The gallery's curator, David Boseman, has been an integral part of this success as well; his ability to manage the business and the staff are also important to the gallery's successful operation. In 1994, George Westmoreland died in an automobile accident. His interest in the gallery reverted to his wife, Judith, who was for six months the sole owner of the gallery. In February of 1995, she sold one-half of her interest to David Boseman, who is her equal partner in the ownership of the business.

Since Mr. Westmoreland's death, the gallery has continued to be a success, but is hampered by a lack of space and out-of-date lighting and interior design.

LOCATION AND ENVIRONMENT

The location of The Westmoreland Gallery is at 2270 Ventura Avenue, West, in the downtown district of Scottsdale. Scottsdale is an affluent community with lots of art patrons who have supported the gallery since its opening. The proposed additions and changes will serve only to enhance its stylish surroundings and clientele.

The gallery is on the first floor of a single-tenant building with ample parking for its customers at the front (on the street) and in the rear (behind the building), and there is a full parking lot located to the right of the building that accommodates parking for other downtown merchants as well as The Westmoreland

Gallery. Apart from the two principal owners, there are six full-time employees and three part-time employees who assist in the daily operations of the business.

COMPETITION

There are several other art galleries in the Scottsdale area. However, there are only two other art galleries that acquire and sell the same quality and style of artistic works as The Westmoreland Gallery. They are:

1. The Howard Gallery, located on Cozumel Lane just five miles south of the city of Scottsdale. This gallery handles only artwork, not any sculpture as The Westmoreland Gallery does. The Howard Gallery is a smaller building with a staff of four people including the owners. Also, the owners of the Howard Gallery have stated that they are not interested in any business expansion.

2. The Moore Gallery, also located in Scottsdale, shows mainly sculpture with an occasional painting. However, their main interest is in promoting local sculptors, not other works of art. They also have a small staff of three employees including the owners. The owners have the gallery up for sale and wish to retire from the business world.

MARKETING PLAN

The business will build its future market on its list of present and past patrons, mounting a referral campaign that will develop new leads and new markets in art and sculpture. Professional art magazines and periodicals have been and will still be used to promote the gallery and individual artists. The gallery hopes to expand its inventory of works after the new renovations, and to move its inventory quicker due to more private showings and an accelerated use of the new, more modern facilities to accent the latest works of art. The better exposure should mean better sales.

Other enclosed documents are:

1. A floor plan of the renovations and changes

2. A profit/loss sheet for the gallery this past year

3. A copy of the mortgage note that is due to be paid off at the end of the fiscal year

4. A list of the potential consignments that are to be showcased in the new surroundings

5. A timetable for the renovations and their completion

6. Copies of all city and building licenses needed to start the work by the contractor

7. Any insurance paperwork needed to cover other works in the building while the renovations are being completed

Financing Proposal for

Author's Book Store

Located at
236 Mountain Highway
Wytheville, Virginia

submitted to

First Bluefield Bank
Pulaski, Virginia

submitted by

ANNA RICHARDS WOOLWINE

SERINA WHITE WOOLWINE

33 The Terraces
Wytheville, VA 24382

WHAT IS OUR BUSINESS?

Author's Book Store is a full-service retail operation, selling the following merchandise at both basic and discount prices: hardcover books, mass-market paperbacks, trade paperbacks, major periodicals, books on tape, a limited supply of greeting cards and stationery, and certain nonbook materials that meet the communications and educational needs of regular customers. The store also maintains a lending library for adults, stocked with best-selling fiction and nonfiction, and a lending library for children, featuring books that fit school needs but are not necessarily purchased for home libraries. Hours are 10:00 A.M. to 6:00 P.M. six days a week, and Wednesday evenings until 9:00.

Our target markets are customers of all ages who work or reside in the Wytheville/Pulaski area, within 15 miles of the store's location. Because of the nature of the population, we feature many books that are historical, environmental, or educational (both fictional and nonfictional), and that appeal to well-educated readers in the medium- to high-income market segment.

Customer service includes a membership discount plan for regular customers who desire it, complimentary gift wrapping, searches for out-of-date and second-hand books, and consultation about appropriate books for readers of all ages.

MARKET ANALYSIS

The population of the Wytheville/Pulaski area exceeds the high-income, well-educated population of 25,000 advocated by the American Booksellers Association as ideal for the successful operation of a bookstore with moderate competition whose potential customers circulate near the location at least once a week in the course of business or normal shopping routines. According to the Chambers of Commerce of the two communities, supplemented by a Nielsen readership survey two years ago, book purchases average four per year for adults and three per year for children in this region. The figures do not include high-volume purchases of certain books by libraries, educational centers, private clubs, or other institutions.

The only two competitors within a 30-mile radius are Waldenbooks, a national chain that has a small retail outlet but largely solicits sales by mail, and a Christian Education bookstore that sells a small selection of popular hardcover and paperback books.

MARKETING PLAN

Author's Book Store focuses largely on individuals and families whose incomes are such that they have little hesitation about making spur-of-the-moment purchases at the point of sale when they spot a title that interests them. The retailer's basic discount is 40 percent for trade books and 45 percent for nonbook merchandise. For the purpose of this business plan, the total cost of goods sold, after computing transportation costs, is 62 percent of gross sales.

Using the recommendations of the American Booksellers Association (ABA), the owners intend to allocate a sum equal to two percent of annual sales for promotion and advertising in the following media:

- Regular newspaper ads in the *Wytheville Times*
- Display ad in the Yellow Pages
- Direct-mail advertising to regular book purchasers and to a list of prospective buyers who fill out in-store cards
- Cooperative advertising in the Pulaski Chamber of Commerce newsletter
- Library and school promotions during Library Week and special educational events

FINANCIAL REQUIREMENTS

The owners of Author's Book Store started the business with their own equity investment of $10,000. To this sum, they are adding a second equity investment of $6,000, and will require an additional sum of $18,000 as a business loan. These funds will be used for the following purposes, to build the business and to increase future sales:

1. The addition of 600 square feet of store space available directly adjacent to the present layout
2. Construction of new shelving and reorganization of existing shelves for the enhanced display of books
3. Redecorating the entire store with a new "literary/historical" theme
4. Design and construction of four displays for the front of the store, respectively for "Best-Selling Novels," "New Nonfiction," "Books for Young People," and "Local History"
5. An "Open House" promotion, with signings by local authors, prize drawings, and refreshments, to inaugurate the store's new image

MEET THE OWNERS

The owners of Author's Book Store are cousins who were born and raised in Austinville, midway between Wytheville and Pulaski. They joined forces three years ago to establish the bookstore when returning to the area after enjoying separate professional careers in other parts of the state.

Anna Richards Woolwine, Ph.D. received her doctorate in English literature and history at William and Mary College in Williamsburg, and for twenty years taught in the English department at the University of Virginia in Charlottesville. She is the author of a biography of the southern poet Mary Ellen Chase, and the editor of two anthologies of works by Virginia writers.

Serena White Woolwine, MA received her undergraduate and graduate degrees at American University in Washington, D.C., where she specialized in marketing. For eighteen years, she held various executive positions in marketing, advertising, and promotion in department stores in Richmond, Virginia, and was an executive vice president in marketing at the time of her retirement and entry into the retail book business.

Business Plan for

"Buy the Book" Bookstore, Inc.

submitted to

Peach State Savings & Loan
Atlanta, Georgia

submitted by

KAREN HARTLEY, PRESIDENT

"Buy the Book" Bookstore, Inc.
P.O. Box 3302
Marietta, GA 30906

STATEMENT OF PURPOSE

"Buy the Book" Bookstore is going to be financed by the owner, Karen Hartley, and her father, William Hartley. The bookstore is to be located in Marietta, Georgia, in an already established shopping mall, the Mulberry Mall at the corner of Wilson Avenue and Evans Street. The store renovations and improvements will be minimal, as the store's previous tenant was a cooking supply firm and the furnishings and shelving will be perfect for a bookstore and its layout. Mr. Hartley as the majority lender in this venture will have insurance to cover liability. The business will be a Sub-chapter "S" Corporation and will conduct business under the corporate name of "Buy the Book" Bookstore, Inc.

DESCRIPTION OF BUSINESS

The primary purpose of the business is to sell books to the Marietta community (population 200,000) and to various educational and religious institutions throughout the area. There will be a total of four full-time employees and six to eight part-time employees. The four full-time employees will include Ms. Hartley, president of the company, her mother Carolyn Hartley, who will oversee the bookkeeping and financial operations of the store, and two long-time friends, Nancy Davis and Julie Crosby, both of whom will assist Ms. Hartley to oversee and carry out the general operations of the store. The part-time employees will be used to fill in on an as-needed basis in all areas of the business. Ms. Hartley's father is a retired sales executive from Barnes and Noble, whose contacts should help the business negotiate with necessary book vendors and supply houses that can furnish the store with its stock. The stock will be books, specialty retail office supplies and papers, book tapes and CDs, some music CDs and tapes, and miscellaneous items related to books and reading. Since Ms. Hartley is herself a former teacher, strong emphasis will be placed on selling to schools and other large educational institutions in order to obtain a reliable and continuous client sales base apart from the local community and its market.

MARKETING PLAN

The business will build its future market on its contacts within the community in three main ways:

1. Through the retail market of the community via the retail store
2. Through the active marketing of the ability of the business to supply various in-state *and* out-of-state educational institutions
3. Through the "cyberspace marketing" of the business by the use of a computer "homepage" that will be originated from the University of Georgia, which has a satellite campus in Marietta. This homepage would be listed on the Internet and would have the latest books on sale through the bookstore. Potential customers could place their order on the homepage directly with their credit card or they could contact the bookstore directly on the toll-free number listed on the homepage and on other printed materials.

LOCATION/ENVIRONMENT/COMPETITION

The "Buy the Book" Bookstore will be located in the Mulberry Mall in Marietta in a marketing environment favorable to prospective purchasers of books. The location is a high-traffic area, making it logical that here will be a high percentage of drop-ins.

The Mulberry Mall is located near the center of town, so the bookstore's exposure to the general retail public will be at its best. The store will be close to other essential facilities that are also located in the mall, such as a mailing and shipping center. There is also a school nearby and the nearest bookstore, which represents the only serious competition, is a chain store located on the other side of town at least ten miles away.

SUPPORTING DOCUMENTATION

A. Personal financial statement, including a lease note between father and daughter
B. Resumes
C. Lease on the building space
D. Copy of the loan or lease note
E. Insurance documentation

Business Plan for

Old Orchard Fruitcakes

submitted to

Wachovia Trust
Palmetto Dunes, SC

submitted by

JOSEPH P. STEVENS
MARIAN DENNIS
JOAN SEAGER

23 Beach Street
Bluffton, South Carolina

DESCRIPTION OF THE BUSINESS ENTERPRISE

During the past three years the company, then known as Old Orchard Bakery, has been reasonably successful selling conventional baking goods to consumers in the towns of Bluffton, Hilton Head, and nearby Sun City. But more and more customers began asking for the popular fruitcakes, not just at Christmastime, but during all seasons of the year. So Marian Dennis, who had started the business baking in her home kitchen, began experimenting with local seasonal fruits that could be used as ingredients in cakes and other recipes, and marketed at other seasons of the year. She tested these on family, friends, and neighbors, and retained only the recipes that received rave notices. Then she used these recipes to create fruitcakes for a variety of religious feasts, national holidays like the Fourth of July and Labor Day, and family events like birthdays and weddings.

Since mass-marketed fruitcakes have received a bad name because they are hard or dry, Marian tested recipes that would avoid these problems, using local fruits that retained their moisture and texture. Her partner, Joe Stevens, attended courses on packaging at a paper mill in Savannah, Georgia, 35 minutes from his home, and learned how to provide packing that would keep their particular ingredients fresh for longer periods of time. The company uses an "Always Tasty, Always Fresh" slogan in its marketing and advertising.

BUSINESS OBJECTIVES

Old Orchard Fruitcakes intends to focus on these essentials of freshness, uniqueness, and flavor that built the business and increased profits in the past, with the added seasonal distinctiveness.

In addition, the company has plans for the following enhancements:

- Specialty fruitcakes baked to order for customers, but at no increase in the average pound-for-pound prices

- Issuing its own discount credit card, in addition to accepting Visa and Master Card

- Seasonal "cake tastings" of both old, established products and new recipes

- Fruitcake-of-the-Month promotions in its marketing area

- An eventual mail-order business, once OOF's packaging materials and techniques have been tried and proven long enough for such a venture

FINANCIAL REQUIREMENTS

Old Orchard Fruitcakes requires equity financing in the total amount of $105,000 for the following purposes, to accomplish the business objectives outlined above:

1. $15,000 to discharge leasing costs for baking equipment, which will then be fully owned

2. $25,000 to establish its new name and build its present and future reputation on past performances

3. $10,000 for inventory purchases

4. $15,000 for the hiring of a part-time advertising and media specialist

5. $20,000 for the expansion of facilities

6. $20,000 for promotion and media

MEDIA PLAN

Old Orchard Fruitcakes will use the last-mentioned figure to expand its very modest current advertising campaign in local newspapers, several regional magazines, and mailings. OOF will also begin publication of a small catalog, which will be used for distribution locally, and selective mailings to prospective customers.

A newsletter is under consideration, which would go to regular customers and business friends, and which would encourage feedback from readers such as suggestions for new kinds of fruitcakes or changes in recipes.

A modest fund will be set aside for a booth at the annual Chamber of Commerce business fair held at the beginning of each year, with the emphasis on OOF's ability to supply fruitcakes for holiday occasions or corporate dinners.

Chapter 3

Plans for Small Service Firms

A key example here is Facility Maintenance Services. The plan describes in detail the elements you need to consider and work into your business plan. These range from a description of an existing business to the current problems, the need for growth and expansion, the nature of the operations, management strategy, and plans relating to such matters as financing, marketing, advertising, and future expectations.

This business plan is in two parts: (1) a condensed presentation, mainly for internal corporate orientation, and (2) a complete, detailed presentation to outside sources necessary for accomplishing the present and future goals of the company.

A Small Business Master Plan for

Arrow Electric

submitted to

Fourth Federal Savings Bank
2991 Central Avenue
Yonkers, NY 10710

submitted from

Donald Hess, President

Matthew Zotti, Electrical Engineer

Marjorie B. Babcock, Treasurer

Scott Furstin, Sales manager

Arlie Dawes, Service manager

2675 Mathews Avenue
Mount Vernon, NY 10552

Description of the Business

Arrow Electric, also referred to by the name of its parent corporation, The Arrow Group, Inc., is an electric contractor, licensed and equipped to undertake a wide range of energy and power projects, including commercial, industrial, and residential installations, computer wiring, repairs, 220-volt changeovers, swimming pool and outdoor lighting, electric dryers and ranges, heating, air conditioning, wiring for heavy machinery, smoke and fire alarm detection installations, and general electrical consultation.

The business was founded in 1951 by the grandfather of the current president, specializing in the field of residential service and installations. In 1974, the owners presented a small business plan to the Fourth Federal Savings Bank to receive financing so service could be extended to commercial customers. And in 1986, a third plan was inaugurated, leading to the certification of Arrow as an installer of wiring and the electrification of industrial equipment and facilities.

Originally confining its operations to the city of Mount Vernon, where it was initially licensed, the company extended its zone of activity to neighboring Yonkers and then Pelham.

PLAN OF ACTION

Arrow Electric now intends to enter a fourth plateau of the electric business by offering high-tech services to customers in the field of computers, data processing, and related spheres. Management reached this decision only after its key personnel had enrolled in and completed a fifty-hour electrical engineering course in computer science at Pace Institute in Westchester and received appropriate Certificates of Completion from the faculty.

Supplementing the personnel orientation program was a plan to utilize 50 percent of the company's R&D accumulated fund, a sum amounting to $7,800, to purchase electronic testing equipment and instrumentation necessary for the installation and servicing of computers. It is estimated that an additional sum of $12,400 will be required during the next six-month period to complete the computer instrumentation program.

Management foresees this last-mentioned sum as an essential part of a loan request for the upgrading of Arrow Electric from a "Class B" electric service organization to a "Class A" entity. Further loan requirements for this purpose would entail:

$38,000 for an electronically equipped mobile service vehicle

$20,000 for laboratory extension facilities

$11,800 for advertising and promotion; and

$32,000 for the salary of an electronic technician

MERCHANDISING PROJECT

Once the proposed financing has been authorized, Arrow Electric intends to undertake an aggressive merchandising campaign to establish its prerogative as an accomplished installation and service arm in all major areas of electric power. For this objective it has developed both internal and external public relations and advertising programs, the latter in collaboration with the Four-Star Advertising Agency, which has handled past Arrow campaigns.

The long-range plan calls for a series of concentrated marketing campaigns in the following sales categories, and in the order listed, with strategies tailored to each different type of prospective customer for the electric business:

1. *Residential*, using past cases to win the confidence of home owners, many of whom have been frustrated by the lack of interest or sloppy practices of local electric service firms.

2. *Commercial*, quoting favorable comments from steady customers in this field, such as retail stores, restaurants, and motels.

3. *Industrial*, emphasizing Arrow's accomplishments in several instances in which the firm was called upon to plan and complete very intricate plant and factory installations.

4. *Computerized installations* and the need for very skilled, specialized attention to detail. The thrust of this campaign (since Arrow is new to this field) will be on the firm's high-tech equipment and depth of recent training.

COMPETITION

Although competition in this field has been described as "tough," even "fierce," any firm that offers steady, reliable service at reasonable rates is likely to stay well ahead of the game. Two strong, regular competitors are:

Westchester Electric Cooperative, which has three offices and a processing plant in Westchester County. Its basic impact is in the installation and servicing of major appliances, which it also sells, retail and wholesale.

QED Electric Corporation, which handles all types of electrical installations, including design and layouts, for residential, commercial, and industrial customers.

A Proposal for

Skylens, Inc.
Aerial Photography
Fairfield Airport
Fairfield, California

proposed to

Capital Ventures
Pacific East Building
Santa Rosa, California

subject

Financing

proposed by

WESTON & WESTON
MANAGEMENT CONSULTANTS

Campus Executive Park
Berkeley, California

DESCRIPTION OF THE BUSINESS

Skylens, Inc., is an aerial photography business that first became airborne in 1987, with one plane, a Piper Cub, hangared at a small private airport near the wine fields of the Napa Valley. Used mostly for pleasure and partly for business, to finance its upkeep, the plane was assigned on its initial missions to take photographs at altitudes ranging from 100 feet to upwards of 20,000 feet. The resultant pictures were useful to vintners in selecting new sites for grape crops and in studying the comparative growth of the vines in different locations.

The business was founded by Charles ("Chick") Laurick as a hobby after he left college during his sophomore year and opened a photography studio in Berkeley. Trying to beat out the competition, represented by over 100 commercial photographers and studios in the region north of San Francisco, he took to the sky and discovered that there were many people in business, as well as residential homeowners, who would commission him to take black-and-white or color pictures of their real estate from the air. He was so successful that by 1990, the first plane had been joined by two others, a second Cub and a Cessna, and he was keeping four fellow pilots and two other photographers in business on regular assignments. They received a great deal of publicity and became known as the "Flying Fools," often risking their necks to take low-level photographs at breakneck speeds.

The business received an unpleasant jolt when its outside accounting firm came up with some shattering figures to show that Skylens had not only failed to make any profit, but was swiftly falling downward in debt. Laurick and his winged partners had failed to pay a large number of creditors and were more than $30,000 in debt to the Internal Revenue Service, the state, and the county for taxes in arrears. Adding to these woes, the Oakland Trust Company, from which Skylens had borrowed $75,000 toward the purchase of its new planes, was calling its note, plus interest and fees.

Through an agreement with one of his major clients, Sonoma Vintners, Laurick was able to obtain a $50,000 advance against the taking of a series of high-level ultraviolet photographs for the better prediction of weather and climate conditions. With this money in hand, he was able to pay off most of his creditors, pay part of the company's back taxes, and convince Oakland Trust not to call the loan.

Thoroughly cowed by his near-tragic financial debacle, Laurick hired a consulting firm, Weston & Weston, and enrolled in an intensive three-month curriculum that was recommended by one of the partners, Hugh Weston. The course covered the economics of establishing a growing business and enabled Laurick to build more solid and enduring operational plans for Skylens. At the same time, he recruited two partners who were knowledgeable in the fields of flying and photography and, with the help of his CPA, established a more dependable rate-and-cost accounting system for billing his clients.

Within one year, Skylens was operating in the black and planning future growth.

A Solid and Workable Investment Plan

Operating now with a gross of more than $3 million a year, Skylens sees many opportunities for soliciting and developing new business in other regions of the Pacific West, notably Southern California, Oregon, and Washington. With the help of their consultant and an independent marketing firm, the partners of the company have made realistic projections and estimated that they can triple their clients within three years and pass the $10 million gross income mark, yet adding only one more plane to the photographic fleet and trade in the original Cub for an upgraded model, probably a Beechcraft.

To accomplish this mission, Skylens is seeking venture capital in the amount of $1,600,000, in return for which it will grant a 15 percent interest in the company and a seat on the corporate board. The partners are open to all financial considerations and alternatives that might achieve this objective.

A Better Business Proposal for

Partyliners

presented to

Big Sky Bank & Trust
Billings, Montana

through Partyliners'
Holiday Development Staff:

JEFF FRANKLIN

BETA DE GURNY

SALLIE JO PINKNEY

MIKE SCHERER

276 Custer Boulevard
Hardin, Montana 59034

WHAT ARE OUR SERVICES?

Partyliners had its start, inauspiciously, three years ago when its four present partners, then seniors at Montana State, joined forces to decorate the gymnasium for a June "Homecoming" weekend. They had so much fun, and received so many raves from students and visitors alike, that they undertook to return to the campus to plan the decorations for a college football dance in October, a Thanksgiving dinner for senior citizens, and a pre-Christmas party for kindergarten tots. They found that they could not only have fun, but make money by buying decorations and refreshments at a big discount and charging a fee for their services.

Since all four graduates had been forced to be on their own at a time when the local economy was at a low ebb and jobs were hard to come by, they decided to merge their assorted creative and entrepreneurial talents under the Partyliners logo and promote what they already knew they could do best. Since then, they have prospered by offering hosts a fine way out of their dilemma of coping with decorations and supplies whenever they were forced into masterminding a big do, for whatever reason. They specialize in creating themes appropriate to the occasion at hand, and locating all the trimmings, no matter how demanding or unique. In fact, they quickly came to love the challenge of zeroing in on the right motifs and the best embellishments for occasions as dissimilar as Mardi Gras, *Cinquo de Mayo*, Rosh Hashana, baby showers, Derby Day, Corn Husking Holler, Custer's Last Stand, Big Sky Breakfast, River Boat Ramble, and an All Day Coffee Break. Decorations are merely the "up-front" part of the job. They often have to locate sources for unusual and difficult-to-find ethnic foods, arrange for top-star rock at rock-bottom prices, tote gargantuan props to remote locations, or make last-minute changes when threatened by party-spoiling weather. They found that clients were not always that easy to please. One wanted them to change the color of trees in the yard to match those of bridesmaid's gowns. Another wanted life-size cartoon figures that could be animated remotely at the touch of a button. And a demanding host specified that they make his desert backyard "bloom" with jungle plants.

Partyliners themes have centered around events as varied as a Parisian ballet, an English garden party, a Low Country oyster roast, a Viennese ball, opening night at a summer theater, mountain climbing, a samba carnival, a Polynesian pig roast, a Passover seder, an African Plains expedition, and river boating.

PLANNED EXPANSION

Partyliners has reached a plateau from which it now cannot move upward without substantial equity investment to help the business to grow vertically and expand horizontally. Its initial gross income ranged from under $1,000 to about $10,000 per job. With personal investments from the four principals, totaling $8,000, to mount an advertising and promotional campaign, the company attracted a number of higher-income assignments and was often billing clients upwards of $15,000 and even $20,000 in two instances. The important factor here was the realization that the larger jobs required no more managerial time and effort on the part of the partners than some of the assignments in the lower price ranges. Time-and-motion studies prepared by an outside efficiency expert verified this assumption.

With all of the statistics and data on hand, Partyliners proposes that it be considered for financing in the amount of $40,000 in two equal segments, for back-to-back special advertising and promotion campaigns to potential corporate sponsors. These would be aimed at large companies and other organizations in Billings, Butte, Great Falls, and Helena, where preliminary research and studies have already targeted more than one hundred possible sponsors who will be celebrating anniversaries or other singular events.

Financial projections indicate that the income from just ten such assignments would be more than enough to liquidate the loan or other financing within a period of just one year.

COMPETITION

Since a successful marketing effort of the kind envisioned would make it possible for Partyliners to expand its operations to cover metropolitan areas in two or more additional states, the competition can be said to be regional, not local. Even so, there are only three other firms whose experience and capabilities even begin to approach those of Partyliners. These are:

Executive Hotels Gala Affairs Group, in Denver, which occasionally accepts outside jobs to set up large galas and jubilees. However, its major thrust is internal, relating to the hotel chain's own events programs.

Theme Parties Unlimited, a Salt Lake City firm that is quite comparable to Partyliners in regard to the size and variety of projects it undertakes.

Universal Decorators, in Helena, Montana, which has a flair for design and visual imagination. However, as the name implies, the firm tends to focus much more on the decorating aspects of an event than on the programming and orchestration.

It is not anticipated that these, or other, competitors hold much threat to the growth or profitability of Partyliners.

Business Plan for

Morrison's Nursery and Lawn Care, Inc.

submitted to

The Sun Bank of Florida
Orlando, Florida
and
The Small Business Administration
Lakeland, Florida Office

submitted by

FRANK MORRISON, JR.

DAVID MORRISON

EDNA J. MORRISON

Route 7, Willow Oak Road
Lakeland, FL 24490

STATEMENT OF PURPOSE

Morrison's Nursery and Lawn Care, Inc. is seeking refinancing for the existing corporation. Following the death of the president and founder, Frank Morrison,

Sr., the business has declined. The sons of the founder, Frank Morrison, Jr. and David Morrison, along with their mother, Edna J. Morrison, want to rebuild and expand the business.

The company seeks $550,000 in an equity loan from the Sun Bank of Florida. With these funds, the business plans to restock its nursery and greatly expand its landscaping business.

DESCRIPTION OF THE BUSINESS

The business was started in 1975 by Frank Morrison, Sr., as a wholesale nursery. During its first nine years, Morrison's was in the black and enjoyed a healthy success on a local level in the community of Lakeland, Florida, located on 150 acres of fine farmland just outside the city proper. Morrison was an experienced nurseryman and was educated at Clemson University in Clemson, South Carolina. Sons Frank, Jr. and David also were educated in the nursery and landscaping business, but never elected to join their father in the business.

In 1990, Frank Morrison, Sr. suffered his first heart attack and had to hire extra employees to help him with his business. However, due to his poor health and a lack of management, the business began to decline to its present state today. When he died seven months ago of a second heart attack, his widow asked her sons to join her in rebuilding the family business.

MARKETING PLAN

The business plans to market itself as a landscape and nursery business, in the hopes of getting more commercial accounts such as shopping malls, hospitals, business centers, and the like. David Morrison is a landscape architect and has a client base from his own business that he is willing to bring to the new business. Frank Morrison, Jr. is an experienced nurseryman, who also has a client list that he is bringing with him from his company as well. The firm plans to market itself in two main ways:

1. Through the local community of Lakeland, Florida

2. Throughout the state of Florida by networking the contacts of the two brothers in the architectural and landscaping business

COMPETITION

There is one other nursery in the Lakeland area, Smith Bros. Nursery and Lawn, Inc., that is a chief competitor of the business. Following Morrison Sr.'s illness and death, the Smith firm acquired many of the key customers of the Morrison business when they became discouraged with the declining management and responsibilities of Morrison's Nursery.

There will be a need for a lot of intense marketing to regain the customers and business that were lost in the last five years. The local newspaper and radio will be essential tools for remedying this problem. However, because of the excellent location of the acreage just outside of Lakeland, the business should enjoy the benefits of its superb soils and convenient access.

Business Plan for
_____

Crown Carpet Cleaners, Inc.

submitted to

The Chase Manhattan Bank
New York, New York 10014

submitted by

JOSEPH CARLUCCI

MARK CARLUCCI

_____

STATEMENT OF PURPOSE

Crown Carpet Cleaners, Inc. is seeking a loan of $250,000 to upgrade and purchase new equipment. The loan would be paid off in a five-year period or earlier if the company's yearly profits allow for it.

The business is also taking out a large insurance policy on the debt to assure that it is paid off should any personal or business problems harm the owners, Joe and Mark Carlucci, or the business, Crown Carpet Cleaners, Inc.

DESCRIPTION OF BUSINESS

Crown Carpet Cleaners, Inc. is an older business (25 years) that has been purchased from the original owner, William Sonoma, by Mark and Joseph Carlucci. Both men are experienced tradesmen in the carpet cleaning business and have new clients to bring to the business. The business already has ten other employees who work in the office (two women) and operate other carpet cleaning machinery (eight men).

The business is located in downtown New York and is operated out of a warehouse/office operation. There are two phone lines and one fax line. The majority of the business is commercial—offices, hotels, banks—and is run on a 24-hour basis. The business is not seasonal but steady throughout the entire year.

COMPETITION

There is moderate competition in the carpet cleaning business in New York. There are three potential competitors in the marketing region where Crown Carpet Cleaners will operate:

1. Stanley Steamer Carpet, located in Manhattan, has eight employees but does not run on a 24-hour basis.

2. Village Carpet Cleaners, located in Greenwich Village, has three employees and is up for sale, but does not have the clientele or equipment to be a strong competitor.

3. O'Brien Carpet Cleaners, located in Queens, has fifteen employees, has the necessary equipment to do cleaning on a 24-hour basis, and is the chief competitor of Crown Carpet Cleaners.

MARKETING PLAN

The business will continue to build its client base through business contacts and advertising in professional and trade publications. Most clients of Crown Carpet Cleaners are commercial, not residential. Also, both of the Carlucci brothers have brought new clients with them to the new business.

Business Plan for

Facility Maintenance Services

submitted to

North Carolina National Bank

submitted by

PARKER SCOTT

ORIN WESLEY

SANDRA CUNNINGHAM

506 River Bend Drive
Durham, North Carolina

■ **PART ONE**

Condensed Presentation of the Business Plan for
FACILITY MAINTENANCE SERVICES

[Sample of a plan condensed for distribution to associates, employees, and others who might be interested in the company and its development.]

COMPANY ANALYSIS

Present Business

Facility Maintenance Services (FMS) provides property management companies with reconditioned apartments for new renters through cleaning, painting, repapering, floor conditioning, and the like. Since rentals are cyclical in nature in the communities served, which are the centers of two major colleges, one of the ever-present problems is to smooth out the workload and provide employees with steady employment. The company has been in business for five years, has forty-five employees, and brings in annual revenues of over $500,000.

Current Problems

The owner directs the operations from his home and handles most of the firm's accounting by hand, a method that is both time-consuming and inefficient. One of the current objectives is to improve the efficiency of the system, analyze costs more accurately, and save time, which can then be directed toward marketing, namely the printing and distribution of flyers under contract with a local printing firm.

Future Growth Areas

An evaluation of the types of services rendered by FMS suggests that there would be substantial growth and income potential if the firm were to expand into minor construction, for example, the repair of buildings (not necessarily all residences) that had been damaged by flood, fire, or vandalism. An advantage to this kind of expansion would be a lessening of dependency on cyclical needs (such as student housing) and an avoidance of the peaks and valleys associated with the region's apartment business. Employees would benefit through a more even flow of work assignments during the course of the entire year.

Office Operations

Facility Maintenance Services functions with two personal computers, IBM-compatible, with appropriate software, word processing, and printing facilities that make desktop publishing feasible for the preparation of information and promotional literature about the firm. Computerization includes such media as DacEasy Accounting, which includes general ledger, accounts payable, accounts receivable, inventory, billing, purchase orders, and other relevant modules; and ProfitWise, which provides easier preparation of reports and guidelines necessary to the conduct of business. However, the office situation would be greatly improved if it were located separately, instead of in the home, which would also be more professionally acceptable for meetings with clients, interviewing prospective employees, and conducting business in general.

Client Information System Analysis

The company has often sent advertising fliers to existing and potential customers. The computers are used only for letters, and there is no mail-merge facility in the word processor. A flexible and thorough Client Information System (CIS) is needed since advertising plays a strategic role in the company's business. Three alternatives are reviewed:

1. Use existing shareware (Contact Plus)
2. Use graphical Personal Information Manager (PD4)
3. Use Database Manager

Contact Plus is an interactive filing system that keeps track of important business contacts by providing a personal detailed calendar for each important client. A history of phone calls, correspondence, and notes is kept for each contact in an easy-to-use format. Contact Plus also functions as an electronic rolodex; keeps track of appointments, tickler dates, phone calls (both outgoing and incoming), and form letters; allows data search; includes an autodialer; and allows the user to classify contacts in a variety of ways using 24 customizable categories. The system also acts as a mailing list manager, whereby one can create customized form letters and send them out to contacts of one's choice. Contact Plus locates important contacts by last name, company name, or by one of the two user-defined index fields specified. One can enter the first few characters of the last name, company name, or user-defined field when searching for a particular contact.

Personal Information Manager is called *PackRat* and is a program that benefits from its use of the Windows environment. Its list of functions includes a phone book, phone log, calendar, to-do list, index card file, time manager, financial manager, project manager, and a scratch pad. Although functional power is a great asset of this package, its primary benefit is its simple and appealing graphical interface.

Database Manager, equipped with an internal programming language is the third alternative. Advantages to this type of software are its flexibility of database design and size along with the ability to customize the software to meet the client's needs. There is a definite trade-off using a database manager as opposed to the "functionally-ready" personal information manager (PIM). A database manager can retain as much information as the client desires but may require programming beyond the software's basic functions.

FoxPro is the recommended database manager. FoxPro is a dBASE-compatible program with a powerful programming language. Maintaining compatibility with dBASE assures effortless data transfers to other software programs (i.e., spreadsheets). This enables FMS to realize the main objectives in using a Client Information System: to integrate client information with the word processor; to quickly produce mass mailings of advertising; and to price information.

MARKETING

The Original Situation

The business is very cyclical, with highs in the summer months and troughs in the winter. During the peak period, demand is very high and clients sometimes become desperate. It is easy to expand the clientele during this period. However, because of a high rate of turnover of apartment office managers, it often happens that the contact is lost. Managers who are contacted during the inactive period often do not feel the urgency and forget by the time maintenance is required. Furthermore, the possibility exists that they would have been replaced by then. Flyers are regularly mailed to apartment complexes and some business is generated from them.

Strategy

The firm needs to build an effective marketing strategy. To do this it has to develop a good knowledge of:

a. *The market:* What is its size? How best to segment it?

b. *The client:* What are the needs of the client? What services are appropriate? Which are the most effective means to communicate with present and potential clients?

c. *Competition:* Who are the main competitors? What is FMS's competitive advantage?

Knowing the various market segments is crucial for success. Knowing which ones to serve is the key to success. Different market segments require different approaches. FMS is presently serving specific low-rent markets. It might be appropriate to study the market in more depth to be able to make comparisons between the different segments. We took a number of different approaches to tackle this problem. We interviewed a few apartment managers to get a feel of what they think. We discussed the potential use of building a database of apartment complexes, contacts, and the like, as discussed in the next section. We also discussed ways of improving the advertising process to make it more cost effective. Presently, flyers are being used as the main form of advertisement. Flyers are useful, but more needs to be done. In this report, we address various methods of promotion and advertising that FMS can use in order to reach the different market segments.

We recommend the use of various forms of promotion and advertising, with tracking to determine the effectiveness and costs of each. A combination of methods can then be used to reach each segment, taking into consideration the cost/benefit of each method and its pertinence. This would be followed by an adjustment of the processes and procedures in order to achieve a better combination of methods for effectively and efficiently reaching the potential clientele.

Advertising and Promotion

Advertising and promotion can be used to reach the clients, induce them to use the service, and maintain contact. Following are some methods that can be used in this market. This list is not intended to be either authoritative or comprehensive; it is only an attempt to share some practical ideas in order to stimulate creative thinking and to find better ways and means to keep in touch with clients. Use of photographs should be encouraged, especially pictures showing FMS employees at work. It is very important to project an image of real professionalism. Therefore, the medium used should be of a high quality and the work done should project an image of excellence.

Functional Promotions

FMS needs to maintain a presence in the offices of apartment complexes. This presence can be maintained by the use of various promotional items that remain in the office even when the current manager leaves. Therefore, objects that stick to the wall or require replenishment can serve this purpose well. While serving a function, these promotions provide a sense of continuity that, in turn, reduces the loss of clients when managers leave. These promotions should properly display a list of services provided by FMS and should include the relevant telephone numbers. Among the media for this purpose are calendars, year planners, rolodex cards, booklets, and folders.

Decorative Promotions

Promotions like decorative pictures with the FMS logo and telephone numbers and services available can complement or replace the functional promotions mentioned above. The same advantages given for functional promotions also apply.

Disposable Promotions

Cheap and attractive promotional items can be used to please the managers and induce them to use the services of FMS when they need them. Again, it is very important to print the telephone numbers and the types of services provided in an attractive manner on these objects, which include pencils, pens, key chains, phone rests, and refrigerator magnets.

Discounts

FMS should also consider giving a discount to first-time users of FMS services. This discount can be justified by the fact that the potential client is unsure of the quality of work and service initially provided by FMS. This method is best used during the winter months when demand is low. During the peak period, clients are usually in urgent need of service and often would even be ready to pay a premium. Discounts can also be used to maintain clients during the winter season. Care must be taken to ensure that the clients do not perceive this gesture negatively. Furthermore, considering the fact that FMS projects an image of being a quality service firm, the giving of discounts may be counterproductive. One possibility is to try this out on a small sample, analyze the outcome, and base future actions accordingly.

Comparisons

The use of these types of advertising and promotional needs requires consideration before decisions can be made. For example, prices of the different options should be gathered and compared with one another. FMS needs to obtain input from present and potential clients in order to get an idea of their preferences. Questionnaires should be used in order to collect more information about the individual clients and their perceptions and expectations.

ADDITIONAL RECOMMENDATIONS

Strategy

At this point in its history, FMS needs to have a clear strategy and well-developed objectives. This study brings to light some areas in which FMS needs to work, including management orientation and training and the use of appropriate reading materials on these topics. Once a clear strategy is formed, a plan can be developed to implement the steps required to achieve the objectives.

Computerization at FMS

The use of computers and electronic data processing at FMS are taken very seriously. Already a number of computer packages are in operation and others are in the installation phase. FMS is undergoing computerization at a fast pace, so much so that there is some danger of too heavy a reliance on hardware and software and too little on the human elements.

Personnel

Personnel is another potential for concern in this area. FMS needs knowledgeable and stable personnel to run the ever-increasing volume and complexity of computer work. The more FMS becomes dependent on the use of computers, the more disruptive the loss of personnel can become. Management needs to learn all software packages in order to maintain continuity. This might be the best approach in the present situation, but as time goes by and more packages are implemented, one might consider other alternatives such as having an additional part-time person working on some of the packages. A graduate student in computer sciences would be an ideal candidate.

Security

Computer security can take various forms but here we limit ourselves to just one. Security copies of the software and data should be made regularly, kept on diskettes, and updated when the software itself is updated. This method should ensure that in case of accidents the latest software can be recovered without problems. People tend to ignore this potential serious problem, and FMS should not make the same mistake. As for data, this should be duplicated at least once a week and stored off the premises. In case of having a lot of input in any one day, extra security copies should be made to prevent loss of data. It is prudent to have a copy of the software and the data stored in a place away from where computing is done because, in case of fire, both the computer and the security copies kept in the same area can be damaged or even destroyed. Money can replace the hardware but only copies stored off-site replace the software and the data.

■ **PART TWO**

Complete Presentation of the Business Plan for
FACILITY MAINTENANCE SERVICES

[The detailed plan as prepared to submit to potential lenders, joint enterprises, or other organizations who are interested in the company and its development.]

COMPANY ANALYSIS

Present Business

Facility Maintenance Services provides a service to property management companies. FMS's primary business is to recondition apartment interiors for new renters. This principally consists of painting and cleaning the interior of apartments between lease agreements. Painting is the primary source of FMS's work and profit, but the cleaning is provided to offer a complete service to the property management companies. Since rentals are cyclical in nature, especially in areas with high college student and faculty populations, FMS needs to smooth out its workload and provide its employees with a steady employment. The business is based in Durham but also does significant work in Greensboro and Winston-Salem. The company has been in business for five years, has approximately forty employees, and in fiscal year 1989 generated revenues of about $500,000.

Current Problems

The owner directs the operations from his home. He also does all of the firm's accounting by hand and contracts out the direct marketing, namely printing and mailing of flyers, to a local printing company. The current method of accounting is both time-consuming and inefficient. The current method of direct marketing is both time-consuming and expensive. FMS's problem is as follows: if the efficiency of the accounting system can be improved, the time spent on accounting can be decreased and costs can be better analyzed. The time saved can be better used by bringing the direct marketing in-house, thereby reducing the marketing costs and improving the efficiency.

Future Growth Area

The owner sees great potential in expanding into minor building construction (primarily repair and rehabilitation) since maintaining a steady stream of work is a major concern. FMS would, for instance, do the drywall reconstruction of a house that has been seriously damaged by fire. An advantage to this expansion into minor construction is that FMS would decrease its dependence on apartment work and thereby avoid the peaks and valleys associated with the apartment business. A disadvantage to this expansion is that FMS will have to increase its marketing efforts and attract a new category of clients.

THE OFFICE WORK

FMS currently has two personal computers (286's/IBM compatible) with VGA displays and hard disks. Current software includes an initial graphical user environment (Microsoft Windows 3.0), spreadsheet (Quattro Pro), payroll system (DacEasy Payroll), client information software (shareware software called Contact Plus) and a word processor (WordPerfect). Although the company has an abundance of software and a great willingness to learn, lack of time and difficulty of systems have prevented full implementation.

Accounting System Analysis

Currently, the company is keeping track of accounting transactions with a combination of handwritten bookkeeping coupled with some spreadsheet analysis. Accounting reports are either limited in scope, or in some cases too time-consuming to produce on a regular basis. Payroll, however, is computerized by using the software DacEasy Payroll.

Our consulting group has performed a software analysis of current accounting packages for the company. The software packages are as follows: DacEasy Accounting, Act1, Peachtree Complete III, ProfitWISE and Bedford Integrated Accounting. The analysis is based on a review by PC Magazine in a recent issue. The accounting packages were reviewed in the areas of General Ledger, Accounts Payable, Accounts Receivable, Billing, and Inventory modules. High priority has been placed on the immediate need for the Accounts Receivable module.

Business Strategy and Financial Proposal

Facility Maintenance Services, acting on the advice of an outside commercial consultant, requests equity financing in the amount of $28,000 over a period of six months in order to upgrade the operation from what is essentially a home-based enterprise to the stature of a professional community business. The requested sum would finance the following basic improvements in the business:

1. Renting a small office in the center of Durham and establishing the company's business at that location

2. Providing the office with the necessary furnishings, equipment, and signage

3. Relocating the existing computers, hardware and software, and communications equipment from home to office

4. Hiring a part-time secretary/receptionist

5. Renting a two-car parking space behind the office, for the convenience of employees and clients

With the fulfillment of these improvements and the improved image of FMS as a professional enterprise, it is anticipated that the business can be doubled within the next two years. According to the firm's consultant, "A more professional profile would be likely to orchestrate a business increase of 20 percent or more in just the first month. Also the more centralized location would be sure to attract many customers that are now missed by FMS because of its anonymous location and/or amateurish standing as a business."

Marketing Plans

Facility Maintenance Services proposes to undertake a complete renovation of its marketing plans, to focus advertising and promotion on year-round, rather than seasonal or cyclical, business operations. The aim will also be to motivate prospective customers, particularly the owners of short-term and temporary residential facilities, to plan ahead for those seasons when their business increases abruptly.

FMS fully realizes that there is a pressing need to build an effective marketing strategy, and that to accomplish this it has to acquire a better knowledge of:

1. *The market:* What is its size? How can it best be segmented?
2. *The clients:* What are their needs? What combinations of services are most appropriate?
3. *Communication:* What are the most effective media and means to communicate with present and prospective clients?
4. *Competition:* Who are the main competitors? What kinds of competitive advantages does FMS have? What kind of disadvantages?

In order to find helpful answers to these questions, FMS has computerized several studies, including an Apartment Maintenance Survey, addressed to the owners and managers of housing units, to determine what kinds of services they use for preparing properties for rentals, and what kinds of deficiencies they find in such services.

ADVERTISING AND PROMOTION

FMS has planned a new and upgraded advertising and promotional campaign, for which the following are some relevant examples:

- Redesigning the FMS logo, to make it more visible and attractive
- Preparing an office window display with "before and after" photographs to dramatize the kinds of improvements that can be made to residences in need of more tender, loving care
- Mailing a flyer to residential owners and managers, to describe FMS in brief, and using an architectural design motif to suggest professionalism
- Running small box/display ads in the real estate section of local newspapers, offering free consultation, and top service at reasonable prices
- Distributing small, inexpensive items that would be kept as reminders (with phone number and address) of FMS services, including rolodex inserts, magnetic business cards, imprinted pencils, and miniature paint brushes

FMS has also been successful in achieving free promotional impact by sending press releases to newspapers and local periodicals with an attached "MoneyBack" coin. The text includes a small chart and a description of two examples of ways in which the cost to clients of FMS services was self-liquidating because it resulted in (a) increased rental fees for apartments that were renovated, and (b) fewer apartment vacancies.

CONCLUSION

Facility Maintenance Services has come a long way in five years. This has been achieved through hard work, determination, and perseverance. Management is looking forward to a period of substantial expansion. The idea of consolidating the past achievements, computerizing the office work, and using computers in order to keep track of the clients is an excellent step in the right direction. Management needs to be relieved of the ever-increasing amount of clerical work. The decision to turn to the use of computers in order to face this challenge should prove to be productive in the future.

Business Plan for

The Old Millstone Restaurant

submitted to

Second National Bank
of Prescott Square, Virginia

submitted by

LIVINGSTON PERRILL, OWNER

AND

RENE C. DUBOIS, EXECUTIVE CHEF

The Mill House
Highland Falls, Virginia

EXECUTIVE SUMMARY

Introduction

In 1992, The Old Millstone Restaurant was founded to provide a fine dining experience for the residents and visitors of the town of Prescott and surrounding Lake Silver communities. The restaurant also attracted customers from the city of Charlotte. The restaurant is an upscale dining facility featuring French and Classic cuisine. The food is defined by high quality and innovative menus offered at reasonable prices. Service provided is attentive and unintimidating in an elegant yet casual atmosphere. The restaurant has developed a loyal following and an excellent reputation for the past three years it has been in business.

The Old Millstone Corporation will purchase The Old Millstone Restaurant from the current owner, who is retiring from the restaurant business. The current owner has scaled back operations from serving lunch and dinners to serving dinners only. The Corporation will reestablish the popular lunch and Sunday brunches while adding full-service catering and a room-service operation to the eighteen-room Davidson Village Inn.

Overall, The Old Millstone Restaurant can be characterized as a high-profile upscale fine dining establishment known for its reputation of quality and a good perceived value.

The purchase price for The Old Millstone Restaurant is $104,000. This includes equipment with a cost basis exceeding $190,000. The purchase will be paid from the following proceeds:

Bank Financing	$ 50,000
Owner Equity	$ 20,000
Seller Note	$ 40,000
Total	$110,000

The additional $6,000 will be used to fund rent deposits and inventory. This will not be sufficient to fund all costs; an additional $25,000 letter of credit to cover the beginning operations deficit and start-up costs will be needed.

The projected cash flows are sufficient to repay all financing needs for the Corporation.

The equipment included in the purchase has a cost basis exceeding $190,000.

CONCLUSION

The Old Millstone Restaurant enjoys an established track record of excellent service for our customers. Their expressions of satisfaction and encouragement are numerous, and we intend to continue our advances and growth in the food service marketplace with more unique and effective fine dining menus and catering services. It will be a pleasure to serve our guests.

Vision/Mission

Present Company

The Old Millstone Restaurant was founded in 1992 and is presently in its growth stage. The Old Millstone Restaurant can best be described as one of the area's finest dining establishments for French and Classic cuisine, offering full food and beverage service. In recent times our key strengths have been an exquisite menu for fine dining, excellence in customer service, a strong management team, and innovative marketing.

The current owner is a well-known world-class chef with an extensive history and reputation as a leader in the culinary arts profession. After a brilliant sixty-year career, the current owner wishes to retire and turn over the operations to new owners. We are ready to continue the standards of excellence set forth by The Old Millstone Restaurant. The restaurant has a dedicated following of clientele and the company is now ready to branch out in new directions.

Management

Most of our management team is in place; however, we will need to retain the assistant chef and wait staff to complete our team. The present sous chef and waiters and waitresses have agreed to remain on staff. We are currently planning on hiring two to three additional employees to fill the positions of additional wait staff, and kitchen personnel for prep/pantry and dishwasher.

Products and Services

At present the business is serving dinner only and is in a mature stage. We feel the current product line and services are in need of extension. By popular demand we plan to re-open for the lunch trade and to introduce a Sunday brunch. We will also introduce full-service catering both on and off the premises. This service is currently being developed and will include all aspects of catering, from gourmet picnics and boxed lunches to formal meals.

Market Environment

The marketplace has been undergoing rapid changes for the past several years. We are now poised to expand the business by offering other services such as those described above. The area is growing and the market has expanded to the surrounding Lake Silver communities as well as customers from the city of Prescott. Now is the time to take advantage of these opportunities and to expand the company's profits.

Pricing and Profitability

Current prices are holding and profits are increasing. With the expansion of services offered we should increase the volume of sales and therefore increase profits.

Customers

Currently customers are frequenting the restaurant for dinner only. Numerous requests have been made that the restaurant open for lunch and for the Sunday brunch offered previously. There are requests for the restaurant to offer catering services both off and on the premises. We wish to capture this market. With the type of food service we offer and with the contacts we have in the industry, we will be particularly well suited for wedding and bridal functions. We will offer catering for all occasions, from boxed picnic lunches to extravagant formal sit-down dinners and receptions.

Distribution

We have one restaurant location in Prescott, Virginia, with 60 percent of the clientele from the surrounding Lake Silver communities and 40 percent from other nearby locales.

Vision and Mission

By the year's end, The Old Millstone Restaurant will be a highly visible company known as one of the very best fine dining restaurants and caterers in the food service industry. We will have developed a diverse menu for all occasions of fine dining and classical catering. We will have marketed these products and services throughout the Lake Silver and Prescott areas. We will be a leader in the restaurant community. Sales after one year will exceed $600,000 and we forecast sales to exceed $700,000 within two years. The Old Millstone Restaurant will actively be promoting full-service dining and catering. We will achieve the forecasted sales through increased operating hours and services not provided by the current owner.

Mission Statement

In order to achieve our vision, The Old Millstone Restaurant commits to the following objective: to provide innovative, practical, and top-quality products that will improve and on all occasions enhance the quality of our guests' dining experience. The most exquisite food, the best service, and a conceptual good value for their money will create a memorable and totally enjoyable experience for consumers with today's hectic and busy lifestyles. We believe our first responsibility is to the customers who use our products and services. Our strong financial position will enable us to produce a high-quality product: exquisite cuisine in an elegant atmosphere.

In carrying out our day-to-day business we strive to:

1. Treat our employees with respect, consideration, and fairness. They are the keys to our success.
2. Follow the philosophy that our customers are number one, to be treated as though they are invited guests in a private home, and more than welcome.
3. Be considered as the leader of fine dining and congenial hospitality in the community.

Through a long-term commitment to this mission, we will be known as a company that cares and produces only the very best of quality and service. Our customers, vendors, and employees see The Old Millstone Restaurant as offering the finest foods and services, totally committed to customer needs, always producing results in the most professional manner.

Goals

In order for The Old Millstone Restaurant to attain its vision described in our mission statement, the following primary strategic goals need to be achieved:

Corporate: Within four months, The Old Millstone Restaurant will have increased sales by adding the lunch trade and by having established a full-service catering operation.

Products: During this period, The Old Millstone Restaurant will also develop Sunday brunches and a full-service catering operation.

Market: Within six months, The Old Millstone Restaurant will expand its market to the regions surrounding the Lake Norman area and to the Charlotte market.

Sales: Each month will see increasing expansion in income.

COMPANY OVERVIEW

Legal Business Description

The Old Millstone, Incorporated; Old Millstone Properties, Inc.; and The Old Millstone Restaurant.

Legal Form of Business

The legal form of Old Millstone is a Subchapter S Corporation.

Legal Business Location

Piedmont Building, 600 Forest Drive, Prescott, Virginia

Management

Our management team consists of two people, whose professional backgrounds consist of over twenty-five years of sales, marketing, public relations, administrative and corporate development, with diverse managerial experience in the food service and retail industries:

Livingston Perrill, President and Secretary

Frank Claflin Essex, Vice President and Treasurer

Stock Allocation

To be determined.

Responsibilities

The president develops and maintains the vision of the company. Oversees marketing, product development, production and finance, and customer service. Approves all financial obligations. Seeks business opportunities and strategic alliances with other companies and organizations. Plans, develops, and establishes policies and objectives of the business organization in accordance with board directives and the company charter. Directs and coordinates financial programs to provide adequate funding for new or continuing operations in order to maximize the return on investments and increase productivity.

The vice president and treasurer manages market planning, advertising, public relations, sales promotion, merchandising, and facilitating staff services. Seeks new markets and conducts market research. Oversees product research and analysis as well as the evaluation of the competition. Identifies and sets strategy for reaching foreign markets. Analyzes sales figures. Directs staffing, training, and performance evaluations to develop and control sales programs. Manages sales programs and distribution by establishing sales territories, quotas, and goals and advises dealers and distributors concerning sales and advertising techniques. Analyzes sales statistics to formulate policy and to assist dealers in promoting sales. Manages working capital including receivables, inventory, cash, and marketable securities. Performs financial forecasting including capital budget, cash budget, pro forma financial statements, external financing requirements, and other financial condition requirements. Directs financial affairs of the organization. Prepares financial analysis of operations for guidance of management. Prepares reports that outline company's financial position in areas of income, expenses, and earnings, based on past, present, and future operations. Directs preparation of budgets and financial forecasts. Arranges for audits of company's accounts.

Outside Support

Additionally, our outside management advisors provide tremendous support for management decisions and creativity:

Armond Rea, Accountant/CPA and Business Consultant

Julia Sussin Trevor, Corporate Attorney

Jocylin Bouton, Data Processing Consultant

Homer Mecklin, M.D., Medical Advisor

Chef's Biography

Rene Cedi DuBois, AOS Degree, Culinary Institute of America. Professional experience includes many different areas in the culinary arts and food service industry. He has been involved as an Executive Chef for over 20 years in a broad spectrum of businesses, from restaurants and country clubs to major hotel corporations with five-star ratings. His past experiences have provided him with a tremendous training background and foundation in executive management covering many diverse areas of the food service and catering industry. He has been recognized as one of America's "Most Outstanding Chefs" with Chefs of America National Registry.

Staffing

The Old Millstone's development team recognizes that additional staff is required to properly implement marketing, sales research, and support functions.

Currently, The Old Millstone Restuarant is composed of two management and four food service and wait staff people. Additional staff may be required at a later date to meet the demands of the projected market over the next five years.

Strategic Alliances

The corporation has formed some very important relationships with major companies in the food service and wedding service industries. The following is a list of existing alliances:

Mecklenburg Bridal Gallery
Charlotte Image Photography
Shelton Florist
Les Pavilion Florist
Dillards Department Store
Belk Department Store
Party Reflections
Cakes by Gayle
Ice Sensation, Inc.
Carolina Bride Magazine
Elegant Bride Magazine

Third-Party Supplier Agreements

We feel we require features and components from outside resources to enhance the attractiveness of the catering services offered to our customers. Because we do not have the resources to supply all equipment necessary for catering, we rely on outside suppliers for products and services to offer full-service functions to our clientele. Wedding cakes, fountains, tents, chairs, tables, and extra linens are such examples of the valuable cooperation with third-party suppliers.

The Old Millstone Restaurant has established relationships with the following: party rentals, florists, cake suppliers, ice carvers, photographers, and musicians, and agreements are being negotiated with other local suppliers and purveyors deemed necessary and beneficial to our success in the field of dining and catering.

MARKET ANALYSIS

Market Definition

In the markets of The Old Millstone Restaurant, currently there are not any other French or Continental fine dining establishments within the immediate vicinity. The closest competitor would be in another town or we would compete with other food service providers on a different scale. Our establishment is the most upscale in fine dining.

The current market suggests that there are no other comparable restaurants offering the services we will provide. The fact that there are an adjacent hotel without food service, numerous surrounding businesses, existing housing in affluential neighborhoods, the community college campus across the street, and nearby construction of more housing and business center developments, assures us that the customer base will provide excellent support for the expanding business.

Market Analysis

Due to growth and competition, independent restaurants must accommodate consumer lifestyle trends. Competing in the current climate, and aware of the changes taking place all over, we must examine trend signals, reevaluate our menus, and improve the ambience to develop and create new concepts. At The Old Millstone Restuarant we plan to offer a diversity in taste and encourage the rediscovery of fine French and classical foods and wines, and we have adjusted the attitude of the fine dining concept.

Using our upscale menu of high quality, innovative, and creative foods, which are sensibly executed and presented for reasonable prices, we have created exceptional service—elegant yet unintimidating, with a casual sense of enjoyment.

Market Segment

Our target market includes the town of Prescott and surrounding Lake Silver communities. In the past as many as 40 percent of the customers also came from the city of Prescott.

Business Risk

We would be unrealistic not to evaluate possible setbacks. The top business risk that The Old Millstone Restaurant faces as it begins to expand in the food service market is restaurant trends and the state of the economy. There may also be some seasonality risks involved. Being located in a college town may also affect the flow of business. We feel the town and surrounding communities will continue to support the business.

MARKETING PLAN

Sales Strategy

The Old Millstone Restuarant's marketing strategy is to enhance, promote, and support the fact that our restaurant offers convenience, quality and value, health and nutrition, a diversity in taste, and a casual attitude that makes our dining experience most enjoyable.

We plan to treat the entire dining experience as a long-term product for customers, with repeat sales on a regular basis. The target market segment we are focusing on are local professional people and their families in the mid-to-high-income bracket, who enjoy dining out on a regular basis at restaurants that offer more than ordinary institutional or fast-food style.

The Old Millstone Restaurant is incorporating plans to sell our food service products through several channels. We will focus on attracting customers from the local business trade, local residents, professionals from the college, corporate travelers, and visitors from area hotels and motels. We will also receive referral business from the outside vendors and businesses we network with regarding our catering services.

The determining factors in choosing these channels are low cost and effectiveness in targeting specific customer markets. Our mix of distribution channels will give us the advantages over our competition of specific customers and providing food service for varying levels of their needs.

ADVERTISING AND PROMOTION

Our advertising and promotion strategy is to position The Old Millstone Restaurant as the leading provider in the market. We will utilize several advertising channels of various media, including newspapers, magazines, dining guides, travel and visitor brochures, outposting our menus and catering services, and networking with cooperative outside vendors.

For the next two years, the company will focus on the following strategies:

Press releases of business events

Display ads in the dining and entertainment sections of local newspapers and magazines

Advertising in the Bell South Real Yellow Pages under appropriate categories defining all of our services

Advertising in the regional Bridal Magazine

Participating in local trade shows

Outposting our services within other local businesses such as hotels, motels, and inns

We anticipate increased sales and profits from increased advertising and increased services offered, and we will maintain the following objectives:

Position The Old Millstone Restaurant as the leading fine dining and catering restaurant in the market

Increase company awareness and brand-name recognition among local businesses and customers

Develop, through market research, significant information to create immediate and long-term marketing plans

Create product advertising programs supporting the better taste, more pleasant atmosphere position

Promote awareness of the company among industry groups and potential customers

Establish an image of The Old Millstone Restaurant as an organization that is professional, completely reliable, and highly positioned in the market

Maximize efficiency in selection and scheduling of published ads in publications to cover the food service and catering markets

Media Strategy

Select primary business publications with high specific market penetration

Schedule adequate frequency of ads to impact market with corporate image and product messages

Where possible, position advertising in or near articles on industry, product reviews, and appropriate editorials

Take advantage of special high-interest issues of major publications when possible

Maximize ad life with monthly and weekly publications

To get the most out of our promotional budget, focus coverage on a sophisticated audience

ADVERTISING CAMPAIGN

The best way to reach our potential customers is to develop an intense advertising campaign promoting our basic premise, theme, and position in the market. To establish and maintain our company image, the delivery and tone of our statements will be understated elegance and excellence.

Ideally, after becoming familiar with our product, many consumers will become regular patrons. Accordingly, The Old Millstone will create a system of research and response to ensure the maximum benefit from our advertising dollars.

Forecasted Statement of Income
for the Seven Months Ending December 31, 1995
and Years Ending December 31, 1996 and 1997

	Comparative Historical Information*			Forecasted		
	1992	1993	1994	1995	1996	1997
Sales	41,350	92,204	151,371	276,883	662,243	763,960
Cost of Sales	(12,184)	(33,178)	(50,934)	(96,909)	(231,785)	(267,386)
Gross Profit	29,166	58,026	100,437	179,974	430,458	496,574
Operating Expenses						
Advertising	283	673	3,161	4,000	6,000	7,200
Chef Salary	10,295	15,215	15,169	15,169	26,004	26,400
Credit Card Fees	1,276	366	3,874	4,458	10,662	12,300
Depreciation	13,683	24,610	18,691	5,583	12,958	14,292
Insurance	225	1,244	1,735	4,000	6,000	7,500
Licenses	5	722	1,055	1,200	1,500	1,750
Linen & Laundry				1,225	2,220	3,000
Miscellaneous	2,680	837	1,527	3,500	6,000	6,600
Office Supplies	2,470	125	2,205	1,250	1,500	1,800
Owner's Salary				35,000	60,000	66,000
Payroll Service				245	456	540
Payroll Taxes		1,471	1,217	4,613	8,142	9,125
Professional Fees		1,087		3,200	2,520	2,700
Rent	24,024	22,410	26,968	15,729	26,964	26,964
Repairs & Maintenance	4,533	251	2,734	4,200	7,200	8,400
Replacements				1,050	2,400	3,600
Sales Tax	1,189	6,927	6,878	19,382	46,357	53,477
Telephone	210	1,656	2,230	1,150	1,800	2,100
Utilities	2,023	5,267	7,116	5,050	8,825	9,125
Wait Staff	438		7,519	10,127	20,425	26,875
Total Operating Expenses	63,334	82,911	102,079	140,130	257,933	289,747
Income From Operations	(34,168)	(24,885)	(1,642)	39,844	172,524	206,827
Other Income and Expenses						
Bank Loan Interest	0	509	0	2,418	4,221	3,328
Owner Financing Interest	0	0	0	1,056	3,780	2,648
Other Income	0	(17,688)	0	0	0	0
	0	(17,179)	0	3,474	8,001	5,976
Net Income	(34,168)	(7,706)	(1,642)	36,370	164,523	200,851

*Based upon current owners tax returns.

Forecasted Statement of Cash Flows
for the Seven Months Ending December 31, 1995
and Years Ending December 31, 1996 and 1997

	1995	1996	1997
CASH FLOW FROM OPERATING ACTIVITIES:			
Net Income	36,370	164,523	200,851
Adjustments to reconcile net income (loss) to net cash provided by operating activities:			
Depreciation	5,583	12,958	14,292
Increase in Accounts Receivable	(494)	(168)	(102)
Increase in Deposits	(2,100)	0	0
Increase in Inventory	(5,000)	0	0
Increase in Accounts Payable	4,759	1,615	979
Net cash provided by (used in) operating activities	39,118	178,929	216,020
CASH FLOWS FROM INVESTING ACTIVITIES:			
Loan Costs	(400)	0	0
Purchase of Equipment	(120,000)	(15,000)	(20,000)
Net cash used in investing activities	(120,400)	(15,000)	(20,000)
CASH FLOWS FROM FINANCING ACTIVITIES:			
Line of Credit	0	0	0
Bank Loan	46,044	(8,527)	(9,421)
Owner Financing	38,793	(3,820)	(4,138)
Capital Contributions	20,000	0	0
Net cash provided by financing activities	104,837	(12,347)	(13,559)
Net increase (decrease) in cash	23,555	151,582	182,461
Cash Beginning	0	23,555	175,137
Cash Ending	23,555	175,137	357,597

Sales Analysis 1995

	Monday	Tuesday	Wednesday	Thursday	Friday	Saturday	Sunday	Weekly Total	Average Price	Average Monthly Sales
Dining—# of people										
Lunch Food	25		35	40	50			150	7.95	4,969
Lunch Alcohol	4		5	6	8			23	5.00	469
Dinner Food	20		28	38	50	70		206	27.95	23,900
Dinner Alcohol	3		4	6	8	11		31	15.00	1,931
Brunch Food							40	40	20.00	3,333
Brunch Alcohol							6	6	7.50	188
										34,880
Catering—# of events										
Wedding Reception						1		1.0	2,800.00	2,800
Room Service–Davidson Inn—# of people										
Breakfast	8		8	8	8			32	8.14	1,085
Dinner	5		5	5	5	5		25	23.40	2,438
										3,523
Average monthly sales										41,203

Seasonality Analysis 1995

	Jan	Feb	March	April	May	June	July	Aug	Sept	Oct	Nov	Dec	Total
Percentage of sales	10.00%	12.00%	9.00%	7.00%	6.00%	5.00%	6.00%	7.00%	8.00%	9.00%	10.00%	11.00%	100.00%
Sales for month	0	0	0	0	0	24,722	29,666	34,610	39,555	44,499	49,443	54,388	276,883

Memorandum to

Stanton Center Review Board
Upper Falls, Kansas

From:

Monica Keller and Susan Tremont

Date:

February 20, 1998

Subject:

*Proposal for establishing
a day care center*

The Situation

Despite the rash of people who think it would be a fine idea to start a small home-based business as a day care center, there are many problems and ramifications. Day care providers need to stay informed of federal programs and proposals because of the direct consequences of new and existing day care businesses. For example, even after a proposal has been approved by the township, major shifts in public attitudes toward the provision of quality child care might occur, often as the result of some unfortunate incident at a day care center in the region.

Although starting a day care business is relatively easy, the legal issues facing the potential day care center operator or in-home provider are complex. Because of recent court cases, day care providers must have a substantial knowledge of the laws for operating a center or providing care in the home.

Child care providers need to have a clear understanding of their relationship with the children and which decisions are theirs to make concerning the children in their care. An important step in precluding lawsuits filed by parents is to require them to sign a consent form that outlines the policies of the center and the procedures to be followed in special situations and emergencies. Also, the responsibilities and expectations of the day care provider and the parents should be clearly understood.

Proper insurance coverage is essential to cover the costs of lawsuits, liabilities, and unexpected expenses. Even though precautions may be taken, accidents can happen. Therefore, the child care provider should be covered with liability insurance in case of an accident resulting in injury. Coverage should include the following:

- General liability, which protects against claims of injury or property damage involving clients

- Fire, business interruption, and crime insurance

- Workers compensation, unemployment insurance, and optional employee benefits such as health and life insurance

BUSINESS PLAN

Having evaluated the above considerations, and having taken extensive training programs at Kansas State University, Monica Keller and Susan Tremont wish to assure the review board that they are fully competent to conduct a day care business. The plan is to use an existing facility, the former children's day center at the First Presbyterian Church of Upper Falls (which has moved to a new building), which can be leased at a modest monthly charge. It is fully equipped and has all the facilities needed for instruction, recreation, refreshments, toilets, and first aid, among other amenities.

BUSINESS NAME

The venture has already been incorporated under the name of Upper Falls Day Care, Inc., a name that has been registered in Greenwood County, using UFDC as its acronym.

CASH FLOW ANALYSIS

Although most businesses require a cash investment to get started, UFDC is already assured of being self-liquidating as a result of tuitions pledged by parents, and with enough funds for two months' supplies and outfittings. Cash flow projections have been made to help determine the following: start-up costs, regular maintenance, and estimated monthly payments by those using the services.

FUNDING REQUIRED

The business plan requires an advance investment of $68,000, to be repaid within a two-year period. The money from this will be utilized for:

1. The immediate purchase of a van to be kept on the property and used mainly for obtaining supplies and emergency transportation, if needed
2. The initial salary for hiring two part-time helpers for a start-up period of four months
3. Payment of insurance premiums for the purposes described above

Future payments by parents and others will adequately compensate for maintenance, depreciation, new equipment, modifications to the building or exterior facilities, taxes, utilities, and of course the remuneration of the owners of the business.

MARKETING

UFDC already has a modest marketing plan to attract potential users of the service. The owners of the business have paid, out of pocket, for leaflets describing the day care center, for signs, for visits with prospective patrons, and for small advertisements in educational newsletters and two weekly newspapers. These payments will not be charged against the company.

SAFETY

In every aspect of the design of the center and its facilities, safety has ranked number one in priority. The center, which was initially approved by the Presbyterian church's Safety Board, was examined very carefully by Safety Consultants, Inc., and certified under all existing regulations of the State of Kansas.

UNIFORMS

Children at the day care center will not be required to wear any special kind of clothing except that which the parents deem to be comfortable, sanitary, and compatible with seasonal and weather conditions. At some future date, however, UFDC intends to make available several items that will be of interest to young children, including caps, T-shirts, and emblems. These will be available at cost plus an overcharge of no more than 10% for procuring and handling.

INCOME PROJECTIONS

The following annual figures, subject to change, provide a realistic profile of the financial structure of the business, estimating from past experiences in this Kansas community the number of children who will be served, on average, and the income to be derived, once the center is in full operation:

10 toddlers @$13/day × 260 days	$ 33,800
24 three-year to school-age children @11.50/day	71,760
28 kindergartners @10.50/day	76,440
Food reimbursement	7,346
Total income	$189,346

It has been highly recommended by all concerned, as well as by several members of the review board, that this proposed venture be approved as a vital service to the community.

A Diversified Business Plan and Application
for Economic Assistance on Behalf of

Rekord Chek Services

1100 Marilla Avenue
Ampora, California

presented to

Pacific Credit Affiliates
Seaward Building
San Juan, California

presented by the Principals of the Business

JOHNSON K. KORMER, OWNER

EMILE KNIGHT KORMER, MANAGER

JANE E. CARDOVA, RESEARCHER

BUSINESS HISTORY

Rekord Chek, commonly known in the field as "The Double K," from the initials of the founders, had its origins when the Kormers, a husband-and-wife team of educational researchers, were selected and commissioned to undertake a major on-campus research project by the University of San Diego. During the course of searching out the necessary data and compiling statistics, they began to realize that many of the strategies and programs for this kind of research were antiquated, poorly classified, and often undependable. So they began to perfect better systems of (a) determining where to seek information, (b) cataloging their findings, and (c) presenting their conclusions in media that were clear and easy to apply to the essentials expressed and outlined.

As the university program neared its completion, Johnson and Emile Kormer prepared for their economic future by surveying community needs in San Diego and Riverside Counties and seeking out prospective clients. They narrowed their search to colleges and universities, banks, government offices, and nonprofit institutions—all of which were constantly in need of accurate and dependable research data for the normal conduct of their operations. When they had compiled a suitable list of prospects, they mailed out a small brochure entitled, "Reliable Research at Your Doorstep," which described the new firm, Rekord Chek Services and outlined the kinds of research, investigation, and analysis that could be expected by clients.

FINANCIAL REQUIREMENTS

Now that the small firm has been functioning successfully and expanding steadily over a period of more than three years, the owner and other principals foresee an excellent opportunity for both horizontal and vertical growth in an area covered by three southern California counties—the two already mentioned plus the eastern portion of Los Angeles County. They base their optimism not on wishful thinking or their own opinions, but on a comprehensive economic study of the region undertaken within the past twelve months by the business school of the University of Southern California. In this 346-page report, some 16 pages were devoted to problems caused, and income lost, because of poor research. More important, a section with the subtitle "The Research Mine—Gold or Iron?" concluded that even when the research was adequate, "the dismal and ineffectual efforts to communicate the findings often left the sponsor with no more conception of the steps to take than if the research had never been undertaken."

Rekord Chek Services has carefully prepared an overview of the situation and has evaluated steps that could be taken to develop the business in a practical and realistic manner. The firm hereby requests a sum of $18,000 as an initial shot in the arm and an additional $17,000 within four to six months. The owner and principals of the firm are certain that the entire sum-whether loan, equity financing, or credit advance—can be liquidated, with interest, within less than eighteen months from the dates of receipt. They base their assumption on the following program aimed at putting this funding to good use.

ECONOMIC APPLICATIONS

Under the formal proposal for future development, the initial sum of $18,000 would be used as follows:

- To use ongoing research to make a list of 1,000 businesses, organizations, and bureaus that could benefit from the capabilities, experience, and facilities of the firm

- To prepare a revised brochure about the firm and its capabilities

- To seek professional consultation in this field by experts knowledgeable about both the business and the demography of the market

Chapter 4

Plans
for
Small
Manufacturers

This chapter contains model business plans for small manufacturing operations, selected to give readers a variety of types and circumstances. One of these plans, however, is presented in a more descriptive fashion, using a number of boxes and sidebars that describe significant elements and factors that must be used as guidelines for this kind of compilation. This particular SBP case history is based on a real plan, changed only to make it shorter, to eliminate some excessive supporting material, and to protect confidentiality by disguising the identity of the original.

The plan, for a manufacturer titled Digital Data Communications, describes an existing facility whose owners propose that they enlarge their business, with sound counsel from SCORE—the Service Corps of Retired Executives.

MANUFACTURING PROPOSALS AND PLANS

If you are creating a business plan in the field of manufacturing you should be familiar with the term *manufacturing engineering*, which may play a significant part in your presentation. Also referred to as *production engineering*, this is the scope of operations that fits into the manufacturing sequence between product design and full-scale production. It encompasses the following:

Process engineering, which develops the logical sequence of manufacturing operations for each product or part

Tool engineering, the adaptation of existing tools and the creation of new ones for the particular job(s) on hand and scheduled

Materials handling, the physical movement of materials and parts from one part of a plant or assembly line to another

Plant engineering, the designing of plant layouts to locate tools, equipment, personnel, and supplies so they can be processed in the most efficient and economical manner

Standards and methods, a quality-control function that assures that each product or component complies with the exact specifications, and that working methods and practices support the specified procedures

The purpose of manufacturing (or production) engineering is to design the product to overcome any problems foreseen in its eventual manufacture. One of the major responsibilities of a production manager in a small- to medium-size manufacturing company is to determine whether (a) to manufacture a product in total or contract with another producer to do so, (b) let out contracts for some of the parts of a product and make the rest and handle the assembly, or (c) obtain all of the parts from an outside producer and just be involved with assembly.

These decisions should be clear and precise in your business plan. They rest on many factors, and therefore you should give prime consideration in your proposal to the following factors, among others:

- Demand for the product, whether short- or long-term

- Permanency of the product, whether it will virtually remain the same over the next few years or require substantial changes to avoid technological obsolescence

- Competitive advantages gained by choice of product design or production equipment

- Integration with other products, materials, and services offered by the company

- Suitability of present manpower and equipment in regard to the end product

- Effect on quality of the product

- Cost of operating and maintaining the production equipment

- Source and availability of capital for each option

These are the kinds of decisions that you, as a small manufacturer, have to make.

ONE WAY TO SCORE: A PLAN-WRITING EXERCISE FOR A SMALL MANUFACTURER

When Melville Parker and his two partners in a small production and marketing business, Digital Data Communications, decided to look for investment support and enlarge their business, they turned to SCORE for counsel and help. SCORE (Service Corps of Retired Executives) advised the DDC team to prepare a detailed business plan for that purpose. Two SCORE representatives then described the nature and purpose of the proposed business plan and gave the three partners an outline for this purpose, in the form of an extended worksheet.

The outline is reprinted below, with the initial rough draft notations of the partners shown in italics. Use this as a model for getting started in the preparation of your own business plan.

I.   History of the Company

    A.   Date and place, including state of incorporation as well as pre-incorporation organizational structure.

    Rock Ridge, PA. Start. Later Upper Falls. Started as sole ownership, later partnership.

    B.   Founding shareholders and directors.

    No directors. Just Melville P. & wife & one daughter.

    C.   Important changes in the structure of company, its management, or its ownership.

    Partnership setup. First with Lucius Goss (p.r. and journalism), *then Bob* Farsley (law). MP as Sr. Partner.

    D.   Company's major successes or achievements in the field to date.

    At start, a good idea, appeal to local business owners. *A* centralized, computerized accounting and *recording service. Then, phasing into* easily made products, for easier *computation and use.*

II.   Business *Summary*

    A.   Principal products or services.

    Easy-to-use forms and graphs, etc. Registered name E-Z *File. Kept increasing numbers and kinds available to clients, customers.*

    B.   Describe the unique features of the business. Compare these with the competition.

    Bought forms at first on discount. Then got equipment and started making own. Not much competition, and we had an edge because we could formulate them to fit client's needs.

    C.   Detailed breakdown of sales or services for the current year and for the past five years.

    Gross sales five years ago only $230m, and up a little next two, but doubling for last three years.

    D.   Breakdown of *sales* by industries.

    Mainly four fields of customers: retailers, jobbers, wholesalers, communicators.

E.   Product brand names, price range, and quality.

E-Z File. Then a "Junior" EZ File for computer nuts. Prices always an edge below competition. Quality OK.

F.   Capital goods versus consumer goods. How cyclical or seasonal?

Mostly consumer. Seasonal simple to anticipate, such as tax time and end-of-year records. When businesses putting data together for a purpose. Also some clients have inventory periods we can meet for them well ahead of time.

G.   Patents, trademarks, and other trade advantages such as geographic or labor advantages.

All E-Z File *names* and *sub-names registered OK.* No labor-intensive needs. In good geo area for kinds of clients we want.

H.   Describe any technological trends.

We have to keep abreast of computer hardware, software, and data-processing equipt improvements & we do.

III.   Manufacturing Plan

A.   Plant location and size. Products.

Near our homes. So no commuting problems for partners or staff. Outskirts of Upper Falls.

All products are printable forms, graphs, etc., plus a move to supply *holders and* dispensers for these, for office use or in plants or on sites.

B.   Describe levels of current operations.

We *should explain* the sequence of operations, such as: where and how to get supplies. Designing forms. Printing operations. Collating and *distribution.*

C.   List auto equipment, including delivery trucks, number of vehicles, and whether rented or owned. What are the lease arrangements?

Not a big deal. Several leased carriers. Staff cars all owned. *Much use* of public transport, readily available.

D.   Depreciation policies.

Plant equipment very *durable.* Less than 5% depreciation per year. ****Important point for getting financing.

E.   Plant efficiency.

High rating, because nothing older than five years.

F. What is the general housekeeping condition?

Tops! Also good point for financing. As owners of business, we all make *damned sure* we keep things neat & tidy. And *in place.*

G. Is the operation job-shop or mass-production oriented?

Mostly J/S. Could see trend toward M/P in five years.

H. Logic for plant locations.

No reason for changing location. Transport and supply points all convenient and cost-reasonable.

I. What future capital expenditures for plant and machinery are planned? How will they be financed?

We need to write our ideas into business plan, in detail. Some damned good new computerized equipment now being developed by *high-tech firms.* State-of-art equipt. would improve customer service and capabilities for enlargement.

This *kind* of financing can pay off all around. Let's emphasize that in the B/P.

IV. Personnel Plan

A. Number of personnel:

Management: 5. Staff: 14. Others: 12–27. Temps: occasional.

B. Union affiliation:

None, except for employees in carriers and services we do business with.

C. Turnover and morale:

Turnover: almost nil. Morale: *high, because* we have excellent personnel facilities, and profit plans for all regular employees.

D. Labor market:

Excellent in our *region—should we* have to enlarge plants *and increase* hiring.

E. Fringe benefits:

All regular insurance for employees. Profit sharing. *Recreational facilities on* site. Small cafeteria. Etc. etc. (details to be *added* to business *plan*).

V.   Products or Services

A brief description of significant materials and supplies, including availability.

As mentioned above. Availability *no* problem. Are the storage and material handling facilities adequate?

Not at present. One reason for business plan is to obtain funding to increase these.

Does the finished inventory have a shelf-life?

Since most products are paper or composition, shelf-life is almost perpetual. Also, non-fading inks used on all printing.

VI. Marketing and Sales

Describe the market. History, size, trend, and your product's position in the market.

DDC is at forefront of service & sales in its marketing region. But market is getting more competitive and we must make this point in our bus/plan: our position could be threatened unless we get the financing needed to maintain state-of-the-art standing.

Is the market at the take-off stage? Project the market back five years and forward five years.

Another strong point to emphasize in bus/plan: With more and more prospective customers moving into our marketing area, we are poised for a take-off. Business doubled in past five years and most likely to continue so in next five.

Where are the products sold, and who is the essential end user?

Our products are all regional—northwestern PA. End users are any & all businesses that need forms, charts, graphs, records, etc., etc. (And what business doesn't????)

Are the products sold by salaried or commissioned sales force, by distributors, by brokers, or ?

Most sales are direct, by co. staffers. However, we should stress we could expand the business if given enough funding to solicit outside brokers, distributors, and independent sales reps.

Number of customers or active accounts.

NOW: 120–150. IF BUS/PLAN GOES INTO EFFECT: 250–400.

Describe any special relationships with customers.

Most are loyal. About 80% of sales is repeat business.

VII. Advertising and Related Costs and Operations

Annual budget and media used.

$40,000+ Would like to triple this in next two years.

Is business seasonal? If so, explain peaks in production, sales, and so forth.

Yes, to the extent that we have to gear up for normal paperwork surges, such as tax dates, annual report deadlines, end-of-year reports, and the like. No problem, though.

With new equipment we are proposing for purchase, we can balance our print runs so it is quite an even flow from month to month over an entire year.

Selling costs as a percentage of revenues. How will these vary with more or less sales volume?

Our plan is to obtain more sales volume and consequently less cost per increment of volume. We can easily accomplish these goals under the new plan.

Customers' primary motivation to purchase your product:

Our ads cite lower cost, more useful working designs of forms, and on-time delivery—to cite only three pluses.

VIII. Competition

A. List major competitors and their pros and cons.

Arrow Office Services. Too national, not much local loyalty.

Barrow & Barrow. Very local. A good firm, but more interested strictly in legal forms.

George and Arthur Jones, Inc. Very cutthroat. Uses questionable tactics. Covers PA, DE, and part of NJ.

B. Is new competition entering the field?

Not yet. And especially not if our new business plan is completed, which will discourage competition.

C. Compare your company's prices with the competition.

Competitive. Plus we give better service.

D. Share of the business you receive by market area.

About 30%. With new funding and equipment, we can expect upwards of 40%.

E. Independent firms, publications, or outside agencies which have evaluated your firm against competitors.

None. But we should consider this for next year as part of our business plan.

F. Effects of regulatory agencies, including government.

Don't know. We should look into this. Maybe incorporate in B/P.

IX. Research and Development

A. Amount or percent of sales spent per annum in the past five (5) years and projected. Compare with competitors. Detail any capitalized R & D costs.

Less than 2% in past. *Should be double?* Needs a new look, and professional study. Have *had only* one *such* study. Two years ago.

B. Number of employees in this area. Advanced college degrees.

Two, but only on part-time basis. Have relied on outside counsel. Question: Is cost of a full-time *R&D* staff worth it to business? *Should consider for BIP.*

C. Percent of current sales generated by past R & D.

Unknown. Needs review and attention.

X. Management

A. Is an organization chart included?

B. Are resumes included?

C. Are references included?

Answer to all three of the above: They will be *included in the Business Plan.*

D. Have credit and personal investigation checks been performed?

Yes, and will be included.

E. Is there an ongoing profit improvement plan? A sound executive incentive program?

These are being developed—outgrowths of earlier programs, but updated and tied to new facilities anticipated.

XI. Graphics

Describe any illustrations, designs, blueprints, diagrams, sketches, or other visualization you will include in your Business Plan.

These will be limited to charts, graphs, and tables.

XII. Check List

Enter all data to be included, either in sections of the Business Plan itself, or in attachments and enclosures:

List of all personnel, salaries, and other germane remuneration.

Directors, other than officers and employees.

Insurance policies—company.

Insurance—individuals.

Financial reports.

Capitalization and equity data sheets.

Debts and lenders.

Technical reports on quality of products.

Other financial and fiscal data.

Business Plan for

Book Producers, Inc.

submitted to

South Carolina National Bank
and
The Small Business Administration
Columbia Branch Office

submitted by

HENRY PARKER

THEODORE YARDLEY

EMIL BUNKER

3312 Pine Tree Avenue
Beaufort, South Carolina 29945
(803) 688-2000

STATEMENT OF PURPOSE

Book Producers, Inc. is seeking a loan of $72,000 to purchase equipment and inventory; lease an office and facilities at 3312 Pine Tree Avenue; undertake necessary improvements and additions; maintain adequate cash reserve; and provide extended working capital to expand from an editorial consulting service into full-scale book production and related services. The requested sum, enhanced by a total of $15,000 equity investment on the part of the three principals, will be sufficient to underwrite the transition from a relatively static professional counseling firm to that of a community-wide service that is greatly in need in the Beaufort County region. It is anticipated, as determined by outside financial consultants, that this transition will result in a company capable of long-term growth and increasing profits.

DESCRIPTION OF BUSINESS

Book Producers, Inc. is a firm engaged in the development of books of all kinds and sizes, starting with an idea and conceptual plan, conducting editorial research, writing, and preparing the work through eleven stages, including the printed product. The company sometimes functions in fewer stages of book development, such as just the writing or design, or it may extend its services to include such activities as distribution, marketing, advertising, and promotion.

The firm's clients may be individuals, publishers, business organizations, corporations, associations, or any party interested in the preparation and use of a book, whether to be sold at a profit, distributed at cost, or given away. The categories may be non-fiction, fiction, or any other genre desired by clients.

The company began business five years ago as a partnership engaged in editorial consultation, working for the most part with the same kinds of clients envisioned as those for future assignments when the transition is complete. It is expected, however, that the enlarged services will enable the company to deal with a greater range of clients, as well as with those that are larger or whose productive demands will be greater.

There are no seasonal variations in this type of business, though some of the clients may specify deadlines based on their need for publications at certain times of the year, such as tie-ins with annual reports or calendar events.

MARKETING PLAN

The company will build its future market on its list of present and past clients, mounting a referral campaign to develop leads to new business. Our objective is threefold: (1) To reach individuals, groups, and organizations whose interests and functions are substantial enough for presentation in book form; (2) to convince these prospective clients that a book, whether large, small, hardcover, or paperback, could be a vital medium in accomplishing their aims; and (3) to assure them that Book Producers, Inc. has the experience, capabilities, and creative skills to provide the kind of publication best suited for their purposes.

COMPETITION

There are four potential competitors in the marketing region in which the company will operate, but none that are close in terms of the experience, staff, and facilities desired:

1. *The Daily Sentinel*, a newspaper that has occasionally produced books and brochures. The publisher is only interested, however, in a limited concept—associating these publications with news or community events.

2. Eagle Press, a printing company long established in the community. Although EP has printed a number of books, it has neither the staff, the expertise, nor the experience to conceive, research, develop, and write full-length books of the type we have in mind.

3. Farley & Associates, Advertising. While this shop has excellent creative and writing talent, it has produced books (or similar) on very few occasions, and those largely adaptations or compilations of already published materials.

4. James & Lee Smithson. This is a team of authors that has occasionally contracted to write business histories and handbooks. But its capabilities are limited and its capacity no more than two book projects a year.

LOCATION AND ENVIRONMENT

Book Producers, Inc. will be situated in a location convenient for both its administrative needs and its research resources. It will lie only two blocks from the center of town, near the Chamber of Commerce, city hall, and the public library. Two of its principals live close to a major university campus and have ready access to the college library, research center, and other facilities that are conducive to the research and development of books and other works in the fields of business, the sciences, technology, and the arts. The office will also be close to other essential facilities such as mailing and shipping centers, printers, and suppliers.

The company's offices will be light, roomy, and attractive both for personnel working for the firm and for clients who attend business meetings to discuss book projects. The surroundings are also appealing, bordered by a small park on one side and a public square on another.

Other major headings for the business plan will include:

PERSONNEL AND EXPERIENCE

FINANCIAL PLAN

FINANCIAL CHART (CONDENSED)

BREAK-EVEN ANALYSIS

PROJECTED INCOME AND EXPENSES, FIRST THREE YEARS

SUMMARY

A Proposal for

_____

Data International ("Optiscope")

1230 Wasatch Building
Logan, Utah

proposed to

Salt Lake Business Associates
Loan Specialists
Provo, Utah

subject

An Investment Opportunity

_____

INTRODUCTION

After three years of primary research and development, Data International is ready to market two unique electronic products, both of which use the same new, patented technology in the field of computerized optic displays. In commercial application, the programmable message that results is valuable in the creation of signs and displays that use a scrolling technique to attract and inform prospective customers. The action, in full color, can easily be coordinated with music and voice patterns that are particularly attractive to young people.

Extensive field research documents the fact that there is a large potential for both commercial and recreational applications of this product in a programmable sign field that already exceeds $2 million in North America and untold potential abroad. Many units of Data International products are purchased by retailers for in-store promotions because they can readily be tailored to sales promotions and "specials" at a moment's notice. This highly versatile and flexible product enjoys distinct cost advantages over other kinds of store displays, many of which are expensive and time-consuming to revise and adjust.

The product has already received highly favorable reviews in *Modern Technology*, *American Business*, and *Promotional Digest*, and has been acclaimed as "a marketing phenomenon that will change the whole way of promoting in-store merchandise."

DESCRIPTION OF THE PRODUCT

The basic product, which is being produced in several different sizes and formats, is a small-sized screen, similar to a TV screen that produces visual displays in response to both the human voice and music, as well as to other sounds that are keyed to trigger its performance. Known as the Optiscope, it projects its graphic presentations in stunning color and alluring sonics, in variations that can be aimed at any age group but are especially fascinating to the young. Adaptations can be rendered within seconds to rivet the attention of almost any definable type of audience, judging by reactions to sight, sound, music, color, and resonance.

To date, there are no known products that are directly competitive to the Optiscope, although comparisons have been made with television, "visual organs," volcanic lights, infinity lights, "rain" lamps, and other devices that use sound and/or light in highly creative ways.

THE FINANCIAL OPPORTUNITY

Data International is incorporated under the laws of the state of Utah and is ready to commence operations, using its unique new computerized optic displays as the basic products in the start-up marketing program. The founders of the company, all with scientific backgrounds and interests, have devoted themselves unstintingly for many years to this project and have made many personal financial sacrifices to achieve this impressive goal. However, it has been obvious from the start that these dedicated individuals would not have adequate financial resources to manufacture and distribute sufficient units for a profitable venture. Thus, they are prepared to offer a one-third share of the corporation for an equity investment of $110,000.

Substantiating data with this investment opportunity plan indicates a strong assurance that, if the projections are met, there will be substantial profits for investors.

CORPORATE PROFILE

Data International was incorporated in Ogden, Utah, on July 6, 1990, as an operating company reorganized from an existing research laboratory. At the time, the company was organized to manufacture and market computerized electronic communications equipment. Within a year, however, management decided to focus on products that, while stemming from the same patents and systems, would be of greater value for advertising and promotional purposes than for industrial communications. The technology on which these products would be based was covered by a U.S. patent under the code name "DA," for which exclusive licensing was assigned to the corporation. The patent status has been tested and found to be valid and active, despite the revision of goals and technological applications.

At the time of the preparation of this business plan, 230 complete units of the basic product have been produced, assembled, and placed in inventory, except for 10 units which have been installed in key locations for continual testing and demonstration purposes. Production reports substantiate the probability that existing manufacturing and assembly capabilities will sustain the capacity of 300 units per month, and that relatively minor refinements, at modest cost, could increase the production rate by 50 percent. It has been estimated that, within a year, the company could be producing 750 units per month, with consequent gross income and profits.

MANAGEMENT PROFILE

The officers of Data International, and their qualifications are as follows:

Edmund Harcourt, President, a research scientist who was instrumental in pushing for the development of the electronic optic system at a time when no one else foresaw its possibilities for visual marketing.

Frederic Travis, Vice President, Engineering, an analog design engineer with eighteen years of experience as a project manager, research scientist, and inventor, who is responsible for fine-tuning the product and readying it for its unique application in a growing market.

Gilbert A. Schlesinger, Vice President, Marketing, a former advertising agency director and corporate marketing manager who oversees the sale, distribution, and installation of the new products

A Promising Business Proposition for

Friendly Walkers

The Old Depot
Roundhouse Square
Valley View, Kentucky

presented to

Heinrich & Hollowell
Investment Bankers
Number Four the Cynthiana Building
Lexington, Kentucky

presented by Friendly Walkers
with the technical support of

ROADWAY CYCLES, LIMITED
Route 62
Doonsboro, Kentucky

ALL YOU NEED TO KNOW ABOUT FRIENDLY WALKERS

We are a small company in the foothills of central Kentucky's Boone Forest region whose founder, Theron Slocum, was a bicycle manufacturer, or more accurately the reconditioner of bicycles for greatly improved performance on mountain trails and navigating other steep and abrupt grades. Mr. Slocum had been a champion of cycle racing on upland courses and had been three times the winner, and four times the runner-up, of the Bluegrass Trans-Mountain Grand

Prix. He was known throughout North America and in Europe for his prowess with the pedal, and was respected for his entrepreneurial skills in the custom building and reconditioning of bicycles.

In 1986, "Mr. Bike," as he was affectionately known in his home town, biked three times a week to the Old Soldier's Home at Reed's Crossing, where he adapted bicycles for elderly patients who needed exercise and recreation but could not operate a standard model. He added a third wheel, for example, for men who had to bicycle very slowly and needed a machine with balance. He devised a sidecar so that one resident could enjoy riding and take along a bedridden pal for the fresh air and sport. He even adapted three bikes for one-legged veterans so they could use a combination of hand pumping and one foot to ride as much as five miles a day.

A momentous breakthrough occurred in 1987 when Theron Slocum, then 84, was asked by the Therapeutic Director of the Home's clinic if he could use his proven mechanical skills to produce a machine for use inside the facility—one that would make a wheelchair patient more ambulatory and self-reliant. Mr. Slocum, within just two weeks of trial and error, testing and development, invented his now-famous "Friendly Walker." He referred to it as "Your next step to freedom." In essence, this was a four-wheeled vehicle in which the user walked, standing up, by gripping two adjustable handlebars, and in which he could navigate any hallway, room, or incline in the facility almost as fast as a perfectly healthy individual could walk. He could rest on a high seat when desired, and could handily carry along books, a newspaper, or personal items in a basket. This ingenious machine even had hand-grip brakes, and one model had, as optional equipment, a battery-operated radio/cassette with earphones.

Shortly after fine-tuning this enterprising invention, and the year before he died, Theron Slocum launched a new business, Friendly Walkers, in partnership with his son, Baddy Slocum, and one of his nephews, Westy Trapp. The younger Slocum had served thirteen years as an automotive technician at the General Motors plant in Lexington, and Trapp was a mechanic who was then operating his own twin auto and boat repair service in Jabez, Kentucky, on the shores of Lake Cumberland.

By the end of the second year in business (and following Theron's death), Slocum and Trapp had designed and were building four different models of their Friendly Walkers.

WHY WE ARE SOLICITING YOUR PARTICIPATION

As a small company, Friendly Walkers is functioning just fine. We sell about ten walkers a month at our shop, which is located in the former railway depot in Valley View. We sell another five or six each month through mail orders that result from ads placed in *Kentucky* magazine. And we have just signed a contract with the Old

Soldier's Home to manufacture eighteen custom-built Friendly Walkers during the coming year. In addition to the two partners, Slocum and Trapp, the company now employs three production workers full-time and two clerical workers part-time.

Friendly Walkers has achieved a position in the industrial world at which it is possible to expand quickly from a small enterprise to a middle-sized business with only a moderate amount of financing. After conferring with our accountant and financial advisor, Tom T. Driscoll, we are convinced that we can grow the business 50 percent in one year's time and 100 percent by the end of two years of increased operations. We can do this with equity financing, a loan, or other financial input of no more than $38,000—which is the sum we are seeking. We should add that we have already placed personal savings amounting to $12,000 in the company account to add to the $38,000.

WHAT YOU NEED TO KNOW ABOUT OUR PROPOSED PLAN OF ACTION

Friendly Walkers has spelled out the company's specific goals and objectives as follows:

1. To increase sales at the Valley View Shop 50 percent within the next twelve months

2. To increase mail-order sales 100 percent during the same period through a 50 percent increase in advertising, mostly in area newspapers

3. To solicit quantity, custom-ordered sales to institutions such as hospitals and nursing homes through a program of editorials and ads in *Bluegrass Institutions Journal*

4. To enlarge the machining and assembly line at the Valley View shop by 400 square feet

5. To design two new models to add to the line, specifically for children who, because of birth defects, disease, or accidents, are unable to walk without assistance

COMPETITION

Friendly Walkers has no local or regional competition in either the manufacture or sale of wheeled walking-assistance equipment. Its only competitors otherwise are two firms that sell such devices by mail:

NobleMotion, Inc., located in Pittsburgh, Pennsylvania, whose "Rover Walker" is sold through hospital and medical supply shops, as well as by mail. Its prices are considerably higher than those of Friendly Walkers.

Handicap House, with retail and wholesale outlets in Los Angeles, Chicago, and New York. This firm is a general supplier of many kinds of products and equipment for people with physical handicaps. It distributes two walkers under the "HH" label, but these are semi-wheeled, and not as mobile as Friendly Walkers.

Business Plan for

Better Breathing Aids (BBA)

presented by

SCOTT TECHNOLOGIES, INC.

Barkley Building
2340 Redondo Drive
Austin, TX 78701

NOTICE: This Business Plan is registered by Scott Technologies, Inc., and contains confidential data of a technological nature that must not be referred to or copied by any parties other than the authorized representatives of Better Breathing Aids. For further information, contact The Secretary, Scott Technologies, Inc., at the above address.

SUMMARY

Scott Technologies, Inc., is a corporation in the biomedical equipment field, serving hospitals and the medical profession for more than thirty years. The company was originally founded as Scott Brothers, Ltd. in the United Kingdom before moving to the United States.

THE SUBSIDIARY. Better Breathing Aids is a new arm of the company, founded in December, 1994, for the specific purpose of researching, developing, and manufacturing portable breathing aids so small that they can be worn on the person as comfortably and almost as inconspicuously as a modern hearing aid.

THE PRODUCTS. BBA sells and distributes a line of five breathing aids of various sizes and capacities, each operated by a single rechargeable battery cell. Accessories make it possible for the user to wear a unit around the neck, in a jacket pocket, strapped to the waist, or on the wrist.

RESEARCH ANALYSIS. Six complete lines of the breathing aids have been hand-crafted, assembled, and submitted to six independent research agencies for testing and evaluation. With the exception of one set that was returned for repair and reassembly, all have met the original specifications and have performed well over a period of six months. They are now ready for market.

THE MARKET. It has been estimated that there are between seven and eight million patients with lung ailments in North America alone who could benefit from the use of properly selected and adjusted Scott aids for better breathing. These range from individuals with chronic ailments like asthma to those whose lungs have been injured in accidents, and patients with advanced cases of lung cancer.

DISTRIBUTION. Better Breathing Aids will be mass-produced in a new plant now being completed in Fort Worth, Texas, and later in a second plant to be built near San Jose, California. They will be distributed to hospitals and lung specialists in small quantities by Sterling Hospital Supply Corp., an affiliate of Scott Technologies, Inc., which will have the responsibility of pretesting each instrument individually and instructing doctors and hospital technicians on their proper adjustment and application for individual patients.

MAINTENANCE AND REPAIR. Each instrument is sold with a one-year total guarantee in the matter of performance and reliability, fully covered by Scott Technologies. The units can also be leased by individuals or distributed by physicians as part of an overall health care treatment plan.

FINANCIAL REQUIREMENTS

Management has decided that $315,000 in equity financing would be required to implement this business plan within the time limitations expected: six to eight months from the date of authorization. The proceeds will be used for the following:

1. Continuing product development and improvement

2. The establishment of production facilities capable of supplying a total of 600 complete breathing aid units per month, in all models

3. Advertising and promotion in medical journals

4. Contingency funds

5. Additional personnel in manufacturing, distribution, and sales

A detailed description of the above requirements has been filed and is available for review at any time.

Current Financial Condition

The parent company, Scott Technologies, Inc., was initially funded with specific objectives in the field of medical technology and has been operating successfully within this sphere of production, showing a profit during the last ten years, as described in its annual reports for the years 1986 through 1995. Although the company has sufficient R&D funds for product development, it was the decision of the Board of Directors that the creation of the Better Breathing Aids division should be reached under a separate and distinct business plan, as outlined and presented herewith.

DEVELOPMENTAL BUSINESS RISKS

No business plan for this venture would be complete without a realistic evaluation of the risks and possible problems that are endemic to almost any venture involving the creation, development, and distribution of a technological aid in the medical field. Basically, the following perils should be considered by a lending or financing institution or party:

1. A better product could be designed and placed on the market by a competitor.

2. The medical profession, which represents the key to approval for patient use, could take the stand that people afflicted with lung ailments should undergo therapeutic exercises rather than use medical accessories.

3. The relatively high cost of breathing aids could limit the market and eradicate any chance of profitable operations in the long run.

4. The products could fail to achieve consumer acceptance because of resistance to any device that labels the user as being in poor health.

5. A foreign competitor could place a breathing aid on the market that was "almost as good," but far cheaper to produce overseas.

It is the considered opinion of the parent company, the developers of the breathing aid, and independent business consultants that the above risks have been fully anticipated and negated and that the venture will succeed as planned.

Business Plan for

Barnegat Builders

35 Jefferson Place
Troy, New York

presented to

The Albany Reconstruction Finance Commission

Harrison State Campus,
Albany, New York

subject

Single-Family Residential Reconstruction

NOTE: This building contractor has been in business in the Albany/Troy region of New York State for 24 years and has been solvent and profitable for all but two years during a recession period in the early 1970s. During its existence the firm has built or renovated more than 250 structures ranging from small residences to office buildings and sports complexes.

STATEMENT OF PURPOSE

Barnegat Builders herewith requests a loan of $90,000 for the purpose of renovating a single-family residence at 342 Pine Tree Boulevard in the town of Waterford, New York. This building, built in 1910 and once a fine old mansion overlooking the Hudson River, has been condemned by the county because of faulty plumbing and wiring and because it has remained unoccupied since the death of the owner four years ago. As a result, substantial remodeling and repairs must be completed before the house can be placed profitably on the market for resale. According to independent inspectors, approved by the county, the house is structurally sound and should easily receive an occupancy certificate once the above-mentioned deficiencies are corrected.

Three local real estate estimates have established the resale value of this residence at a range of $250-300,000 when the intended restoration has been completed. Barnegat Builders has purchased the property, on speculation, for $85,000, and thus feels assured that the venture will be profitable and that the requested loan can quickly be repaid. An independent real estate study of the area has indicated that four comparable homes along the Hudson in this region, some eighty years old but in good condition, have sold recently for $267,000, $290,000, $298,000, and $310,000 respectively. Current real estate sales and related activities indicate that, realistically, the house will be sold within six to ten months of the start of construction and renovation.

Economics of the Venture

Terms of the projected sale: Lenders in this region have been lending 80% of the appraised value of a first mortgage. Buyers expect to make a down payment of 10-15% of the selling price, the terms on which this business plan is projected.

Title to the property: As evidenced by preliminary reports and policy of title insurance, Barnegat Builders presently owns all rights.

Costs to renovate the property: Based on work to be completed by the employees of our firm and/or low bidders from other companies, the costs will total:

Plumbing, including water and gas pipe, new water heater, faucets, and toilets:	$3,200
Electrical work, pulling new wiring throughout the house, and the installation of outlets and boxes:	$5,430
Roof and gutters, including new shingling, sealing, and rain spouts, with high-quality copper:	$12,100
Flooring and carpeting, wall to wall, with suitable replacements of boards and molding:	$4,980
Kitchen cabinets, new installations, as well as the rebuilding of existing shelves and storage:	$3,980
Range and refrigerator, replacements:	$2,700
Painting and wallpapering:	$3,800
Miscellaneous repairs and renovation:	$5,000
TOTAL COSTS:	$41,190

PROFIT AND LOSS FORECAST

Expected sale price (minimum)

Less 6% commission

Net proceeds

Less:

Cost to acquire house

Cost of renovation

Building permits and fees

Carrying costs (10 months maximum)

Interest and loan fees

Developer overhead

   Total project cost

Projected profit of the venture:

Business Plan for a Small Manufacturer

Apex Packaging, Inc.

presented to

    Fourth Dakota Bank & Trust

presented by

    THE PRESIDENT AND BOARD OF DIRECTORS

    Company Headquarters
    256 North Avenue
    Grand Forks, ND 58201

WHY ARE WE IN BUSINESS?

Apex Packaging, which annually does upward of $5 million in business in its marketing region, was formed in 1976 when small local producers of products and materials began to thrive but had problems packaging their merchandise as it was being readied for market. The solution came when the Apex Paper Company saw the growing need and established a separate department to produce paper packaging materials and advise customers about ways to package their products in wrappings that were both protective and appealing.

Over a period of several years, however, the paper company found that many of the packaging needs were becoming highly specialized, thus placing heavy demands on the overworked subsidiary and resulting in annual losses to the corporation. Then, in 1983, the vice president in charge of packaging, Thomas Tilletson, formed a group of investors and offered to purchase the subsidiary in a deal that included the plant, its packaging machinery, and existing supplies. With his brother, David Tilletson, and the latter's son, David, Jr., he assumed the presidency of a new company, Apex Packaging, retained those employees who wanted to continue in the business, and hired a packaging designer from Chicago, Lawrence Harvey, who had held positions in that field with the St. Regis Paper Company and Zellerbach.

Under the Apex label, the company has continued to meet the needs of manufacturers who require packaging for their products.

What Business Are We In?

We are essentially a three-part company, offering:

1. *Service:* consultation and design

2. *Products*: materials and units in which other products and materials can be contained

3. *Distribution*: the means of moving the packaged goods from the producer to the user

We could also be classified as a manufacturer, since we are concerned with the production of the materials that are used for packaging, such as paper, plastics, cloth, and metal. However, the decision was made shortly after the formation of Apex that we would not become directly involved with producing these materials. Rather, it was elected, and formulated in the company's certificate of incorporation, that Apex would rely entirely on *outside* sources and resources for the materials used in its packaging. The decision was based on lessons learned in the 1970s when manufacturing demands were pinpointed as one of the problems causing the original paper company to suffer annual deficits.

STATEMENT OF REQUEST

Although Apex Packaging has shown corporate profits for the past three years, changing economic conditions in the company's marketing region indicate that the profit trend is sliding downward gradually and that steps must be taken to offset this undesirable situation. Consequently, in 1995 the board of directors authorized the hiring of an industrial consulting firm to survey Apex's operations and to evaluate the changes and needs in the market for packaging services and products. This study has now been completed, highlighting the following trends:

- Producers want packaging that meets specifications for strength, water-proofing, and other protective qualities, but they are insisting on lighter weight in order to minimize postage and other shipping costs.

- Manufacturers of consumer products are selecting richer color combinations in product packaging, but at the same time resist having to pay more for the look of quality.

- Packaging today must be biodegradable, recyclable, and otherwise in keeping with ever-stricter environmental laws.

In order to meet these revolutions in the marketplace and remain competitive, Apex Packaging requires a loan or other funding in the amount of $125,000, 20 percent of which must be used within six months and the balance over a period of two years. This entire sum would be devoted to packaging research, to seek the best solutions and alternatives for addressing these manufacturing and operational problems.

MARKETING

The officers and board of Apex take the position that successful marketing starts with management. We have to know our materials, products, distribution, customers, and competition. We have taken steps to evaluate our market—past, present, and future—and schedule reviews of this market every six months. Such reviews are tailored to focus on the following questions:

1. What is the current primary market?
2. What is the current secondary market?
3. How has the market changed in the past six months?
4. What aspects of the market are seasonal?

5. Are production goals responsive to the needs?

6. Do market changes require any reorganization of, or additions to, current personnel?

For reference purposes, Apex lists marketing information according to the Standard Industrial Classification (SIC) of the pertinent products and industries, published by the Superintendent of Documents of the Government Printing Office.

COMPETITION

Apex Packaging has two major competitors in its general marketing area:

1. Allied Paper Company, which is also a supplier of materials for Apex. Allied is a much broader company, dealing in all kinds of paper manufacturing and sales, and maintains one small division that is specialized in the packaging field.

2. Northern Corrugated, Inc., which was originally established (as the name implies) for the production and sale of corrugated packing materials. The company, however, has been gradually enlarging its facilities to market other types of packages and materials.

Apex is currently undertaking a market study to determine whether there are other competitors entering this field or with plans to compete in the Apex marketing area. The study will also determine the percentage of market penetration and dollar sales in the market, and the loss in sales of each company as a result of competition by the other companies. Each company will also be rated in terms of its strengths and weaknesses, marketing characteristics, new product development, and adaptability to changing market conditions.

PRODUCTION

It has been determined that only a small percentage of funds requested for improvement will be required for production and distribution, since these operations have remained fairly consistent during the past two years. In fact, the steady process of upgrading and keeping abreast of technological changes has largely been taken care of by modest price increases paid by customers for products, materials, and services. The largest monetary increase has been the cost of raw materials, traditionally built into the price structure and readily acceptable to customers, old and new alike.

Business Prospectus for

Safer Swords
A Small Toy Maker

presented to

Alliance Manufacturing Association
and
Carolina Lenders, Inc.
Greensboro, North Carolina

presented by

GRENVILLE ASSOCIATES
Pinehurst, North Carolina

CURRENT SITUATION ANALYSIS

A toy given the amusing name of the Wacky Whacker began as an idea of a fencing coach, Ron Miller, and is in effect a foam sword originally designed to function as a practice fencing weapon. However, given the safety and durability of the product, it also serves as a children's toy. Safer Swords, Inc. was established as a small business by the coach to market the foam sword, and was sold on a small scale at fencing meets and through catalogs. Having been awarded a patent, it can now be distributed on a national and international level.

As a start-up company, Safer Swords, Inc. has a number of marketing strengths:

- The design allows it to be multi-marketed, not only as a fencing practice item, but as a toy, for sport, and as a souvenir.

- The innovative product design of the Wacky Whacker makes it one of the safest and most durable products of its kind in the toy industry. The fencing model is unique to the fencing and sporting goods industry as a useful practice weapon.

- Coach Miller's reputation in the fencing world gives Safer Swords a strong competitive advantage in the fencing market for a quality, proven product.

- The coach's contacts in the fencing industry have given him a leadership position in this emerging market for foam fencing weapons.

- Given the patent, Safer Swords is fairly protected from competitors duplicating and marketing the product.

As a small, inexperienced company, however, trying to compete in a large toy industry, Safer Swords has some inherent weaknesses when compared to its competition:

- It is difficult for Safer Swords to make a name and presence in the overcrowded toy industry (limited volume, marketing and advertising resources, etc.), given its financial constraints and minimal visibility.

- Limited distribution channels and contacts make it difficult to market the product on a large scale.

- Adequate product volume may be a problem given Safer Swords' limited control over foam supply and production.

- Safer Swords' unit cost may be significantly higher than a large competitor that could mass-produce the toy internally, if it could circumvent the patent.

- Safer Swords has a limited product line at this time, though the foam sword can serve in many markets.

- Safer Swords does not have the resources of a large toy manufacturer to protect it should a lawsuit arise because of product liability.

- Safer Swords needs to select a few markets to determine a clear strategic direction in developing its position, given its limited resources, as opposed to trying to experiment in every opportunity that arises.

Safer Swords has many opportunities to consider, given its strengths:

- Demand appears strong in both the toy and fencing markets for the Wacky Whacker.

- Safer Swords can diversify its product line to include accessories and related products, such as foam body guards and face masks.

The management would like to reap the benefits of sales of its unique product, working within the parameters of the following constraints:

- Limited time to devote to market penetration
- Minimal personal money to invest up front
- Ability to reinvest profits
- Willingness to give up control of day-to-day operations

INDUSTRY

The Industry Structure

The American toy industry is responsible for about $12 billion in sales, with increases of about 5 percent each year in the mid-1990s. The industry is composed of many thousands of firms, but dominated by several large companies, which account for about 80 percent of the total industry sales.

The Industry Driving Forces and Key Success Factors

Every industry has certain "driving forces" or dominant market influences that substantially impact firms within the industry. Understanding these driving forces allows a firm to develop a strategic plan that will more effectively address the crucial business issues. The driving forces at work in the toy industry, for small firms in particular, include the following:

- *Product innovations.*

- *Product line diversity.* The toy industry is a faddish business. Product innovations and the expansion of product lines allow a firm to develop new markets, reduce risk through diversification, and profit from innovations.

- *Marketing innovations.* Numerous toy companies leverage their successes through marketing innovations, such as licensing agreements and joint agreements with retailers. On a smaller scale, Safer Swords could develop an agreement with schools or a minor league sports team to promote its products.

- *Changes in cost and efficiency.* Reductions in product cost and increased efficiency will reduce financial risk, increase profitability, and allow the firm to defend its marketing position against competition.

- *Changes in who buys and how they use products.* The Wacky Whacker is a good example of how the purchasers and users of a product can be composed of separate markets. The marketing plan can be geared to allocate efficiently the limited resources across the market segments.

Key success factors are elements that have a crucial impact on whether a firm will achieve healthy profits and industry success. Some key success factors in the toy industry for a small firm include:

- Low production costs

- Successful product innovations

- Strong distribution channels
- Strong merchandising skills
- Alliance or joint venture with a global toy company

Price-Cost-Profit Economics

The industry's profitability and general well-being is greatly affected by the general nature of the economy, as well as demand/supply product balance in the industry. But this product, being moderately priced, may be less sensitive to a weak economy than a much more expensive toy. A small firm can succeed by exploiting its unique advantages, particularly nontraditional marketing, niche markets untapped by large companies, and low overhead.

COMPETITION

There are other products on the market that are competitive, or noncompetitive but that affect customer purchases so they buy other kinds of toys and recreational equipment. Therefore, the Wacky Whacker must be promoted for its special appeal against items made and marketed by the large companies in the toy and recreational field.

CUSTOMER ANALYSIS

Who buys?

The Wacky Whacker ("WW") is segmented into two distinct markets:

a. Fencers who use the WW as a training tool. This primary use of the Whacker is that it enables fencers to practice in hot conditions without wearing all their gear.

b. People who use the WW as a toy. Customers range from small children (ages 5 and up) to adults.

Where sold?

Present sales: The Whacker can currently be purchased at three distinctly different retail stores: a toy shop, sporting goods store, and a card shop. The inventor has also had success selling it "on the street," at events like the Junior Fencing Olympics, where he set up a booth and sold many. Additionally, the Whacker was used as part of the winners' awards, thus increasing the product's exposure greatly.

In addition, the Whacker is sold through mail order, appealing both to fencers and other sports enthusiasts and to parents and children. It is promoted in this market as both a training tool and a toy.

Potential future customers:

- Retail through other local sporting good stores and local toy stores
- Retail through national toy stores such as Toys 'R Us
- Convenience stores, grocery stores, "dollar" stores, etc.
- Sporting good trade shows
- Sports promotions, at football and other games
- Halloween/costume stores
- Fencing supply distributors

Future Distribution channels: Supermarkets, drugstores, and price clubs.

Influences of Buying

One of the selling features of the WW is its packaging. Since there is no protective wrapping, browsers can pick up the WW and hit a friend or a wall, getting instant gratification while in the store. To a large extent then, the WW represents an impulse purchase. Prominent display is crucial.

As for mail-order customers, they perceive the Whacker as a humorous device, which will give them great satisfaction. When people see other people using the WW, its appeal increases greatly. Thus, setting up a stand at, say, a football game appeals to a large audience and should lead to great sales.

Price

The Wacky Whacker is competitively priced, in regard to other toys, games, and recreational items, and is a durable product.

Marketing Basics and Analytical Tools

This section outlines a few marketing ideas that Safer Swords may find helpful.

Five Steps of Marketing Management

ANALYZING MARKETING OPPORTUNITIES: This step entails gathering information about the marketing micro- and macroenvironments. The microenvironment includes all participants that could affect the company's ability to produce and sell the product (suppliers, marketing intermediaries, customers, and competitors). The macroenvironment includes broad demographic, economic, legal, and technological trends.

RESEARCHING AND SELECTING TARGET MARKETS: The task here is to estimate the market's overall size, growth, and profitability. Usually this involves dividing the market into major market segments, evaluating them, and selecting and targeting those market segments that the company can best serve.

DESIGNING MARKETING STRATEGIES: Once a target market is chosen, the company needs to develop a differentiating and positioning strategy for that target market. The company must define how it will differ from its primary competitors. This step should include life cycle planning for modification of strategy at different stages of the product's life cycle.

PLANNING MARKETING PROGRAMS: This step includes (1) deciding what level of marketing expenditures are necessary to attain marketing goals, and (2) deciding how to divide the marketing budget among the four primary marketing tools: product, price, place, and promotion.

ORGANIZING, IMPLEMENTING, AND CONTROLLING MARKETING EFFORT: The company must identify who will organize the marketing resources and how the marketing program will be implemented and controlled. In a small company, one person may be responsible for all three tasks. Feedback and control procedures include annual planning and variance analysis, profitability analysis, and strategic control.

Recommendation

We recommend that Safer Swords pursue a partnership arrangement with a small- to medium-size toy company for the following reasons:

- *Flexibility:* A partnership arrangement allows Safer Swords to capitalize on its own strengths and experience as well those of the partner.

- *Time commitment:* Relative to the distribution option, a partnership option requires a smaller time commitment.

- *Risk:* Rather than Safer Swords assuming all of the financial risk, the partners share the risk.

- *Capital:* If the partner assumes responsibility for all marketing, the largest investment of Safer Swords would be inventory. Depending on the partnership agreement, distribution may be the responsibility of either party.

- *Upside potential:* In contrast to a licensing agreement, a partnership arrangement would preserve the upside profit potential of Safer Swords.

- *Staffing:* In a partnership arrangement, additional staff is probably not required.

- *Hands-on experience:* This option will allow management to broaden their business experience by actively participating in operations. This prepares management to take a more active role, if so desired, when the agreement expires.

Because of management's experience and familiarity with the fencing market and distribution channels, we recommend that Safer Swords maintain manufacturing and marketing control in this segment. Thus, the partnership agreement should be limited to the toy and promotion segments. Safer Swords needs to hire an attorney who has specific experience with licensing, partnership, and distribution contracts to ensure it is well protected and maximum benefits are obtained in a contract.

IMPLEMENTATION

The following represents the recommended implementation plan for the partnership option:

1. *Identify potential partners.* First, identify a list of criteria for an ideal partner. For example, the partner should have a current product line that complements Safer Swords' product. Other criteria may relate to the size of the potential partner (in revenues or number of products), profitability, size of sales force, and geographic strengths and weaknesses. Second, a list of toy companies from a toy industry association or other source should be obtained and the list narrowed according to the identified criteria.

2. *Prepare for negotiation.* Through research into standard partnership agreements, identify Safer Swords' criteria for an acceptable partnership (i.e., the profit sharing arrangement). While Safer Swords should consult with an attorney in developing any legal agreement, the following are items the company may want to address:

- Specific responsibilities of each party

- The point at which title passes from one party to another

- Specific definition of each market segment

- Provision for extension/termination/alteration of the partnership agreement

- Duration of the agreement

3. *Contact potential partners.* Be aware that this requires Safer Swords' management to sell the idea of a partnership arrangement. Some of the companies contacted may have never considered a partnership agreement while others may be involved in numerous such arrangements.

4. *Evaluate potential partners and select.* In addition to how well each partner meets the pre-identified criteria, interpersonal considerations play an important role in any successful partnership.

5. *Develop plan with the chosen partner.* After a partner has been selected, and while the legal arrangements are being finalized, jointly develop an action plan for bringing the product to market. Developing a detailed plan before finalizing the legal agreement may help identify specific issues that need to be addressed. It is important to understand that there is a distinction between the legal and business aspects of the relationship.

Contingency Plan

In the event the partnership option requires more resources than management chooses to commit, licensing may represent a viable alternative. While the profit potential of a licensing arrangement is smaller than that of a partnership, this option entails a limited commitment of time and money and greatly reduces the risk borne by Safer Swords.

Business Plan for

Chat Cards, Inc.

presented to

Pine Tree Investors, Inc.
Deep Valley Center
Gaylesville, Vermont

presented by

JAMES ARCHER
THOMAS FULTON
MARIA OLDER
River Building
West Lebanon, NH 03784

DESCRIPTION OF EXISTING BUSINESS

NOTE: See also this description in the case history of Twin State Printing, pages 197–200.

Known until last year as "Four Guys Printing," the firm functioned for two decades as a commercial print shop, meeting the limited needs of businesses in the area and occasionally supplying consumers with letterheads, labels, and other common stationery needs. In an attempt to expand, the four owners discussed the possibilities of investing in a printing franchise, such as Insty Prints or ExpressPrint, but decided that (a) the investment was too unmanageable and (b) the stipulations were too restrictive. During a reorganization, two of the owners retired from the business and three entrepreneurs joined, to form Twin State Printing. The newcomers brought additional experiences and capabilities, thus making it possible to undertake more complex printing jobs and expand the market considerably.

In addition to conventional printing jobs, Twin State Printing expects to form subsidiaries that would be unique in their marketing and merchandising potential, but require nothing more than sound printing and distribution facilities to be successful. One of these ventures is Chat Cards, Inc.

GOALS AND OBJECTIVES

The major purpose of the new company is to produce, advertise, and market packages of cards, slightly larger than conventional playing cards, with various kinds of word games and questions. Some would require specific answers and some would simply be conversation stimulators. Over a period of time, Chat Cards, Inc., intends to produce an increasing variety of cards, with the themes aimed at different age groups and people with different interests. One of the first in the series would be business-oriented, and could carry the business logo or imprint of a company, as an advertising medium. Several of the cards would be tailored so that the question asked required an answer directly identifying the advertiser.

Financing Required

No new money is needed for the above purpose, since the printing firm itself is already in existence and capable of producing the cards quickly, easily, and at low cost. An initial fund of $175,000 is required for the following purposes, after which the enterprise will become self-liquidating as cards and advertising are sold to clients:

Adding a print-run adapter to existing equipment.

Hiring a researcher, writer, and editor to initiate ideas for the themes and contents of cards in the series and prepare the texts.

Hiring two salespersons, on a salary and commission basis, to market the concept and supplies of cards to prospective advertisers.

Advertising in local media, including newspapers, regional periodicals, and the *Yellow Pages*.

Distribution of samples at business and commercial meetings and seminars.

Qualifications of the Principals

James Archer has been in the printing business for ten years, and has specialized in the kinds of printing and online processing necessary for the Chat Cards. This has included playing cards, business cards, labels, tags, and novelties, among other items.

Thomas Fulton has had extensive experience in advertising and marketing for twelve years, and has a long list of satisfied clients who would also be prospective purchasers of Chat Cards in quantity.

Maria Older is an art director with experience that would make her highly qualified to lay out and design the Chat Cards, as well as advertising campaigns to sell and market them to clients.

The firm has also engaged the services of Mittendorf and Small, graphics specialists in Springfield, Massachusetts, to serve as consultants whenever their assistance and expertise may be required. M&S has an enviable record of service with large corporations, small businesses, and government agencies, and is also serving as consultants to Twin State Printing.

COMPETITION

There is at the present time no direct competition to the Chat Cards concept in the company's marketing regions. However, since it is anticipated that other printers may see the value of the Chat Cards and try to imitate them, the company is taking positive action to protect its patent rights and copyrights.

Business Plan for a Small Manufacturer

Stinkeraser, Inc.

presented to

United Trust & Development Company

presented by

THE INVENTOR OF THE PRODUCT
TAKAMI ILLUIA, M.D.
and
THORSON VEEDING
IPIMA LABORATORIES
Kailua Acres
Kauai, Hawaii

NATURE OF THE INVENTION

Without giving away any trade secrets, the invention has been described by an objective testing service as "a unique mass of brownish material that can be as soft as putty or as hard as an eraser, and applied by gently rubbing it over surfaces that have for one reason or another acquired an unpleasant odor." This action almost instantly, and permanently, removes the odor and in its place releases a fresh woodland scent that is pleasant and fragrant. The material was developed by its inventor, Dr. Illuia, a medical research scientist, who was experimenting with medical compounds derived from wild palm trees native to the islands of Hawaii. In the course of investigation, he noticed that one amalgam not only had medicinal qualities he was seeking, but also tended to neutralize chemical odors in the section of the laboratory where he was working.

Experiments with the neutralization of other odors, such as those in the kitchen, like onion, garlic, and cabbage, proved to be equally successful, as did treatments applied to his two dogs to get rid of "doggy" odors.

STATEMENT OF REQUEST

The plan of action is for the creation and organization of a small company, with Dr. Illuia as the researcher and developer of products and Mr. Veeding as the administrator of the company and the marketing director. Another manager will be hired whose major role will be to design and produce packaging that meets specifications for strength, waterproofing, and other protective qualities, is lightweight in order to minimize postage and other shipping costs, and is attractive for consumer presentations and displays.

In order to meet the financial needs for starting the company and being competitive in the marketplace, Stinkeraser, Inc., requires funding in the amount of $145,000, 50 percent of which must be used to establish the business and the balance to cover general needs over a period of two years.

MARKETING

The founders of the company are convinced that successful marketing starts with management and careful attention to research, product development, marketing, distribution, customers, and competition. The principals have taken concrete steps to evaluate the market, and intend to review this market on a quarterly basis. Such reviews will ask the following questions:

1. What is the current primary market?

2. How will the market change, whether seasonally or gradually?

3. What aspects of the market are specialized?

4. What production goals will be set?

5. What personnel requirements are expected?

COMPETITION

At present, there are no serious competitors in the Pacific market area where the company will do most of its initial business. However, as the company expands, it will encounter competition in other marketing regions. These are the various manufacturers of air fresheners and deodorants with brand names like *Glade, Out, Wizard,* and *PineSol*—all produced and distributed by large commercial manufacturers rather than small businesses.

Degan & Roth, a consulting firm hired by Dr. Illuia, is currently making a market study to determine whether there are other competitors—especially small and relatively unknown companies—in his marketing area, or with plans to enter it. The study will also determine the size of the market for Stinkeraser products.

PRODUCTION

It is estimated that the company can be in production large enough to start test-marketing within two months of receiving initial funding, can achieve 50 percent of its potential distribution within one year, and can be in full-scale production and merchandising within two years.

Chapter 5

Plans
for
Home-Based
Enterprises

As in the preceding chapter, this chapter contains a variety of model business plans. These are shorter than most because they are based on limited enterprises of the type often referred to as a "cottage industry."

One of these is selected for more detailed examination, its nature introduced by a descriptive quote. "Homework has taken on new meaning for more than ten million Americans," reports Carol Eliason, speaking for the Research Management Corporation of Falls Church, Virginia. "The drive for economic self-sufficiency has motivated large numbers of persons to market their skills and talents for profit from home. Our increasingly service-oriented economy offers a widening spectrum of opportunities for customized and personalized small-business growth."

Elements in this particular model plan include:

- Information gathering, to determine what kinds of home-based businesses could be successful for the reader

- Research, to eliminate some choices and focus on others, based on legal and tax issues, proper space utilization, consumer demand, and the talents and qualifications of the entrepreneurs

- The entrepreneurial personality, with a checklist to determine whether the developer of the proposed enterprise really has the personal traits and interests to undertake the venture

- Selection, a list of home-based products and services that are customarily desired by consumers, including such things as secretarial aids, handicrafts, repair work, art, instruction, mail-order services, and recreational sales

- Time management, and the necessity for preparing schedules and deadlines, as well as anticipating time requirements for the services offered

- The work site, determining what part of the main residence, cellar, garage, outbuildings, yard, or other space will be feasible and available for the business in mind

- Legal and legislative restrictions, to learn what operations can and cannot be conducted on the premises in question

- Insurance research, finding out what changes in coverage, or additions or new policies, are needed to conduct the desired business

- Overall homesite evaluation and location to determine such matters as customer convenience, parking, nearby competition, traffic flow, available utilities, taxes, police and fire services, security, employee convenience, environmental factors, and transportation

The chapter also discusses the marketing plan, the management plan, the operations plan, and a financial summary.

Business Plan for a Home-Based Business

Computerized Office Services

submitted to

First Union National Bank of South Carolina
and
The Small Business Administration
Hilton Head Island Office

submitted by

ALICE M. RICHEY

P.O. Box 3015
Hilton Head Island, SC 29928-0015

STATEMENT OF PURPOSE

Computerized Office Services is seeking a loan of $10,000 for start-up purposes. Ms. Richey, who is the sole proprietor of this home-based business, expects to repay the loan within a three-year period or less. Her goal is to build up a steady nonseasonal client base that will sustain the business and pay off the loan. Ms. Richey has already invested $10,000 of her personal savings in furnishing her office and purchasing high-tech electronic data processing, communications, and printing equipment.

DESCRIPTION OF THE BUSINESS

The business, called Computerized Office Services, is the creation of Alice Richey, a former paralegal/secretary. The primary purpose of the business is to consult, train, and service the needs of the computer-literate community of Hilton Head Island, South Carolina. Ms. Richey hopes to serve both the needs of the business and consumer community of the island and surrounding Low Country regions.

Because of her business training, technical knowledge, and understanding of computers and other data processing equipment, Ms. Richey envisions carving a substantial niche in this state-of-the-art market. To her knowledge, there is no other single computerized business that offers the range of services that her operations and facilities can provide. However, Ms. Richey's long-term goal is to concentrate her efforts on the teaching and consulting aspects of her business, rather than the service area. This is the area of the business profile that shows the most promise and that has, indeed, been forecast by experts in the field as the way the business should be trending.

COS does not intend to market computers, but rather to advise clients about equipment and computer systems that would be most beneficial to their needs. By using this approach, Ms. Richey assumes the position of an unbiased consultant who can impartially recommend various brands of computers to her clients. Other services such as word processing, technological research, and hands-on classroom review will also be offered.

LOCATION AND ENVIRONMENT

The business is a home-based enterprise and is located in an office at Ms. Richey's home in the prestigious Sea Pines Plantation sector of Hilton Head Island. This is a locale where the escalation of business enterprises has been little short of phenomenal and where technical and technological assistance to local managers has been greatly lacking and in short supply. As a Chamber of Commerce report stated, "Firms that can offer reliable and continuously updated service in the field of data processing will find many clients knocking at their doors."

COS enjoys a distinct advantage over many professional services in that its business phone line will be located at the residence, as well as a fax and a private line. All computer equipment will be on site also. The goal of COS is to remain a home-based business, literally offering 24-hour, fully licensed service to its clients.

COMPETITION

To date, other than two computer sales and service stores located on Hilton Head Island, there is no other business that offers the range of services that

Computerized Office Services provides. Because of the distinctive nature of the business, it may be an added service for the other computer businesses to use in a complementary manner, since there is such a lack of available computer instructors and consultants in the Beaufort County region.

Ms. Richey has chosen at the start of her business to provide services in consulting, services, and training so that she can maintain a realistic perspective of where the computer industry is going and what the needs of businesses and consumers alike really are in today's highly competitive marketplace.

MARKETING

Because of its limited budget, the business will rely on "word of mouth" by clients for its advertising and promotion—an option that has been productive in the past. Later, small newspaper ads will be placed in the *Island Packet* and other local periodicals.

Proposal for Financial Assistance in the Development of

Absentee Administrators, Inc.

proposed to

West Gulf Coastal Bank

subject

Our New Home-Based Business Venture

proposed by

MARTIN AND MIRANDA TRAVIS

DESCRIPTION OF THE BUSINESS

Absentee Administrators is a small, home-based business that is flexible enough to serve a range of customers, from the "mom & pop" category to those with organizations staffed by upwards of twenty employees. Its purpose, as epitomized by its advertising slogan, *"You Take the Vacation, We Take the Work,"* is to provide experienced, reliable management for the owners of small businesses who need R&R (Rest & Recreation), but who have become chained to their daily grind and do not seem able to get away to enjoy the profits of their labors.

The founders of Absentee Administrators are a husband-and-wife team, each of whom achieved top management positions during some thirty years in their respective executive careers. They have impeccable credentials as managers, are familiar with executive and management requirements in many fields of business, and have served as commercial and industrial consultants to more than fifty top business clients. Their new business is based on a three-part strategy, which not only provides their clients with the R&R period desired, but affords them with an appropriate opportunity to provide counsel, if desired.

Phase 1: For a period of one to two weeks before a client leaves the business in the capable hands of Absentee Administrators, the Travises act as their corporate shadows to determine the needs and nature of the business. During this period, they make a complete log of what has been done and has to be done during the hiatus of the owners.

Phase 2: The Travises, singly or jointly, remain on the job during the time their clients are away and handle the complete administration of the business. They assume full responsibility for the handling of every facet of the assignment, as specified in the log that has been written up during phase 1.

Phase 3: The Travises not only turn the reins back to their clients, but provide pertinent and objective counsel regarding business improvements that could be made. This counsel is based on their observations during the interim period and their own experience in the improvement of business operations and functions in the past.

STATEMENT OF REQUIREMENTS

As a brand new venture, Absentee Administrators requires a small amount of funding, in the amount of $20,000, for the following purposes:

$4,000 for the preparation of a brochure and mailing piece describing the business and what it can accomplish for clients

$3,200 for an electronic data processing system and computer, for basic administration

$2,000 for office installations and improvement

$500 for additional phone and communications installations in the home-based office

$6,000 for local advertising over an initial period of two months. It is anticipated that a percentage of client fees will sustain the advertising and promotional effort in the future

$700 for an open house and lunches, for public relations purposes, to alert business editors and commentators to the new service

$3,600 for secretarial services during an initial three-month period

COMPETITION

There is no known service that is deemed to be at all competitive in this field of business.

Financing Proposal for

Med Transcripts, Inc.

submitted to

First Massachusetts Lenders
Old State House
Boston, Massachusetts

submitted from

MEDICAL RESOURCES GROUP

27 Pilgrim Street
Hingham, MA 02043

AMELIA HART
JESSICA MEADOWS
TRACY KIRKLAND

DESCRIPTION OF THE BUSINESS

Med Transcripts is a comprehensive recording and transcription service for professionals and professional offices, particularly in the field of medicine and health. It was founded four years ago by two biomedical researchers who were assisting physicians, surgeons, dentists, and other medical specialists in transcribing tapes and who realized that standard secretarial services were not adequate to the job. For one thing, these lacked the knowledge and insight to detect errors in medical phraseology and the spelling of pharmaceutical and diagnostic terms. Hence, transcripts tended to contain numerous errors, particularly if texts were typed from audiocassettes.

The ultimate product is a visual copy of medical exam histories, diagnoses, patient chart data, statistics, physicians' speeches, convention notes, psychiatric tapings, specialized physiological and psychological reports, and the like.

The procedure consists of listening to audiotapes, or in some cases telephone instructions or electronic messages, typing the aural communications on a computer disk, and then printing the reports on paper. These printouts are not complete until they have been proofread and, in many cases, edited. Professional transcriptionists, whether medical, legal, industrial, or business, were traditionally paid by the line, page, or character count. Med Transcripts, however, evolved a "package" system for its clients, with the charges evaluated in broader terms, and including the very important factor of proofing and editing.

THE NEED

Med Transcripts is in a current position where it can more than double its list of clients, influx of business, and income through a plan of action that has been developed with its business consultant, Reed & Breyer of Dedham, Massachusetts, a professional industrial consulting firm with numerous blue chip clients in the Boston area. It has been estimated that the firm will need financial backing, whether loan or equity investment, in the amount of $20-25,000, which sum will be applied over a period of six months to the following improvements:

1. Upgrading of the present Dell Ultrascan system to a series 600, Word Perfect and Windows capabilities to increase the speed of reception and transmission

2. Addition of two medical/technical software systems, ProTech and MedTech, to eliminate spelling and statistical errors

3. Addition to the staff of a part-time stenographer with a T-35a rating, qualified in medical terminology

4. Addition to the present printing unit, Hewlett Packard 500, of a Panasonic Microlaser printer with a capacity of 12 pages per minute and 4.5 MB of memory

5. Implementation of an initial advertising and marketing campaign as described in the report that follows

ADVERTISING AND MARKETING

Med Transcripts (M/T) has been advertising regularly in local and regional medical and professional journals such as *Massachusetts Medicine* and *Bay State Practitioner*. It plans to augment the number of insertions in the media, as well as to increase the size of its placement in Boston area *Yellow Pages*.

The marketing plan envisions a doubling of the list of individual practitioners, hospitals, and group practices through the services of its present source, Multiplex Mailing Lists, and improvements in the brochure and mail-return cards now sent to these addressees. The new brochure will add the following facts, calculated to recruit new clients, document the increased capabilities of the service, and build client confidence in the ability of M/T to provide the most dependable and accurate transcription service in the entire Bay State area:

- Descriptions of the computer hardware and software available

- Brief biographies of the owners and staff members of the firm and their respective qualifications

- Quotations from regular clients regarding their complete satisfaction with the firm's speed, accuracy, and pricing

- A list of "special packages" available to clients to relieve them of transcription chores, records, and accounting

COMPETITION

Med Transcripts is in direct competition with only two other transcription services in its marketing area:

United Association of Legal Secretaries maintains a medical secretarial service in Boston. This office, however, is general in nature and, while very experienced, reliable, and reasonably priced, cannot expect to retain the same kind of insight that is the specialty of M/T.

The Medical Reporters Group is an affiliation of researchers, reporters, and writers in the medical field who maintain an office and engage in a considerable amount of transcript work for hospitals and medical practitioners. While it offers a greater range of communications services than M/T, its weakness lies in the proficiency (or lack thereof) of whomever may be selected by the group for any given assignment.

The difficulty of offering a truly reliable and dependable transcription service can be seen in the fact that no less than five other local firms in this field have gone out of business in just the past two years.

Small Business Plan for

Thomas J. Webster, Landscape Artist

submitted to

> Nation's Bank of South Carolina
> *Charleston Office*

submitted by

> THOMAS J. WEBSTER
> *234 Crow's Nest Road*
> *Summerville, SC 29903*

STATEMENT OF PURPOSE

Tom Webster, a trained landscape architect, is seeking a loan of $25,000 for computer equipment and other drafting equipment related to his business. This will enable him to promote his business more effectively, keep better records, prepare lists of stocks on hand and any descriptions necessary, and make quicker adjustments to any changes in the financial records.

DESCRIPTION OF BUSINESS

Thomas J. Webster is a landscape architect who has been working in the partnership of Gordon and Hermann, Inc. and now wishes to start his own landscape architectural firm out of his home-based office. With the loan funds that he is seeking from the bank and S.B.A., he hopes to build his own new client base and work for himself. Due to his creative talents and contacts, he has two contracts for two new projects in the Charleston area, a golf course and a new church in Summerville.

Mr. Webster has been in the Charleston area for over fifteen years and has many business contacts to his credit. He has an excellent reputation in the community and hopes to stay in Charleston for many years to come. He will be the only person working in his office and he hopes to keep his business a home-based business.

LOCATION AND ENVIRONMENT

Tom Webster's office will be located primarily at his home in Summerville, at 234 Crow's Nest Road. He will have a computer, fax line, business line, drafting table, plotter, printer, and drafting tools. He will be using a courier service for his deliveries. He will also be using a cellular phone for his calling out of the home-based office. He will be the only employee and does not plan to move his office out of the home.

COMPETITION

There are other competitors in the landscape architectural field in the Charleston area. However, the field is not saturated and there is a high demand for architects in the area due to the heavy population growth in the county. Mr. Webster feels that his competition is not great and that his contacts from his previous work and the two new contracts that he has already will give his business a good start and a foundation for more new business.

MARKETING PLAN

Mr. Webster plans to market his business by "word of mouth" in the beginning and then he hopes to advertise in various trade publications throughout the state. He will also have an ad in the Yellow Pages of the phone book.

Other enclosed documents should be:

1. Copies of the two new contracts for work

2. References from work and from friends

3. Any insurance documentation

4. A resume

5. A personal financial statement

6. Examples of any past work

Business Plan for

Barbara J. Maniotis, Legal Assistant

submitted to

Small Business Administration
of St. Paul, MN

submitted by

Barbara J. Maniotis
1414 Walker Street
St. Paul, MN 40052

STATEMENT OF PURPOSE

Barbara J. Maniotis is seeking a loan of $15,000 from the Small Business Administration of St. Paul, Minnesota to purchase computer equipment for her home-based business.

Mrs. Maniotis is a certified and trained "real estate" paralegal. Mrs. Maniotis plans to prepare real estate packages in her home office for several one- and two-person law firms. The requested funds would be sufficient for a period of eighteen months to assist in starting her business.

DESCRIPTION OF BUSINESS

Mrs. Maniotis plans to prepare real estate and some tax packages from her home office using a computer, fax machine, copy machine, and delivery service for the following six small law firms:

Williams & Harper, P.A.

Winslow, Nelson & James, P.A.

William P. Cooper, Attorney at Law

Tillison & Tillison, P.A.

Maddox, Foreman and Lester, P.A.

Her work will be on a contract basis only. She will assist the attorneys with closings, but she will essentially work for herself.

She will also prepare closing and settlement statements for the closing banks as well:

First Union of Minnesota

Nationsbank of Minnesota

Trust Company of St. Paul

Fleet Finance of Minnesota

Apart from preparing the closing packages in her home, Mrs. Maniotis will be going to the local courthouse and will be preparing title searches.

LOCATION AND ENVIRONMENT

The location and environment for Mrs. Maniotis's business will be primarily in her home office. She lives in the center of St. Paul, Minnesota and is in close proximity to all of her clients. She will be the only person using her office.

COMPETITION

To date, there is little or no competition in her field for this kind of new business venture. Most paralegals and legal assistants still work out of law offices. Her venture is new and unique.

MARKETING PLAN

The marketing plan is simple, mainly promotion through word of mouth and the placement of information in local business journals and the business sections of local newspapers. Because she is a legal assistant working under a lawyer's direction, she cannot advertise on her own.
Other enclosed documents should be:

1. Certification of legal training

2. Insurance paperwork

3. Personal financial statement

4. Business and personal references

Chapter 6

Plans for Research Organizations

SMALL BUSINESS RESEARCH

One of the most common fields of small business research is directed at the design and manufacture of products and parts, especially those that can be made locally and tailored for regional use at prices that are competitive with those of large national manufacturers. Small enterprises that intend to submit business plans to financial institutions or private investors must be knowledgeable about the principles and responsibilities of research and development.

Popularly known as R&D, this aspect of scientific investigation and planning is often a substantial component of a company's makeup, particularly in those fields where a competitive edge depends on new breakthroughs or innovative improvements to existing products and services. R&D is essential in every small business that has a stake in technological development and scientific know-how. It has been estimated that there are some 8,000 government, university, independent, nonprofit, and commercial research centers of standing in almost 150 nations around the globe, and as many as 13,000 nonprofit research and development companies in the United States and Canada alone.

With this in mind, entrepreneurs who want to venture into this field must have more than the usual qualifications and skills if they expect to survive in the marketplace. One of the most common fields of research is directed at the evolution, planning, design, and manufacture of products, parts, and related materials and accessories. Production engineering, for example, is almost totally devoted to the physical and mechanical means of developing products that will meet market demands, satisfy purchasers and users, and turn a substantial profit for the manufacturer, with a minimum of delay and replacement or repair of defective merchandise. Like all forms of research, this field of investigation, experimentation, and study depends on a very close working knowledge of new technologies and state-of-the-art techniques. In the pharmaceutical industry, research is directed not only at the materials, equipment, and tools for the processing of medical and health products, but at the components that must be examined, blended, and analyzed in laboratory programs that may take many months, even years, of endless testing. In the food and beverage industry, a large proportion of research is likely to be not only investigating in culinary laboratories, but inquiring into the needs and preferences of consumers. And in the service industries, the thrust of research may be almost entirely in the field, tracking down statistics and records to determine what kinds of services are in demand, where, and during what chronological periods or seasons of the year.

In recent years, strong focus in industry has been on operations research, particularly in the field where researchers approach problems and proposed projects by constructing models of facilities and systems for advance study. Such models, which constitute the heart of operations research, might be expressed in computer simulations, or composites thereof, but without having to create expensive physical and material prototypes. In each case, objectives must be considered and stated carefully in order to achieve the intended research responses, and this preliminary planning stage has been recognized as perhaps the most important phase of this type of research and development. Researchers in this field often apply the "game theory" technique, which, as the name implies, pits several "opponents" against each other in simulation, the objective being to study the advantages and drawbacks of various competitive approaches. The game theory could be used, for example, to help a small manufacturer of consumer products to determine which channels of distribution used by competing marketers would sell the most merchandise for profit in a given period of time, or in the long run.

Technological developments, the enormous spread of computers, and the increasing importance of commercial innovation have played strong roles in bringing research and development from its rather limited base in large industry to a position of prominence in some areas of small business. In addition, there has been a rapid escalation of small private research firms, which can often exist because of assistance from government-sponsored R&D agencies and industry-oriented units in the science departments of major universities and academic research institutes.

Another essential area of business research, particularly for applications in advertising, marketing, public relations, and other communications, focuses strongly on demographics, the in-depth study of people and populations in the area where a company is doing business. This field of study looks at the population from the standpoint of age, race, gender, marital and family status, income, ethnic background, religious faith, employment, nationality, and other personal characteristics, and attempts to associate these data with economic factors such as consumer needs and demands, buying habits, discretionary spending, brand loyalty, and the like.

Related to this is personnel research, which studies people and the work environment, with a view to improving on-the-job conditions and attracting a higher caliber of employee. This is obviously important when a small business can do enough research to attract better and more reliable employees in an area than its competitors.

This chapter, though short, presents the business plans of several small enterprises engaged in the field of research.

A VITAL RESOURCE

If you are contemplating the preparation and presentation of a business plan in almost any field of small business, you should be aware of the resources and assistance you can get through the Association of Small Business Development Centers, which have offices in every state in the United States. ASBDC can be particularly helpful in matters relating to research and development, whether for the benefit of the whole company or just one segment of it.

SBDC, for example,

- Helped a scientist in Indiana to obtain a $50,000 grant to establish a scientific laboratory as a small business that later began to serve major corporations, such as DuPont, Boeing, and Polaroid

- Provided guidance for a Michigan company to conduct agricultural studies and revive a food processing plant that had failed, thus greatly improving the economic stability of a small rural town

- Provided loans and technological studies to a metal processing company that wanted to double its capacity and spread its operations into the production of plastic products

- Made it possible for a cooperative venture in Massachusetts to expand a waste-collection business into a recycling company with the capabilities for providing service to three adjoining communities

- Assisted an adult language school in obtaining state funding to establish branch centers and curricula throughout several counties in the metropolitan New York City area

- Supplied feasibility studies that enabled two entrepreneurs to start and support a technical research center to investigate new applications for forest products in upstate New Hampshire, thus revitalizing a dying industry and providing jobs for the inhabitants of a small township

- Helped two engineers in Georgia to start a diagnostic research firm to improve the performance of commercial air conditioning equipment in local offices and factories in the Atlanta area.

For further information on Small Business Development Centers and how they can assist your small business, whether in research or any other field, see the Appendix, page 265.

New Business Plan for

An Environmental Research Facility

To Be Located

> At the Junction of the Wilmington
> and Skidaway Rivers at Thunderbolt
> In the Vicinity of Savannah, Georgia

a proposal to

> Wachovia Bank

proposed by

> THE DEVELOPERS OF THE PLAN
>
> *Peach State Research Consultants, Limited*
> *The Port Royal Ecological Study Group*

THE NEED FOR THE PROPOSED ENVIRONMENTAL FACILITY

During the past decade, there has been increasing evidence that the Low Country wetlands of Georgia and adjacent South Carolina coastal regions are being seriously threatened by a growing list of ecological "enemies." These include:

Heavy population expansions along southern shores

The boom in residential building

Increasing wastes from commercial and industrial installations

Climatic changes, particularly alternating floods and drought and tropical storms

The weak enforcement of antipollution regulations and restrictions

A lack of public education about the local and regional environment

Two organizations directly concerned with programs to protect the environment, Peach State Research Consultants (PSRC) and the Port Royal Ecological Study Group (PRESG), have made intensive studies of the deteriorating situations and have evolved a plan of action. The plan focuses on the initial need for an environmental research facility, tentatively referred to as simply ERF, and hereby initiates a proposal and request for funds and authorization to launch this venture within the next twelve to eighteen months.

WHY A RESEARCH FACILITY?

Exhaustive research and investigations by PSRC and PRESG have demonstrated without doubt that *the lack of specific knowledge* about wetland problems has blocked all significant steps to take positive and recuperative action. Why?

Legislators neither introduce nor support enough laws and regulations to protect the environment because they are ignorant of the principles involved.

Environmental laws are low on the priority lists of local governments and violations are overlooked because law enforcement agencies are too busy fighting crime.

Preservation and antipollution agencies are at the top of the list when it comes to budget cutbacks and thus are seriously understaffed.

Areas in and near wetlands are increasingly overdeveloped because authorities issue too many building permits without realizing the extent of the natural destruction that will take place.

WHAT WILL BE THE PURPOSE OF THE PROPOSED INSTITUTION?

The Environmental Research Facility (ERF) will be established for one basic reason: to investigate and report on all of the situations, causes, and circumstances that (a) contribute to the health of and improve the quality of the existing wetlands, and (b) threaten the wetlands and hasten environmental deterioration. The findings of the research programs and all related factors will be publicized regularly and widely in an ERF newsletter to be published monthly, a quarterly summary, and an annual report. These will be mailed to both specialized and broad readerships, including legislators, government officials, commercial and industrial associations, the media, and the general public. The thrust of the newsletters and reports, and all other ERF publications, will be *education*. Each issue will, in fact, concentrate on a different segment of the audience, to present data and statistics that particularly affect them and their spheres of activity. Thus, for example, one issue might be devoted to *legislative* matters, another to *population* trends, and a third to *developments*.

As a program aired on SAV-TV explained, "If people *know* what hurts them, they'll take steps to do something to alleviate the pain. If they don't know, they won't act."

THE FINANCIAL NEED

The evaluations of PSRC and PRESG, supported by economic projects made by their accounting firm, Tregor and Rowe, signify that the cost of the proposed research facility will be not more than $4 million and not less than $3.5 million. With this in mind, the proposers hereby request a public service loan of $2.7 million, judging that the difference will be covered by funds available through the following sources: state agencies, county agencies, regional corporations, educational institutions, environmental associations, and an intended public drive for donations. These sources will also account for maintenance costs after the facility is built.

The sum of $2.7 million will be used for the following implementations of the plan, which will be described in detail in an accounting statement to be submitted separately to Wachovia by Tregor and Rowe:

1. A research center, 2,200 square feet in size and properly equipped, to be situated on donated land at the junction of the Wilmington and Skidaway Rivers.

2. A four-wheeled Land Rover, or equivalent, for exploration and investigation.

3. A 16-foot, shallow-draft boat with an inboard motor, suitable for navigating wetland areas for research purposes, without threat to the ecology.

4. A small press and accessories for the publication of newsletters and reports; and related communications installations.

Small Business Plan for a Mobile Electronics Service

Right Connections

submitted to

First Bank & Trust Company
Omaha, Nebraska

submitted by

DOUGLAS REMINGTON
SARAH JANE DEMING
ANTHONY J. PERUTTI

Right Connections, Inc.
26A Burlington Building
Council Bluffs, Nebraska

DESCRIPTION OF THE ENTERPRISE

Right Connections, Inc., is a brand-new service geared to serve clients in the Omaha metropolitan region, and later in outlying suburbs as the need arises. It was established by three partners with educational backgrounds in scientific research, two of whom had served with the R&D departments of electronic corporations, and all of whom have brought to the business the experience of more than ten years selling television sets, computers, and other electronic equipment at the retail level. Before starting the business, they enrolled in the University of Nebraska adult education course in electronics research, for which they received certification following 134 hours of classroom training.

Right Connections evolved because the three principals were research-motivated and fully aware of the problems so many customers had when trying to purchase, hook up, and program sophisticated electronic units ranging from simple telephone message machines to videotape players, computers, compact disk players, stereos, fax machines, printers, and other state-of-the-art products. Even the best installation handbooks and owner's guides were usually Greek to the purchasers and of little help when equipment broke down or could not be satisfactorily adjusted for peak performance.

Making house calls with a mobile unit, the three principals spend their time visiting customers on call, whether to make installations, clean and tune equipment, test for defective wiring, or make necessary repairs and adjustments.

STATEMENT OF PURPOSE

The company requires financial assistance in the amount of $46,000 in order to purchase a van and equip it as a mobile unit, which will have not only tools and instruments for electronic testing and repair, but shelves for products and a fold-out display at the rear. It was perceived early on after the three entrepreneurs established their on-site installation and repair service that they were constantly dealing with people who were *prospective customers* and who would make purchases on the spot if they so desired—especially accessories or embellishments to equipment being serviced.

At the present time, the firm books an average of seven house calls a day, handles an equal number of service jobs in the Council Bluffs shop, and is handling as many as twelve work orders for repairs on electronic equipment brought in from the field. It is estimated that a minimum of one out of every four service customers is a good prospect for the purchase of accessories under repair, and one in ten will have an interest in purchasing a major item of electronic equipment. Thus, the display and availability of merchandise cannot fail to move a considerable number of goods each week.

Right Connections enjoys an unexpected advantage over many other firms in the field of electronics servicing: By proving their service capabilities *before* selling products, they win over many prospects who are hesitant about buying merchandise that is just going to add to their maintenance woes. As one satisfied customer explained, "I didn't want to have anything more to do with those 'high-tech' products that I can't deal with until I discovered a company that could assure me I'd enjoy them and have no more breakdown headaches. If there is the slightest hint of a malfunction, I get on the phone and in no time Doug or Sarah Jane or Tony are at the front door and my problems fly out the back door."

The company has any number of similar customer citations to support the above contentions, which makes it apparent that the proposed maintenance and repair combo van will be well worth the investment.

A PROJECTION FOR THE FUTURE

Although the business operations of Right Connections have been limited to consumers, the future plans for the company include the development of a research department and the eventual offering of services to businesses and corporations in the marketing area. These services will include the following:

- Development of corporate technical research programs in the electronics field

- Analyses of company-wide electronic equipment

- Consultation on electronic-related problems and methods of improving existing systems

- Publication of a newsletter, *Electronics Research*, to acquaint management with the latest developments in the burgeoning electronics field

Small Business Plan for

The AIDS Research Center, Inc.

A Research Center established for the research and study of the HIV and AIDS Viruses

submitted to

A. F. Harris Foundation of Atlanta, Georgia

(A Private Foundation established for the funding of Medical Research)

submitted by

MARY E. HARRIS

The Harris Foundation
Atlanta, Georgia

THE FOUNDERS OF THE AIDS RESEARCH CENTER

The AIDS Research Center is a research organization founded by the following three principals:

William G. Patterson, M.D., PhD., Director of Immunological Studies at Emory University, and Harvard Fellow in Advanced Research Studies, a graduate of the University of Pennsylvania School of Medicine and Jefferson School of

Medicine. He is also a practicing physician at North Fulton County Hospital in Atlanta, Georgia.

Sheila Whittaker, M.D., PhD., Immunologist at Emory Hospital in Atlanta, and former member of the President's Council of Physicians for AIDS Research and Studies. A graduate of the Yale School of Medicine, she is a physician at the Emory University School of Research and Immunology.

Terence D. Minot, M.D., PhD., Immunologist at the University of Georgia and member of the staff at Emory University in Atlanta. He attended the College of Physicians at Cambridge University in Oxford, England, and the Bristol School of Medicine, Bristol, England. He served a residency at the Sussex Hospital in England and the Jefferson Hospital in Philadelphia, and is a member of the staff at Emory University Hospital.

RESEARCH PLAN

The AIDS Research Center of Atlanta will conduct intense private research for the private business community, private and public pharmaceutical companies, and for the National Institutes of Health in Washington, D.C. and the Centers for Disease Control in Atlanta, Georgia.

All information collected from research and for future research will be amassed with private funding secured from A. F. Harris Foundation, which is also located in Atlanta, Georgia. There will be a board of eight directors that direct and oversee the administration of the research center as well as administer the distribution of the information gained from the center's research activities.

The research center will have an initial staff of forty-two people, with the object of expanding the staff to one hundred people after the first year of operation.

CLIENT/PATIENT BASE

Patients will be admitted to the research center from both the public and private sectors throughout the U.S. and the world. Both private and public medical assistance will be accepted. The research center will be listed as a Medicare and Medicaid provider in order to serve the needs of both indigent and elderly patients. Pediatric services will also be provided.

A Plan for

The Health & Fitness Institute
of Norton, Utah

A REVOLUTIONARY NEW AND HEALTHY METHOD
TO CHANGE AND MODIFY EATING
HABITS AND TO PROMOTE A
HEALTHY LIFESTYLE

THE FOUNDERS

The Health & Fitness Institute of Norton, Utah is a for-profit business designed to aid individuals through behavioral modification and education in changing their eating habits and living a healthy lifestyle.

The Health & Fitness Center is owned and funded by KBL Partnership, Ltd. The partnership consists of Charles Kimble, David Barrett, and Thomas Lewis. Their qualifications are as follows:

Charles A. Kimble, M.D., PhD., the University of Utah and Duke University. Internist and Clinical Psychologist.

David H. Barrett, M.D., PhD., the Ohio State University School of Medicine and Department of Psychology.

Thomas P. Lewis, M.B.A., Wharton School of Business, J.D., Wake Forest University School of Law. Corporate Attorney. A.A. in Accounting, Wake Forest University.

THE CURRICULUM

Each enrollee or patient upon entering the program will be evaluated both mentally and physically. Based on the results of this evaluation, a specifically designed diet and health program will be created for each individual staying at the Institute.

The fitness and health program will be held for a period of eight weeks, during which all participants will attend healthy living classes and lectures, and participate in customized workout programs integrated with a healthy diet specifically designed for their health needs and goals.

There will be an initial staff of sixty health care professionals who will conduct the program. Individuals as well as groups of thirty or less will be permitted to participate in a group-structured health program.

A plan for a second Health and Fitness Institute will be discussed after the third year of operation.

FINANCIAL NEEDS

The business plan calls for a grant of $50,000 from the medical service funds, and a loan of $100,000 to establish the Institute and see it through its initial year of operation. Federal assistance will also be required at a later date if the Institute is to assist participants who are indigent but require continuing rehabilitative treatment of this nature.

Chapter 7

Plans
for
Educational
Institutions

This chapter simulates the preceding one on research, in that it briefs the reader on the standard categories of a conventional small business plan, but then focuses on those functional areas and situations that are advantageous because of the nature of the enterprise. These benefits cover such subjects as:

- Private grants from universities and other large educational institutions

- Grants and support from public institutions and the government at all levels

- Tax relief

- Consultation and advisory services at cost, or in some cases free

- The use of educators and technical specialists "on loan," with all or most of the cost being assumed by the institution supplying the instructors

- The provision of classroom, facilities, and equipment to the small business owners at little or no cost

- Publicity, promotion, and sometimes marketing assistance by larger teaching institutions who see the small firm as being supplemental to their own educational goals

- Promising opportunities for future growth, especially if the educational subject areas concerned are ones that are likely to expand, whether nationwide or regionally

Following this short introductory text, five model plans are presented in the field of private educational institutions.

Professional Plan for a Private Instructional Institution

Keyboard Tutorials

submitted to

The Educational Council
State Collegiate System

East Campus
Canton, Ohio

submitted by

HARRISON G. JEFFERSON, M.A.
JUDITH COWLE LAFFERTY, M.S.

Alliance Computers, Inc.
Suite 45A
100 Central Avenue
Alliance, Ohio

DECLARATION OF INTENT

It is the goal of the petitioners, Harris G. Jefferson, M.A., and Judith Cowle Lafferty, M.S., to obtain a grant of $11,000 for the following purpose: to establish a private adult education program, tentatively entitled Keyboard Tutorials, for the benefit of adults of any age who would like to be more knowledgeable about computers and other aspects of electronic data processing (EDP) systems. As owners and managers of a retail computer store, Mr. Jefferson and Ms. Lafferty have discovered firsthand that very few of the purchasers of hardware and software, and electronics products in general, have even the most rudimentary concept of what they are buying, though they may have invested hundreds, if not thousands, of dollars in state-of-the-art equipment. They have also discovered that, astonishingly, many owners of expensive computers will never get beyond the basic stages of use and will never explore the real capabilities of their machines. As they expressed it to a journalist interviewer, "It's like buying an airplane and running it back and forth around the landing strip without ever getting into the air."

The purpose of the petitioners is to establish a practical course in computer functioning, operation, and programming for owners or users of electronic data processing equipment of all kinds. The curriculum will be practical, with hands-on instructions for using computers to best advantage. One of the advantages of the course is that it will be conducted in an actual, functional computer retail store, where the students will have every opportunity to observe and familiarize themselves with some of the latest products available, as well as older models still in common use. Classes will be divided into three tiers, to be selected at the desire of the student after conferring with the instructors to determine the skills, capabilities, and objectives of the student: (1) Beginner, (2) Intermediate, and (3) Advanced.

Students will not be required to supply any materials or do homework, with the exception of those who specifically request worksheets or programs they can use for practice on their own home computers.

Students who complete a course satisfactorily will be awarded a "Certificate of Completion," which will specify the subjects covered by the student, the amount of time committed to classes and other instruction, and the degree of proficiency achieved.

QUALIFICATIONS OF THE INSTRUCTORS

The faculty for Keyboard Tutorials will be formed by the following members:

Harrison G. Jefferson, M.A., who received his master's degree in communications at the University of Ohio in 1978, taught writing and research courses at Meredith Junior College, Lancaster, Indiana, and for eight years has been a co-owner and manager of Alliance Computers, a retail store dealing in electronic data processing products in Alliance, Ohio.

Judith Cowle Lafferty, M.S., who received her master's degree in computer science at Purdue University in 1981, was an instructor in the science department of the university for seven years, and for the past six years has been a co-owner and manager of Alliance Computers.

Kevin Allbright, an experienced computer technician who has had more than twelve years of experience in the installation, repair, and maintenance of electronics products of many kinds, including all major brands of electronic data processing equipment.

Dorothy Ann Kemper, CPA, who will serve as the new school's bookkeeper, auditor, and treasurer.

Proposal and Plan for a Nonprofit Educational Venture

The Cultural Council of the Cumberlands

The Transition of a Small Neighborhood Enterprise into a
Broad Community Institution to be located in Nashville, Tennessee

presented by

THE NASHVILLE ART LEAGUE

THE SOUTHERN CHORAL SOCIETY

THE BEAUMONT ORCHESTRA

THE CENTRAL TENNESSEE FRIENDS OF THE LIBRARY

THE OAK HILL GARDEN SOCIETY

THE MUNICIPAL SCHOOL COUNCIL

THE MUSIC ROW JAZZ GROUP

THE PLANTATION PLAYHOUSE

UPCOUNTRY HANDCRAFTERS

presented to

HARDESTY & WADE PUBLIC RELATIONS

26 Charlotte Avenue
Nashville, TN 37205

STATE OF THE ARTS

Although Nashville, Tennessee, has long been known for its country music, and has become a mecca for tourists from around the world who come to visit famed Opryland, listen to singers and bands galore, and enjoy music and entertainment during all seasons of the year, many other aspects of music and the arts have existed only as fragmented, neighborhood entities. Thus, there have been dozens of small musical groups, theatrical societies, art leagues, crafts circles, and the like throughout the very broad stretches of the city and its tangential communities.

In the 1970s, efforts were made to join these scattered cultural and talent organizations under a central council. And, indeed, certification was granted for such a movement and office space was offered at cost in a public building near the state capitol. The timing, however, proved to be unfortunate, during a period when downtown Nashville was in the throes of financial difficulties and the attention of community leaders was directed more at economic development than the enhancement of the cultural arts. Thus, all endeavors in the direction of cultural consolidation were put on hold for what was intended to be a "short spell," but proved to be of long duration.

CONSOLIDATED STATEMENT OF GOALS

The Cultural Council of the Cumberlands has now been proposed as the parent organization to be formed and to include all of those activities, entities, and programs that could favorably be considered to be cultural in nature and aimed at the enrichment and enlightenment of the public. In essence, what has popularly been termed the "CCC" will be both an organization on paper, with a large membership, and a physical structure suitable for presentation of the arts in all forms.

Musical productions, theater, ballet, dance, painting, sculpture, song, symphony, art leagues, galleries, lectures, museums, and more have been alive and thriving for generations in the Cumberlands region. Alone and together, they have enriched the population with live stage performances, art exhibits, concerts, benefits, holiday specials, and tours on both a year-round and seasonal basis. Environmental, historical, and professional museums have also played important roles in the education, orientation, and recreation of area residents and have hosted events and programs of continuing interest. While many of these institutions, both public and private, are permanent and self-sustaining, they would benefit immeasurably from association with the many arts through the proposed cultural council.

STATEMENT OF FINANCING

During the past ten months, The Cultural Council of the Cumberlands has received accreditation as a municipal nonprofit institution, conceived for the public good and dedicated to the enhancement of culture in all phases and all levels within the geographical and political boundaries of the city of Nashville. As an authorized and certified entity, CCC has been engaged in private and public fund-raising during this period and expects by year's end to have on hand, or pledged, a total sum of $3 million, to be used toward the design and construction of a Family Pavilion for the Visual and Performing Arts, with facilities for events, activities, programs, and performances in the fields of all of the organizations participating in the venture and listed as members.

The land, 7.3 acres adjacent to Shelby Park, east of the central city, has been donated by the Country Music Foundation, with a grant for total maintenance fees from a private individual who prefers to remain anonymous.

Consultation with designers, architects, city planners, and professional consultants has resulted in the acceptance of a firm figure for the sum required to supplement the $3 million previously mentioned for the design and construction of the building. That figure has been realistically established as $4,560,000.

The purpose of this plan is to request a loan of that size, to be received in three equal installments over a period of 12 months from the time of approval.

FUTURE FINANCING

Professional estimates agree that all future financing will be adequately supplied through the following:

- Membership fees for individuals, groups, and corporate sponsors
- Donations by individuals, groups, and sponsors
- Receipts from sales of tickets for individual programs and events
- The sale of art, crafts, and other creations through the center's gift shop and mail-order service

ACTIVE PARTICIPANT ORGANIZATIONS

The following organizations have enrolled as active members of The Cultural Council of the Cumberlands:

The Nashville Art League

The Southern Choral Society

The Beaumont Orchestra

The Central Tennessee Friends of the Library

The Oak Hill Garden Society

The Municipal School Council

The Music Row Jazz Group

The Plantation Playhouse

Upcountry Handcrafters

The Confederate Barbershoppers

The Cultural Center of the University of Tennessee

Opryland Singers

The Nashville Board of Museums

Kensington School of Talent

The Environmentalists League

Cumberland River Entertainers

Arts & Crafts Institute

Organizational Proposal for a Private Educational Institution

Career Blazers

*Located on a Suburban Campus
on the South Bend River
Near the Town of Elmsford, Ohio*

presented to

Central Ohio State Bank & Trust Company
and the Ohio State Board of Education

presented by

PRINCIPALS:

GEOFFREY JAMES HOWE, PH.D.
ELEANOR GAINES JUDGE, PH.D.
MARCUS R. PLENARY, M.B.A.
JESSICA DOYLE HALSTEAD, M.A.
LUCIAN C. SCOTT, L.L.D.

STATEMENT OF PURPOSE

The faculty and board of Career Blazers, a private school of business established in 1982, have plans for a major expansion to meet the rapidly growing needs of students throughout the state of Ohio, long known for its emphasis on higher learning. Originally founded as a supplemental educational arm to assist students in other schools who were having classroom difficulties or required additional credits, Career Blazers has been completely reorganized as an accredited junior college for individuals who have completed high school and want advanced training in computers, data processing, and related subjects.

Career Blazers seeks immediate funding in the range of $200-220,000 to purchase a bank of computers and terminals for classroom use and to cover the salaries and benefits of two additional faculty members with advanced degrees in data processing technology. An additional sum of $50,000 will be required at the end of one year to enlarge two existing classrooms and one office on campus. The college owns ample land in its present location and requires no expansion of real estate to maintain or enhance the natural beauty of its existing environment.

DESCRIPTION OF THE EDUCATIONAL FACILITIES AND PERSONNEL

The campus consists of an administrative office building, four classrooms in an adjoining structure, two faculty residences, and a separate auditorium, which also houses a 20,000-volume library, study rooms, and three student workshops. Although the college has no sports or recreational facilities per se, it enjoys a participatory arrangement with the town of Elmsford, whereby its students can use the town recreation center and playing fields, regardless of their residential origins.

With an emphasis on the use of computers and electronic data processing, the curriculum is designed to serve individuals who desire to develop their careers in the business field, but most particularly in the following disciplines: accounting, advertising, legal services, management, marketing, merchandising, office administration, and training. Permanent members of the administration and faculty include:

Geoffrey James Howe, Ph.D., President

Eleanor Gaines Judge, Ph.D., Curriculum Supervisor

Marcus R. Plenary, M.B.A., Computer Systems Analyst

Jessica Doyle Halstead, M.A., Instructor

Lucian C. Scott, L.L.D., Instructor and Consultant

Arlene C. Stahl, B.S., Instructor

Henry Clements, B.S., Instructor

Rosemary S. Downes, M.A., Librarian, Research Associate

Based on an average annual enrollment of 223 students, the school anticipates a 50 percent increase within three years.

SOURCES OF GROWTH

A number of developments in the Elmsford and Central Ohio region are clear indications that the school will continue to thrive and can anticipate steady enrollment and growth. These include:

- The influx of new industries, some of whose managers have expressed concern about the labor market and being able to hire employees who are well trained in computer technology
- The recent decision of the University of Ohio to phase out one of its branches located fifteen miles south of Elmsford
- The rapidly escalating use of computers and electronic data processing in all operational areas of business, commerce, and industry
- The certification of the school as one that is now eligible under the State of Ohio Grants and Scholarships Program to request financial help for its students in need

A Proposal for

The Newbury Academy
New Milford, Connecticut

proposed to

Bank of New England
10 Old Dominion Highway
West Hartford, Connecticut

proposed by

THE HEADMASTER, THE BOARD OF REGENTS

purpose

Mortgage application

PROFILE OF THE INSTITUTION

The Newbury Academy is a private, nondenominational residential institution that was founded in 1963 as a tutorial school to ready male students at the eighth-, ninth-, and tenth-grade level for proficiencies and examinations that would permit them to apply for entry into some of the state's more prestigious college preparatory schools, such as Kent, Choate, Taft, and Hotchkiss. At the time of its founding by Alistair Harvey Conkling, Ph.D., former Dean of Admissions at Trinity University in Hartford, Connecticut, the school consisted of a headmaster, assistant headmaster, seven faculty members, a small administrative and housekeeping staff, and sixty-five students.

Newbury is situated on twenty-two acres along the banks of the Housatonic River, housed in six buildings that had once been a Roman Catholic retreat. Shortly after its founding, Dr. Conkling purchased an adjacent twelve-acre farm as his private residence, but with a plan to produce vegetables and dairy products at cost for use by the school kitchen and dining hall.

In 1989, following the death of Dr. Conkling, who bequeathed the entire farm and land to the school, Newbury Academy was reorganized as a college preparatory school in its own right and no longer specializing in tutorial education. By then, the enrollment had risen to 109 residential students and 18 day students. At that time, after considerable recruitment efforts, the Newbury Alumni Association, in coordination with the Newbury Board of Regents, selected a husband-and-wife team of educators, Amanda Guthrie Shannock, Ph.D., and Harvey A. Shannock, Jr., LL.D., to serve as joint headmasters.

Another very important milestone in the history of Newbury Academy occurred two years later when the Board—following a plan that had been in everyone's mind at the time of the headmasters' selection—authorized the school to become coeducational. Two of the existing dormitories were enlarged and the first contingent of female students—thirty in all—arrived on campus in September, 1993. That fall, Newbury Academy celebrated its thirtieth anniversary by undertaking a six-month alumni fund drive.

THE PRESSING NEED

Newbury Academy is now at the crossroads. Although the alumni Anniversary Fund drive was successful, and although the academy has received a special educational grant from the New England Preparatory School Foundation and a modest loan from the Nutmeg State Bank of Stamford, Newbury is critically in need of a twenty-year trust mortgage, or equivalent, in the amount of no less than $565,000. It has been found, since the school went coeducational in 1993, that the dormitory facilities are inadequate to meet the needs of the transition that has taken place, and that there are only three alternatives: (1) to obtain the necessary financing to add to existing funds and build a new dormitory, (2) to reduce the number of students, or (3) to backtrack and return to a single-sex institution.

The second alternative must, almost automatically, be ruled out on economic grounds. To reduce the number of students would reduce the school's income to a degree that might threaten its very existence.

The third alternative, while possible, would be a major setback in the educational concept and planning of the academy. Furthermore, it goes strongly against the current trends of today's teaching institutions to further coeducational programs and curricula at all academic levels, both private and public alike.

It is the decision of the headmasters, the faculty, and the Board that the only possible course of action is the first one.

ARCHITECTURAL IMPROVEMENT PLAN

Newbury Academy plans to use the proposed mortgage income plus existing developmental funds to mount a $900,000, two-year building program. This would include:

- A new dormitory capable of housing and servicing fifty female students
- An expansion to the existing field house to provide a separate locker room, showers, and toilet facilities for girls
- A fifty-seat bus for the use of girls' teams when they are traveling to other schools for athletic contests

With the above additions and improvements, Newbury Academy will be in a class with other fine coeducational schools in the New England region.

Small Business Plan for

Jeffrey Hart Motivational School for Successful Living

submitted to

First Union Bank of Seattle

1145 Harbourshore Drive
Seattle, WA 33401

submitted by

J.H. ENTERPRISES, INC.

P.O. Box 6601
Seattle, WA 33402

THE PLAN: A SCHOOL TO INSTRUCT AND INSPIRE

Renowned motivational speaker and leader, Jeffrey W. Hart, Ph.D., who has been inspiring millions for the past twenty years, wishes to create a private learning center to help people gain their full potential in life through a positive mental attitude and fundamental time-tested methods of leadership and creativity that will aid any man or woman in their journey through life's most difficult moments.

The first motivational center will be located in downtown Seattle near the center of commerce and industry. Due to this prime location, the motivational center hopes to attract members of the business community who are interested in gaining new insight into their career goals as well as learning new skills that will take them to their goals in both their personal and professional lives.

Apart from the daily seminars conducted by Dr. Hart and his staff, motivational media such as books, learning materials, audiotapes, videotapes, and support materials will be available to the public through our Web site on the Internet and our color catalog.

FINANCIAL ASSISTANCE

Financial funding will come from a loan provided by the First Union National Bank of Seattle in the amount of $650,000. As the venture grows the company plans to go public and will issue shares of stock as the corporate debt is paid off. There will be a board of directors to oversee the fiscal operations as well as the growth of the venture as a whole.

Dr. Hart's main interest will be teaching and creating the support materials needed for the school. He will also be in charge of hiring and training other motivational instructors. The initial number of students for the first year will be 10,000, with an increase of 20 percent in attendance per year.

The second motivational school is planned for Alberta, Canada with the intent of instructing the same number of students yearly. The Canadian motivational school will accept primarily Canadian and non-U.S. students. Instruction will be given in French, German, English, and Spanish.

Chapter 8

Plans for Franchise Coordination

Samples of standard small business plans are included, covering franchise operations that will be familiar to most readers. A brief introductory text describes the ways in which the structure and purposes of such plans may differ from those for one-of-a-kind business ventures.

The objective of this chapter is to show readers who are interested in franchises how to prepare the best possible small business plan for their own use and development. Entrepreneurs are advised to study the business plan prepared by the franchise organization with great care, asking questions or obtaining further information if necessary. They should not stop there, however, but transfer the data and objectives into their own small business plan with whatever additions and modifications are necessary.

PLANNING A FRANCHISE VENTURE

Writing a business plan for a franchise is somewhat different from writing one for your own individual business. What you may be doing actually—depending on the franchise management—is completing an application and focusing on facts that will sell you as a person qualified to own and manage the operation in your location. But you still have a lot of homework to do first.

Fortunately, there are many books on the subject that you can select from (see Bibliography pages 263–266). Make it a point, too, to contact one of several associations in this field, such as the International Franchise Association. I try to interview people in your area who have operated franchises successfully for several years, to get an idea of the "good news" and the "bad news."

Here are some professional opinions you should think about, pro and con:

Advantages

Reduction of chances of failure. You can buy into a business concept that has already been tried and proven.

Standardized products and operations. You don't have to worry about whether the products will sell or the system will work.

187

Standardized accounting. You have everything spelled out for you, as well as forms and directions for all financial administrative functions.

Discount purchasing. You can compete with large national chains through the collective buying power of the franchiser.

Consultant services. You can turn to the franchiser for solutions to problems and answers to questions.

Training and orientation. You don't start your business until you have completed a practical, down-to-earth educational and training program.

Advertising. Your name and brands will already be well known, locally as well as nationally.

Financial assistance. You can obtain financing from some franchisers, or at least a payment plan that fits your capabilities.

Sales and marketing assistance. You can quickly learn the selling and merchandising techniques that have been successful and can be incorporated into your own franchise.

Point-of-sale materials. You don't have to worry about designing and printing posters, leaflets, banners, or other graphics because they will be supplied in whatever quantities you care to order—with new materials regularly being produced to tie in with seasonal promotions or holidays.

Advance Planning. You will be periodically supplied with business forecasts and statistics so you can know what to expect in regard to new products or services or sales projections.

Disadvantages

High cost. The franchises that are popular and most likely to keep succeeding and making profits are expensive to purchase.

Royalties. You will be saddled with royalties, often two to six percent a month.

Less management control. Since you will be, in effect, promoting another company's name and concept, you must follow the guidelines and policies specified by the franchiser.

Problems beyond your control. If the franchiser runs into difficulties, such as liabilities, lawsuits, or a dropoff in consumer interest, you too will feel the impact of these problems, and without being able to do much about it.

A Proposal for

Office Arsenal, Inc.

100 Palm City Mall
Savannah, Georgia

proposed to

Commercial Trading Bank International

37 South Wall Street
Brooklyn, New York

subject

General Reorganizational Plan

Being a business plan for the changeover of the company from a member of a commercial franchise to the status of an independent retailer.

DESCRIPTION OF THE BUSINESS ENTERPRISE

For the past nine years, Office Arsenal has been a member of a national franchise chain of more than 120 stores in thirty states in the United States. Its business has been the retailing of a very wide range of office supplies at discount prices. Such supplies included in the past, and will include in the future, computers and accessories, office machines and supplies, office furniture, audio-visual equipment and accessories, storage files and accessories, calendars and appointment books, accounting and business forms, stationery of every style and description, writing instruments, electronic organizers and calculators, janitorial supplies, communications boards and signs, telephones and other communications equipment, books and tapes, and mailroom packaging supplies and implements.

Office Arsenal is also in the mail-order business, with approximately 40 percent of its business attributed to sales through its catalogs and special mailings, not only across America but throughout North, Central, and South America. The company promotes thousands of name-brand office products both in-store and in-catalog, and urges customers to "Shop by Phone, Fax, Agent, or in Person." It promotes to customers the facts that:

You can save up to 75% every day

You do not have to join a club to get discounts

You can count on next-day delivery

You can shop at any time seven days a week

You are guaranteed a refund if dissatisfied

BUSINESS OBJECTIVES

Office Arsenal intends to focus on the same principles that have steadily built the business and increased profits during all nine years of the organization's existence. In addition, the company's management has plans for the following enhancements:

- Upgrading its employees at all levels and in all departments through training and orientation programs under the guidance of the School of Business of the University of Georgia

- Issuing its own discount credit card, in addition to accepting all national and regional credit cards

- Monthly open-house invitations, with refreshments, during which the public can meet store officials and department heads and make suggestions about the improvement of products and services, and any other matters that are relevant to their needs

- Staffing, equipping, and opening a new office department that will offer customers such services as copying, faxing, packaging, mailing, transcribing, printing, and much more—and all at the lowest prices in town

- Inaugurating a "Comparative Shopper" service, which will provide weekly comparisons of prices of key office-supply products with the prices of other major retailers and suppliers in the southern Georgia region. These will be posted in a central store area, as well as next to appropriate product selection shelves and display bays

FINANCIAL REQUIREMENTS

Office Arsenal requires equity financing in the total amount of $370,000, for the following purposes, to accomplish the business objectives outlined above:

1. $75,000 to discharge all obligations and remaining indebtedness to the parent franchise, Office Depot of America, Inc., and its divisions and subsidiaries

2. $95,000 to establish its new name and build a separate reputation, as described in the following Marketing Plan of Action

3. $100,000 for the purchase of part of its inventory from the franchise and for new independent inventory purchases

4. $40,000 for the hiring of new staff personnel (this seemingly small sum is supplemented by existing personnel recruitment funds)

5. $60,000 for the expansion of facilities to incorporate the enhanced inventory and new services described

MARKETING PLAN OF ACTION

Through its internal merchandising department and its external advertising and marketing agency, Southland Advertising Associates of Macon, Georgia, Office Arsenal will apply the above earmarked funds to the following programs for the recruitment of customers and the growth of the business:

1. A series of weekly "Highlight" advertisements in the retail sections of the Savannah *News-Press, Pennysaver,* and *Tell-N-Sell Shopper.*

2. A revision of the seasonal catalog to enhance its image and appeal, and to contain spot illustrations of products throughout its 160 pages.

3. Participation in, and partial sponsorship of, a new Chamber of Commerce "Boost the Business" gala, to be held at the Hotel Hyatt Regency Room, on the River Front, in mid-October of each year.

4. A "House Calls" consultation service, in which customers and prospective customers can request visits by experienced representatives of Office Arsenal to discuss any and all aspects of office complementation, improvement, and related functions—at no charge to the customer.

5. Free transportation to and from the store for customers whose businesses or homes lie within a radius of twenty miles from the Palm City Mall.

Business Proposal for the Establishment
of a Unique Personnel Agency

People . . . People . . . People

submitted to

The First National Bank of Dover
Dover, Delaware

submitted by

BETSY BATTER ASSOCIATES

34 Old Colony Road
Little Creek, Delaware

INTRODUCTION AND REQUEST FOR FUNDS

The personnel recruitment firm of Betsy Batter Associates herewith requests a business loan of $12,000 for the establishment of a subsidiary to be entitled People . . . People . . . People, which will be a partnership under the direction of two principals of the parent company. The new firm will be unique in that it will recruit individuals for positions that are full-time, but only for limited periods ranging from six months to three years. Thus, it will be catering to organizations that need qualified employees for special projects that will start and end on specified dates. Examples might be a public relations specialist for a two-year program leading up to the celebration of a corporate anniversary, or a sales promotion manager to supervise a ten-month introduction of a new product, or a biochemist to operate a scientific laboratory research program under a three-year grant.

The $12,000 financing will enable the parent company to open a separate department in its present office and equip it with the necessary communications and bookkeeping installations for the conduct of business. It is expected that the additional income generated from current clients and prospective clients of the parent firm will put the venture on a profitable basis within three months of its inception, at which time the loan will be repaid.

PRINCIPALS

The two partners who will manage People . . . People . . . People, the new subsidiary, are:

Ellen Schell Darney, who served for ten years as the assistant personnel manager for DuPont & Company, and who for five years thereafter was the owner and manager of the Darney Placement Agency in New Castle, Delaware.

Sumner Todd, a former research analyst for personnel development for Delaware Bay Industries, Inc., and the author of two professional guidebooks on labor recruitment.

These two specialists will function independently from the parent company, but will have the option of using Betsy Batter as a consultant at any time. Ms. Batter, the owner and founder of the parent company, has managed her own business for seven years and before that was a partner in the Bay Area Personnel Agency in Baltimore.

ANTICIPATED BUSINESS RANGE

When planning the new business, Ms. Batter based her business projections on the size and nature of Betsy Batter Associates over a three-year period, as evaluated by her accounting firm, Harvey & Hall of Dover. Her specialty during this documented period of operation was women reentering the workforce after completing family-raising responsibilities, which comprised about 40 percent of her business. The remaining 60 percent was more general in nature, though largely the recruitment of employees for corporations in the Dover area.

Harvey & Hall documented the fact that Betsy Batter Associates had made 6,819 placements during the three-year period and had received a gross of $190,000. An additional income of $23,000 was received from the firm's assignments as a recruiting and personnel consultant. An analysis of these figures revealed that more than 28 percent of the placements were for employees who were hired on a limited-term basis.

These data led Ms. Batter to decide that a specialty arm of the firm would be active and profitable. Furthermore, it would be in a field in which there appeared to be no competition. An added benefit was the fact that promotion and publicity for the unique subsidiary would also bring the parent firm to the attention of past, current, and prospective clients.

COMPETITION

The parent company, Betsy Batter Associates, numbers the following as its chief competitors within a practical operational range of 25 miles:

Dover Personnel, Inc., which has been a leading agency in the region for 25 years, but which has not been recently aggressive in trying to extend its business

Campus Personnel, Ltd., which specializes almost entirely in recruiting and placing teachers and educational employees in schools and colleges throughout the state of Delaware

Strictly Business, whose focus is on technical supervisory people, mainly in the middle-management range

The Woodward Organization, which tends to conduct its business in non-profit and public-service fields, since its owner and founder is personally committed and dedicated to ventures for the public good

As indicated above, People . . . People . . . People has no known direct competition in its unique field of limited-period employment.

A Proposed Business Plan for

Southeastern Marketing

The Continental Building
23 Forest Drive
Wilmington, NC 28401

purpose

The Relocation of a Direct Mailing Firm

DESCRIPTION OF THE BUSINESS

Southeastern Marketing, known popularly to our associates during two decades of operation as "The User Friendly People," offers a complete array of direct mail services to customers ranging from individuals with personal needs to large corporations demanding a wide variety of applications. SM offers, for example:

- Lettershop operations, automated or personal, including sorting, folding, sealing, inserting, tabbing, labeling, collating, and metering

- Creative design, at the hands of experienced graphics designers in-house and talented artists on call

- Persuasive copywriting by wordsmiths who have proven skills in many fields, including advertising, editorial, promotion, and public relations

- Professional research, to document statistics and other data to be published by clients, or to compile specialized mailing lists for target marketing campaigns

- Database operations, including list maintenance, U.S. Postal Certification, and ZIP processing

- Addressing via all media, including ink-jet, laser, Cheshire labels, and pressure-sensitive labels

- Personalized packaging, labeling, and distribution

- Fulfillment, including data entry, follow-up, and response analysis

- Membership and credit card embossing

STATEMENT OF PURPOSE

Southeastern Marketing has conducted commercial and industrial studies to determine the part played by *location* in the development of business and the relationship to company growth and profits. It has been concluded beyond question, both through internal studies by management and through surveys made by an outside consultant, that the company would benefit, financially and structurally, through a move from its present location in the Continental Building to a different location. The site selected is a smaller building, suitable for single occupancy, in the southeastern section of the city, closer to the waterfront. Indications are that (a) the location would be more convenient for present customers, and (b) the location would attract new customers from this busy industrial sector.

For the purpose of relocation, Southeastern Marketing seeks a loan of $160,000 for the following purposes:

- Shutdown of existing facilities

- Preparation and enlargement of new facilities for the existing company departments

- Preparation of facilities for two new departments, to expand SM's capabilities in the service of customers and the development of new business

- Moving and transportation costs

It is anticipated that 40 percent of the above sum would be needed immediately, and the balance over the course of six months, at the end of which time the move would be made.

Summary of Factors Considered

In evaluating the business situation and making plans for the future, management took into account the following factors:

1. *The market.* It was increasingly evident that the market for the company's kind of enterprises was gradually shifting from the northwestern area of the city to the southeast, and that prosperity would lie in a completely different perimeter than that which existed when SM was founded a generation ago.

2. *The labor force.* Although there has been relatively little change in personnel recruitment options during the past decade, it was easily seen that the intended new location would be more favorable for transportation and commuting for employees. This situation would have a twofold benefit: simplifying the recruitment of full-time and part-time employees, and saving time and improving the efficiency of the workforce.

3. *Transportation.* Over and beyond the commuting benefits above, management foresaw in the proposed move both an improvement in the availability and speed of transportation for delivery purposes, and a lessening of transit costs for the receipt and delivery of customers' parcels.

4. *Raw materials.* Proximity to waterway sites, as well as to highway and railway facilities, would result in the expediting of supplies required for the normal conduct of business.

5. *Image.* It was evident that Southeastern Marketing would have a better, more respected image in the eyes of the public and customers alike in its own well-marked building, where the company name and logo could be prominently displayed on the exterior and in the entrance.

6. *Ecological quality.* Although not overly weighted in various considerations, it was deemed to be a fact that the company could more conveniently and inexpensively comply with municipal and state environmental regulations in the proposed new location than in the old one.

Amended Business Plan for
_____

Twin State Printing

for the attention of

Twin State Investors, Inc.
Hanover, NH
White River, VT

presented by

OLGA GREGORIEFF
ARTHUR TREMONT
JEFF DONALDSON
RUTH JAMES LAMBERT
ARTHUR TREMONT, JR.

Connecticut River Landing
West Lebanon, NH 03784
_____

DESCRIPTION OF EXISTING BUSINESS

Known until last year as Four Guys Printing, the firm functioned for two decades as a commercial print shop, meeting the limited needs of businesses in the area and occasionally supplying consumers with letterheads, labels, and other common stationery needs. In an attempt to expand, the four owners discussed the possibilities of investing in a printing franchise, such as Insty Prints or ExpressPrint, but decided that (a) the investment was too unmanageable and (b) the stipulations were too restrictive. During a reorganization, two of the owners retired from the business and three entrepreneurs joined, to form Twin State Printing. The newcomers brought additional experiences and capabilities, thus making it possible to undertake more complex printing jobs and expand the market considerably.

Under its new label and reorganized procedures, Twin State Printing expects to be able to offer a very wide range of services, including not only letterheads and other stationery on order, but business forms, posters, reductions and enlargements, tickets, commercial offset, single- and multicolor printing, screen printing, promotional materials, and catalogs. As its new brochure states, "We aim to be the fastest print shop in the Upper Connecticut River Valley, with computerized typesetting and page layout, offering a complete service from start to finish, with high-volume multicolor work as easily and satisfactorily handled as the most basic printing job."

GOALS AND OBJECTIVES

In order to make the transition from an old-line print shop to a technologically acceptable printing plant, Twin State Printing requires an investment of $145,000 for the following purposes:

- Updated printing equipment

- Expansion of facilities

- Training

- Consultation

- Advertising and promotion

A special accumulative fund of $6,900, which was established some years ago, has already been expended on a professional evaluation of equipment and architectural plans and renderings for the proposed face-lifting. However, since much of this is visualization, rather than technological improvement, the next financial step must incorporate sufficient investment to add professional substance to the new image. A major part of the proposed investment—roughly 75 percent—would be for the following:

Screen printing equipment capable of utilizing heat transfers and printing on cloth, such as T-shirts, banners, bags, and ornamental hangings

Computerized instrumentation, capable of instant transmission and high reliability

Color uniformity and tone controls

Composition/offset prep for typesetting

Reorganization and upgrading of the darkroom

QUALIFICATIONS OF THE PRINCIPALS

Recognizing that the personnel structure of the business is perhaps even more important than the capabilities of the equipment and the modernization of the installations, Twin State Printing has assembled a highly qualified, well-balanced team of professionals to provide top-notch services to all customers, regardless of the size of the job or the complexity of the requirements. Our professional staff includes:

Olga Gregorieff, President, holding her master's degree in business administration from the Tuck School of Business at Dartmouth, and having six years of experience as a corporate business administrator

Arthur Tremont, Operations Manager, with more than twenty years experience as a master printer in four different types of printing plants

Jeff Donaldson, Supervisor, an expert in paper manufacture and printing procedures, and former manager of a commercial paper plant

Ruth James Lambert, Treasurer, a CPA with accounting degrees from Babson

Arthur Tremont, Jr., Designer, with a master's degree in design engineering from the University of Vermont, and eight years of experience as an art director at two Boston advertising agencies

Under this experienced staff, it is expected that there will be no fewer than six printing journeymen available on a full- or part-time basis to handle whatever jobs are undertaken on a seasonal schedule.

The firm has also engaged the services of Mittendorf and Small, graphics specialists in Springfield, Massachusetts, to serve as consultants whenever their assistance and expertise may be required. M&S has an enviable record of service with large corporations, small businesses, and government agencies.

MARKETING PLANS

Twin State Printing has staked its future on building a name for itself, not just in its current marketing area, but in a wide circumference of regions that include Sullivan and Grafton counties in New Hampshire and Windham and Windsor counties in Vermont. Through the services of its advertising agency, Jackson Associates in Burlington, Vermont, TSP also expects to place bids for major printing jobs, such as yearbooks and catalogs, with colleges and universities in Massachusetts, New Hampshire, and Vermont. Jackson Associates specializes in educational advertising and numbers among its clients more than twenty colleges and private schools in New England.

One of the firm's most recent ventures has been a catalyst for environmental protection and recycling programs in the Connecticut River/Twin State region. Two of its officers, Olga Gregorieff and Arthur Tremont, Jr., were recently cited by both the governors of Vermont and New Hampshire for their pioneering programs to recycle paper and other printing media. As a result, the company was awarded the government's "GREEN E" for its participation in this field of endeavor and has been authorized to display the familiar pine tree symbol on its offices and vehicles. The company is also contributing ten work hours a week by its staff for the environmental protection research program being undertaken by the University of Vermont.

COMPETITION

As in many other locations around the country, competition in the printing industry is not only keen but often frenzied. Small print shops blossom and fail with the seasons. A dozen or more national chains start, stop, and continue franchises in every city and town where they can get a foothold. Many small printers, whether franchised or otherwise, cut their prices recklessly, just to stay in business. And many customers become wary of the printing industry in general when their jobs are handled too rapidly and with resultant errors and waste.

Twin State Printing has survived because of its emphasis over the years on accuracy and dependability. Consequently, it has outlived the competition and expects continuously to do so. Its major competitors, of a permanent nature, are:

Minuteman Press, of Lebanon, NH, which is affiliated with a national chain and promotes speed and economy rather than the ability to handle major job orders

Yankee Press, of Brattleboro, VT, which is largely involved with the printing of books and catalogs and deals only occasionally in short runs or small orders

Business Plan for
_____

Scoops Ice Cream Store and Yogurt Shoppe

submitted to

Nationsbank of California

submitted by

ALAN TORRES, OWNER

ALICIA TORRES, OWNER

3342 Fernando Way
Los Angeles, California 44051
_____

STATEMENT OF PURPOSE

Alan Torres and Alicia Torres, owners and managers of Scoops Ice Cream & Yogurt Shoppe, want to open a second store in San Francisco, California. They are seeking an additional $200,000 in loan funds to rent and stock the second store. Existing equipment at the Los Angeles store will be moved and shared with the new store. New equipment will be purchased for the San Francisco store when the business is profitable and can sustain itself.

DESCRIPTION OF THE BUSINESS

The business has been in existence since 1990 and has shown a profit every year since it opened. Mr. Torres, now a U.S. Citizen, had his own ice cream business in Spain and applied his knowledge of the retail ice cream business to his business in Los Angeles. His wife, Alicia Torres, is his partner in the business. All of the ice cream and yogurt sold through the business is made on the premises. Apart from the retail store, Mr. Torres has contracts with several high-end restaurants in the Los Angeles area that include his ice creams and yogurts on their menus. Someday, Mr. Torres hopes to market his ice creams and yogurts nationwide on a mass scale.

There are no seasonal variations in the business; the level of business is constant. The business has six other employees, three full-time and three part-time.

LOCATION AND ENVIRONMENT

The current location for the Los Angeles store is on Fernando Way, which is three streets north of the fashionable "Rodeo Drive." Because of this location, the business enjoys a steady upscale clientele as well as a steady tourist business all year long.

The new store in San Francisco would be located in an equally exposed tourist-oriented and upscale section of town, called Wilkins Street, which intersects with the famous "cable car district" of the city. The business already supplies ice cream and yogurt to ten restaurants in the area, so the quality and the uniqueness of the product is known in the area.

COMPETITION

There are several other ice cream and yogurt stores in the area, but none of the other businesses cater to the "gourmet" style of ice cream and yogurt.

The other businesses that may be competitors are:

1. Baskin-Robbins store

2. TCYB Yogurt store

3. Warner's Ice Cream store (a locally owned store)

Most of the competitors are chain-operated stores and are located throughout the city of San Francisco. Warner's Ice Cream store is the only true competition; however, they are located on the south side of the city and are not in the present area. They also do not market their products through the same channels of distribution.

MARKETING

The business plans to market itself through the radio, newspaper, and various printed circulars and brochures distributed to the general public and the tourist population.

Additional exposure for the Scoops business will occur through the restaurants the business supplies with ice cream and yogurt. The business's ice creams and yogurts will be listed on the menus of the participating restaurants.

Mr. Torres plans to market the Scoops name as the primary identification for the product. Mr. Torres has already copyrighted the Scoops name and logo. He also has future plans for a Scoops ice cream bar as well as other product ideas.

Other documentation should include:

1. A lease agreement for the new store space

2. A profit/loss sheet or statement for the business

3. Copies of other loan agreements or notes that the business currently holds or has paid off

4. If needed, credit references from vendors, banks, investors, and others who are knowledgeable about the company

A Media Business Prospectus for

The Lean Times
A Diet-Oriented Periodical

presented to

Media Franchisers International
Burlington Building
Greensboro, North Carolina

presented by

LT Publications, Inc.
Durham, North Carolina

INTRODUCTION

The Lean Times is a diet-oriented magazine published in Durham, North Carolina, and distributed free in the area known as "The Triangle," which comprises Durham, Raleigh, and Chapel Hill. This periodical was first published in 1987 as a sole proprietorship, presenting articles and graphics on diet and health in general and weight loss and maintenance in particular. From the standpoint of economics, the periodical's income and overall profitability has always depended on paid advertising rather than subscriptions or a cover price. The production costs were kept low from the start, by running offset in newsprint, with a minimum of color and no glossy pages or inserts.

In its statement of concept, it was stated that "*The Lean Times* will be positioned as an editorial magazine geared to the diet-conscious market. Although many general health magazines are now being published, none are directly targeting the overall diet market."

According to the magazine's prospectus, each year surveys indicate that more Americans than ever are overweight—almost 65 percent of the population, to be exact, as defined in a Harris poll. Applying this statistic locally, the publisher was not unrealistic to expect that two out of every three individuals in the Triangle Area *should* be interested in the subject matter of *The Lean Times*. Future indications were that an even greater percentage of the population would—or should—be concerned about weight, as the population percentages continued to rise.

A MODEST PROPOSAL

Based on feedback and statistics from professional associations in the media field, such as the Magazine Publishers of America, the publisher of *The Lean Times* began, a year ago, to analyze the publication's previous five years of circulation and consider the pros and cons of changes and expansion beyond the existing operation. An initial goal, for example, was to expand the magazine on a regional basis, primarily through the Piedmont or Carolinas. Based on a survey of advertisers, however, it was determined that advertising—and hence financial—strength had to come from the Triangle area alone. Therefore, regional expansion might discourage local advertisers, while not replacing them enough with regional advertisers.

The conclusion reached was that the most promising expansion would take place if *The Lean Times* were to become a national diet magazine. Such augmentation would require a greatly expanded staff, for both editorial and advertising purposes, and a total change in the current format, including:

- Converting from free to paid subscription
- Changing from newsprint to glossy production
- Switching from local to national advertisers
- Increasing the use of color and graphics.

It has been estimated by outside consultants recommended by the National Association of Magazine Publishers that *The Lean Times* seek equity financing in the amount of $750,000 to plan and complete the proposed expansion.

A sum of $300,000 has already been pledged by LT Publications, Inc., of Durham, North Carolina, the parent corporation, which also publishes one other regional magazine, two sports publications, travel guides, and automotive handbooks. It is expected that additional funding in the amount of $200,000 will be obtained through a printing company, a mail-order service, and other local enterprises that have expressed interest in participating in the formation of the revised magazine.

Thus, for all practical purposes relating to this business plan, the total amount of equity funding requested by the publisher of *The Lean Times* is $250,000. It has been estimated that all such debts can be discharged by the magazine within three years, based on anticipated annual revenues from advertisers and subscribers.

A Proposal For a Franchise Transition

Although *The Lean Times* is capable of proceeding on its own, as outlined in this presentation, it is proposed that consideration be given to an affiliation of this diet-oriented periodical with Media Franchisers International. Specifically, such an alliance could be in the form of a partnership with MFI's subsidiary, the "Pounds Off" line of generic food products. It is further proposed that the magazine become a subsidiary, mainly for the purpose of sharing consumer lists and mailings, but retain its independent standing.

Market Analysis: Target Audience

New diet programs and weight-loss centers are blossoming across the country. Weight Watchers, for example, led the market at the start of the 1990s with revenues of $1.5 billion, while several other weight-conscious companies found their sales doubling in just two or three years. All of the trends are working in favor of *The Lean Times,* as America's weight problems become more pervasive and transcend all demographic categories, and as the money spent by consumers on weight problems continues to escalate.

The primary segment of the diet market that the magazine will target is described as female, aged 25-45, above average in education, and enjoying an above-average household income. For purposes of comparison, *The Lifestyle Market Analyst* categorizes American adults according to their interests. Four of their major classifications are similar to the magazine's target: Health Foods, Vitamins, Physical Fitness, and Self-Improvement.

According to the American Association of Advertisers in a recent study, the magazine industry is healthy, with more than 3,000 major publications in print and a few hundred new titles added each year. According to the Magazine Publishers of America, the data represent "an impressive show of faith in the future of the magazine industry." Profit figures are heartening as well, showing steady increases in advertising pages, increased per-page revenues for national advertisers, and profit margins for magazine publishers of about 15 percent.

COMPETITION

A number of periodicals have been categorized as potential competitors of the nationalized version of *The Lean Times*. The majority are commonly classified as health magazines, focusing on a total mind-and-body concept of well being. Examples are *Health, American Health, Weight Watchers*, and *Prevention*.

A related classification is that of fashion, as it relates to the figures of women interested in clothes and their looks. Examples of competitors in this category are *Vogue, Cosmopolitan*, and *Shape*.

While there are many health-oriented magazines in national circulation today, only one can be considered a diet magazine, and that is *Weight Watchers*. It is specialized, however, in that it has a reputation for primarily advertising and promoting Weight Watchers food products and diet programs. Thus, it can truly be stated that there is no independent national magazine that is for, and about, dieters.

The Lean Times has the opportunity to be the first magazine to fill this unique niche.

Small Business Plan for

Window Sealers, Inc.
of Santa Fe, New Mexico

submitted to

First National Bank of Santa Fe
1232 West Driftwood Street
Santa Fe, NM 40501
(612) 534-0909

submitted by

DAVID AND JAMES YELLMAN
P.O. Box 2056
Santa Fe, NM 40501

WHO WE ARE

David and James Yellman are experienced glassmen who have worked for Imperial Glass of Santa Fe for the last five years. They also have had vast experience since their childhood because their uncle, Martin Yellman, had his own glass shop and had both David and James working for him from an early age.

The goal of the new enterprise, Window Sealers, Inc., is to provide a general all purpose glass business and on-site glass and window tinting service. Apart from the everyday glass repair job, the Yellman brothers hope to provide services to many members of the artistic community of Santa Fe. At present, there is no glass company in Santa Fe that assists the various art galleries and artists with their artistic glass creations and gallery presentations. Window Sealers, Inc. hopes to fill this need and to expand the market for all kinds of glass work throughout the Santa Fe area.

A future plan is to expand the business to other areas in the United States through the use of the Internet to promote their products for glass and glass-care. Window Sealers, Inc. also plans to do business as The World of Glass on the Internet through their promotion of artistic glass and mirrored objects of art.

FINANCING

Funding will be secured from the initial start-up loan of $125,000 from the First National Bank of Santa Fe, which will be repaid in a five-year period. These funds will be used to rent a shop, equip a glass truck, and build a start-up inventory for the glass business. All licenses and fees will be paid through this also. Because of existing contacts and work history, the Yellmans have established a more-than-sufficient client base for the present and future.

Chapter 9

Plans for Nonprofit Ventures

Model plans are presented in their entirety; one of these is selected for a close-in examination, the objective being to show how each segment is similar to, or differs from, an SBP for an enterprise that is intended for profit.

A sidebar or panel defines the "nonprofit" status and structure and what criteria must be met to qualify in this category of business. It is emphasized here that such plans are necessary even for ventures that are not intended for profit.

Laws That Could Affect Business Status and Procedures

Small businesses submitting plans for *nonprofit* ventures have to evaluate their operations and policies very carefully to make sure they qualify in this category. And, in any case, it is important for you to be aware of regulations and restrictions that might affect the business venture you are proposing. The following laws and federal regulations are those that are most common in business and industry, listed alphabetically and not in any order of priority:

- Age Discrimination in Employment Act
- Civil Rights Act
- Clayton Act
- Consumer Credit Protection Act
- Consumer Products Safety Act
- Employee Retirement Income Security Act
- Equal Credit Opportunity Act
- Equal Employment Opportunity Act
- Equal Pay Regulations
- Fair Credit Billing Act
- Fair Credit Reporting Regulations
- Fair Debt Collection Regulations
- Fair Labor Standards Act
- Fair Packaging and Labeling Act
- Federal Trade Commission Act

- Federal Wages and Hours Regulations
- Federal Warranty Regulations
- Fibrous Materials Regulations
- Flammable Fabrics Regulations
- Food, Drug, and Cosmetic Act
- Hazardous Substances Regulations
- National Labor Relations Regulations
- Natural Materials Regulations
- Occupational Safety and Health Act
- Pure Food and Drug Act
- Robinson-Patman Act
- Sherman Antitrust Act
- Social Security Regulations
- Wheeler-Lea Act

Business Plan for a Small, Home-Based Business

Rib Ticklers

Located at
25 Hedgerow Drive
Morgan Hill, California

presented by

Ernestine Case Rollin, MD (ret.)
Owner and Operator
A Modest Request for a Grant

presented to

California Department of Commerce
Volunteer Service Bureau
Capastrano Building
San Jose, California

DESCRIPTION OF THE VENTURE

Rib Ticklers is a one-person, nonprofit venture on the part of a retired physician who is also a journalist and author of articles in professional medical journals, newspapers, and consumer health magazines. It started three years ago when the founder, just retired from active practice, volunteered at the local hospital in the town where she had been a resident for eighteen years to make visitations to elderly patients in the nursing home facility. Finding that many of these residents were depressed and/or noncommunicative, she typed up pages of jokes and amusing stories, which she read to some of the home's occupants and distributed to others.

This stratagem proved to be surprisingly effective, so much so that the next step was the creation of a four-page *LaughLetter*, which started as a textual printout on Dr. Rollin's word processor and in later issues was embellished with caricatures, cartoons, and other simple illustrations that could be composed on *Windows* software. When this humorous newsletter was distributed, it was often received with such gusto that recipients ran off copies on the office copying machine and passed them around to friends and colleagues.

It quickly became obvious that *LaughLetter* should have a much wider distribution, since its ameliorative effect was immediate and positive in the case of patients who were despondent or withdrawn.

A Practical Plan

Rib Ticklers has been established as a bona fide nonprofit partnership, certified to operate in the San Jose, California area, with headquarters in Morgan Hill. The founder has been joined by three other volunteers, all of whom work on a part-time basis, with a minimum of fifteen hours a week. Two of these new staff members are writers, and one is a professional illustrator, all accustomed to working with word processors and computers. Together, they have now prepared and distributed more than sixteen weekly issues of *LaughLetter*, and have increased the circulation from less than 100 copies to more than 800.

It is hereby requested that the Volunteer Service Bureau provide an annual grant to Rib Ticklers of $4,800, to be used toward the continuous publication and distribution of this humor newsletter. The sum requested would be used almost totally for postage and distribution, which in the past has been entirely out of the pockets of the founder and the other volunteers. It should be borne in mind that the cost of paper and printing has been underwritten thus far by three local printers, who have committed themselves to the project as a public service. Local hospitals, nursing homes, and several doctors' offices have pitched in freely to assure wider distribution and to publicize the venture in the hope of obtaining contributions toward the cost of production.

An Evolving Plan of Action

Realizing that growth, while a beneficial goal for all concerned, is increasingly costly, the staff of *LaughLetter* has designed the prototype for an income-producing venture that might eventually make the entire business self-liquidating. This is a start-up kit, with reproductions of ten past newsletters, a supply of one hundred jokes and thirty amusing stories, and samples of illustrations. The kit, which has been market-tested in mailings to twenty potential subscribers, has been well received and promises to meet the expectations of the staff. The plan is to sell these start-up kits for $25 and annual subscriptions to a continuing supply of materials for $60. The intended purchasers would be volunteer organizations, hospitals, and senior citizens' groups from coast to coast so that they, too, could "brighten the corner" of many a nursing home and senior center.

While it is not expected that the sale of this unique product will ever place Rib Ticklers in jeopardy of losing its nonprofit status, it is possible that the grant being requested by the company could be considerably decreased, if not eliminated, in the long run.

Business Plan for

Greenridge Urgent Care Center

submitted to

Muskegon National Bank
Muskegon, Michigan
and
Kent County Hospital Board
Grand Rapids, Michigan

submitted by

STEVEN S. CATCHWOOD, MBA
MARIAN MOORE DENNISON, MD
HARRISON SMART, MD
DONNA PERTS-SMYTH, CPA

Grand Rapids Medical Associates, Inc.
Shelby Building
Grand Rapids, MI 49502

STATEMENT OF OBJECTIVES

Greenridge Urgent Care Center is the new name for an existing medical center established ten years ago in Grand Rapids by a group of five physicians engaged in general medical practice. The organization encountered financial and organizational difficulties a year ago, following the death of the founder, the retirement of one physician, and the move of another to the West Coast. At that time, it was decided that the center could perform a more vital service to the community if it were reorganized to handle patients in much greater need of immediate attention and care, rather than standard examinations, preventive medicine, and routine treatment. To achieve this goal, the two remaining physicians enrolled in medical university courses in urgent care procedures and therapy and brought in as partners two specialists with broad experience in this field. Together, they created the concept of Greenridge Urgent Care Center and laid out plans for staffing and equipping the facility for that purpose.

The principals in this venture have accumulated $30,000 in personal equity funds to achieve their goal. The plan presented herewith anticipates a further financing need of $78,000 to restructure the interior of the existing building, purchase or lease urgent care medical equipment, and hire a technician experienced in emergency medical procedures.

DESCRIPTION OF PROFESSIONAL SERVICES

Greenridge Urgent Care Center is backed by a seven-day-a-week, 24-hour emergency department and staffed with residency-trained board-certified emergency physicians. Physician consultants are also on call, so that the Center represents more than thirty medical specialties and subspecialties, from gynecology and gerontology to plastic surgery and sports medicine. As a state medical journal was quoted, "Greenridge can attract the finest generalists, specialists, and staffers because it is located in the heart of a region that lures the best professionals from around the country, not only because of the attractive living conditions but the access to the finest technology."

Greenridge has already built a reputation in the field of cardiac diagnosis, treatment, and rehabilitation capabilities, for example. It also boasts a highly advanced multidisciplinary cancer care program. And it offers complex neurosurgery capabilities and facilities for treating life-threatening injuries from accidents of all kinds. The Center is closely affiliated with both the Grand Rapids and Lansing hospitals for continuing care, laboratory testing, radiology, and all state-of-the-art technological advances.

COMPETITION

There are only three urgent care facilities in Kent County, the nearest one being some thirty-five miles from Greenridge. Although these are recognized as having excellent facilities and highly capable staffs, they are not considered to be very competitive. For one thing, they are outside of the radius for the quick aid and transportation of patients in need of immediate attention. More important, rather than nearing any kind of saturation point, urgent care facilities are in short supply in the region. In fact, a recent report from the office of the medical examiner of the State of Michigan asserted that "Our attention must be given to the establishment of additional urgent care facilities, particularly in the central region of the state."

The medical situation prompting the medical examiner's survey and report was one of the reasons why Greenridge Urgent Care Center came into being and why it is imperative that this kind of high-tech facility be given every chance to serve the public more quickly and effectively than in the past.

PERSONNEL

The key staff members are as follows:

Steven S. Catchwood, M.B.A.
    B.S., medical administration, Johns Hopkins,
    M.B.A., University of Chicago

Marian Moore Dennison, M.D.
    Specialist in cardiac diagnosis,
    Resident consultant, Muskegon Hospital

Harrison Smart, M.D.
    Specialist in oncology,
    Resident at Grand Rapids Hospital

Benjamin Stein, M.D.
    Chief of surgery, specialist in accident
    trauma and sports injuries

Sandra Hollowell, M.D.
    Gynecologist

Donna Perts-Smyth, CPA
    Treasurer

Medical Affiliates, Inc.
    Consultants for laboratory testing and diagnosis

A Financial Plan and Proposal to

The South Street Center

Redonda Wharf Building
South Bay Street
Tacoma, Washington

submitted to

> The National Endowment for the Arts
> and The American Fine Arts Association

submitted for

> an Arts Program and a Center for the Disadvantaged

submitted by

> THE ROW HOUSE FELLOWSHIP
> *1879 Riverton Heights*
> *Seattle, WA 98106*

> Committee for the Arts
>
> DONALD R. KOMISTRA, M.A.
> GERALDINE TUBBS BEECHER, PH.D.
> T. HUSTON LEONARD, M.ART.
> CHERYL PICKENS SMITHERS

PAST HISTORY AND PRESENT NEED

The Row House Fellowship is a volunteer organization composed of members who have deep interests in the creative and performing arts, and who are committed to establishing facilities for the disadvantaged so they can participate in all areas of the arts at little or no cost to themselves. In the past, the RHF has been instrumental in obtaining more than 200 grants and fellowships for needy artists, writers, and performers to help them develop their talents; has secured funds to build studios, galleries, and theaters for more than a dozen projects in the State of Washington; and has sponsored eleven public exhibits of art and sculpture by promising minority artists in the Seattle/Tacoma area.

Through the generosity of two contributors who prefer to remain anonymous, the Fellowship has acquired twelve unoccupied buildings along the South Street bay and wharf area, ten of which are now being converted into row houses for the indigent. The donors have supplied the necessary funds for cleaning up the area, providing exterior lighting, and reconditioning the buildings for suitable occupancy.

After considerable discussion, a review of the area, and an evaluation of costs, the directors of The Row House Fellowship have authorized the Committee for the Arts to apply for financial aid to renovate the two remaining row houses and convert them into a place where artists can work and children can learn art in all of its media.

This paper is a plan for financial assistance.

WHAT SUM WE NEED AND HOW WE PROPOSE TO SPEND IT

The Row House Fellowship urgently needs the sum of $25,000 as seed money, which it is hereby requesting from The National Foundation for the Arts, either through an NFA grant or from an affiliated organization or corporate sponsors. The grant, if received, will be used as follows:

$20,000 for the rehabilitation of two currently unoccupied buildings on South Bay Street, which will be joined together as one structure to be used as an art center, with three studios, two classrooms, an exhibit hall, a kitchenette, and three restrooms. This sum is for the restoration of the exterior and interior of the existing structures, the reinforcement of walls, ceilings, roof, and supporting beams, and the installation of heating and air conditioning equipment. As for labor, we have been assured that the city's nonprofit museums and galleries will supply a cadre of volunteer carpenters, electricians, painters, plumbers, and other skilled workers at no cost, and thus we can keep the sum required at a bare minimum.

$5,000 for the purchase of art supplies and materials and teaching aids, in an amount sufficient to establish and maintain Fellowship programs for the first six months of operation. A special grant from the Pacific Coast Art Foundation, along with funds from donors on the RHF lists, will cover the expense of these materials thereafter.

The Committee for the Arts will supply volunteer instructors and consultants for the events and activities of this Center.

A Proposal Regarding Spiritual Financing for

The Magdalene Ministry of Healing
Number Three Alomogorda Place
Ayoka, New Mexico

to the fund-raising council of

The National Congress of Churches
2614 I Street, NW
Washington, D.C. 20001

a presentation from

THE COMMUNITY ECUMENICAL CHURCH
South Park Drive
Artesia, New Mexico

Under the sponsorship of

PASTOR LESTOR U. LINCOLN, NJ
COMMUNITY ECUMENICAL CHURCH
Artesia, New Mexico

FATHER HIDALGO GOMEZ, II, FS
CHURCH OF THE HOLY SEPULCHRE
Las Cruces, New Mexico

THE REVEREND JAKOB BIERMEISTER
UNITED LUTHERAN CHURCH
Hobbs, New Mexico

DR. PETER SCOTT TERHUNE
ADVISOR, CHRISTIAN HEALING MINISTRIES
Albuquerque, New Mexico

WHO ARE WE?

The Magdalene Ministry of Healing (MMH), founded in St. Louis, Missouri in 1972, is a church-oriented, community-minded brotherhood of many faiths whose members are volunteers engaged in serving as lay ministers, in order to relieve and complement ordained ministers as they strive to meet the sometimes overwhelming personal needs of their congregations. MMH ministers undertake such ameliorating actions as visiting the sick, transporting the handicapped to doctors, church services, concerts, classes, and other events and places that they would otherwise not be able to attend. One of their most vital and enduring responsibilities is to act as caregivers and simply to sit and listen while their care receivers find therapeutic benefits in being able to unburden themselves and find a sympathetic ear.

MMH ministers, though laypersons, are required to make many commitments regarding their time and responsibilities, including being available night and day for services, limiting the times they are away on vacation or for other reasons, and maintaining the strictest confidentiality about the identity and problems of their care receivers. Furthermore, they cannot be registered as official representatives of MMH until they have completed sixty hours of church-provided training, engaged an equal amount of time completing home studies and homework, and attended three two-day weekend retreats. MMH ministers are men and women in ages from the early thirties to the late seventies—single individuals for the most part, but sometimes joining as couples.

The Community Ecumenical Church in Artesia is the regional sponsor of the MMH movement at the start of this program, after which sponsorship will rotate in turn to the Church of the Holy Sepulchre in Las Cruces, the United Lutheran Church in Hobbs, and other churches to be announced.

Although the pastors of these churches are leaders in furthering the good works of the MMH movement, the actual training programs are conducted by ordained associate ministers, qualified lay ministers, or laypersons who want to dedicate themselves to the needs and responsibilities of the program. All of these leaders, known as Cluster Guides, must undergo a rigid sixteen-day training program at the MMH headquarters in St. Louis, Missouri, make careful studies of four reference works on the subject, and write a 2,000-word commentary on the obligations and accountabilities of leadership.

WHAT DO WE NEED?

The Magdalene Ministry of Healing is applying to The National Congress of Churches for a share of NCC's discretionary funds in order to expand and further its work and goals. The joint clergy of the current sponsoring churches and the MMH administrators agree in principle that a "matching grant" program would be the most reasonable, impartial, and equitable means of securing funds and thus address this request in that spirit. The Ministry's current fund drive in all regional churches that would benefit from the program expect to receive congregational pledges totalling $6,000 by the time the campaign is concluded at year's end, and two special $500 bequests, for a total of $7,000.

This proposal respectfully requests that the National Congress of Churches allocate a like amount from its discretionary funds at the beginning of next year to the work of The Magdalene Ministry of Healing.

How Will We Spend Our Funds?

The administrators of the MMH program have carefully evaluated all phases of its mission, both short-term and long-range, and evolved a financial plan that would be most effective in achieving the Ministry's goals. Assuming that the treasurer will have $14,000 to work with (the MMH's $7,000 from fund raising, plus the matching grant), the following sums would be allocated:

1. $2,000 for coordination and administration
2. $6,000 for training Cluster Guides and the lay ministers
3. $3,000 for literature, both for educational use and for orienting congregations and communities about the Ministry
4. $1,000 for transportation
5. $1,000 for medical aid to care receivers who are ill, when crises arrive
6. $1,000 for the MMH basic emergency fund

All intended expenditures would, of course, be shown to the National Congress of Churches for financial review before any actions were taken.

Financial Proposal for

Multiply the Gift

submitted to

Gulf Coast Bank & Trust Company

submitted by

James Baer, Barbara Keeley
Gordon Genette, Joyce Rising
Millie Gustavson
430 Palmetto Lane
Baton Rouge, LA 70804

Statement of Goals

The following business plan has been prepared and presented as a planning, operating, and policy guide for the founders and principals of the organization known as Multiply the Gift, as well as a financial proposal to the Gulf Coast Bank & Trust Company.

The listed persons, operators of the program, are hereby requesting a commercial loan of $18,000. This sum, together with a $6,000 equity investment by the operators, will be sufficient to rent suitable space, purchase office equipment, provide secretarial help, hire transportation, and cover other start-up costs for an initial period of six months. It is estimated, on the basis of consultation with experienced advisors in the investment and accounting fields, that the organization will be able to be self-sustaining at the end of that period and discharge all indebtedness—whether loans or otherwise—in a period of no more than one year from the date on which such financial help is provided. Working capital will then sustain the business—a nonprofit venture for the public good—indefinitely.

DEFINITION OF THE VENTURE

Multiply the Gift was created some ten years ago as a church program to help raise money for the missions of two community churches in a small town near New Orleans. The idea was to solicit church members to serve as volunteers who would produce products—mainly food items—for sale at church-sponsored events. The income from sales, minus repayments to volunteers for costs incurred, were pooled and used to help support the missions. Over a period of several years, the nature of the offerings was broadened to include products other than foods, such as arts and crafts objects, bird houses, paintings, personalized stationery, and the like.

Participants also began to donate services, depending on their individual skills and interests. These included bridge lessons, local historical tours, handyman services, tutoring, and the manufacture of various household goods. Bringing a considerable amount of imagination to the expanding program, volunteers came up with such intuitive ideas as providing music and skits for parties, supervising kiddy parties, poetry reading sessions, charter fishing trips, and writing speeches.

FUNCTIONAL OPERATIONS

Multiply the Gift is located at the Palmetto Lane address, occupying one room of a small office building and using the parking area and occupant's facilities at cost. The office is open three afternoons a week, from 1:00 to 5:00, staffed by a secretary and one volunteer. It now serves six area churches and, with the intended financing, will be able to serve at least ten more churches, as well as any community nonprofit institutions wishing to mount this kind of fund-raising campaign.

It is expected—and hoped—that the increasing success of this nonprofit venture will make it possible to establish a string of other M/G subsidiaries throughout the state, and possibly in adjoining states. In anticipation of this kind of growth, several volunteers with writing skills are already preparing guidelines for churches and other potential sponsors, and have been authoring a directory of services. The latter will be a loose-leaf publication, so that it can easily be kept complete and updated as new products and services are made available.

PERSONNEL

The principals of Multiply the Gift, in whose names this financial proposal is being presented, are:

James Baer, President, a qualified fund-raiser by profession

Barbara Keeley, Recruitment Director, a corporate personnel manager

Gordon Genette, Treasurer, a CPA and financial consultant

Joyce Rising, Public Relations Manager, an advertising executive

Millie Gustavson, Communications, a journalist and author

Additional staff members are recruited on a part-time basis as the needs arise. In general the pastors of churches or the heads of other nonprofit organizations coordinating their fund raising with M/G serve as temporary Project Directors during active campaign periods.

COMPETITION

There is no direct competition for the Multiply the Gift organization, since it is unique in its concept and manner of conducting fund-raising campaigns. However, indirect competition could be said to be any and all nonprofit community groups and organizations engaged in fund raising for worthy causes.

Canine Companions, Inc.

Providing Dogs for Disabled People

submitted to

The Small Business Administration
of Houston, Texas

submitted by

JULIE AND DENISE MORROW
HAPPY TAILS KENNELS

Houston, Texas

WHO WE ARE

Julie and Denise Morrow are owners of the "Happy Tails" Kennel located on the west side of Houston, Texas, a well-established full-service breeding and boarding kennel that specializes in breeding Yellow Labrador Retrievers. Apart from being breeders, Julie and Denise Morrow are accomplished dog trainers and run an AKC-sanctioned Dog Obedience School at the kennel as well.

In establishing Canine Companions, Inc., the Morrow sisters hope to use Labrador Retrievers and other dogs that would be otherwise unsuitable for show purposes and train them to aid disabled individuals who have a need for a guide dog or an aid dog to help them with everyday tasks. Also dogs who are still unacceptable as aid dogs will be given to seniors who desire a canine friend or companion in their lives.

FINANCING

Canine Companions, Inc. will be run on a nonprofit basis with all donations, fees, and monies raised going to the training and placement of the dogs with their companions. Outside dogs will be donated from area shelters, humane associations, breeders, and other kennels. Dogs of certain breeds will be considered for training and placement. The health regimens of the dogs in the program will be supervised by Dr. Dan Harper, D.V.M., of Houston, Texas, himself a dog breeder and partner in the enterprise.

Chapter 10

Plans
for
Importers/
Exporters

DO YOU KNOW HOW TO EXPLORE FOREIGN MARKETS EFFECTIVELY?

Before you prepare a small business plan in the export/import field, do your homework to make sure you know the categories to emphasize. You can turn to the SBA, SCORE, and other national resources, and to associations like the National Foreign Trade Council if you are taken with the idea of looking beyond the borders of America to expand your business. You should also communicate with government agencies in the field of commerce. Just for starters, here is what the NFT has to say, as a preface to going global:

> The reasons to explore foreign markets for your product or service are numerous and tempting. Selling overseas broadens your market, forces you to be more competitive, and might well reduce your per-unit cost of production. It can help to hedge against recession or a change in demand at home. Foreign marketing may even extend the life of a good product that is beginning to lose ground at home, perhaps because a competitor has arrived on the scene. In short, "going foreign" might boost your bottom line.

But exporting is not all a bed of roses. There are numerous reasons against it. For instance, it's not the solution for dumping excess inventory. Then too, the ups and downs of the dollar can make pricing a nightmare. And, of course, you may be faced with knotty and unfamiliar embargos and other constraints.

If you have a quality, marketable product that you can sell at a competitive price, and if you do your homework, going global should not be much riskier than trying to enter a new geographic market in the United States. Many small companies—even home-based ones-have succeeded abroad. To decide whether exporting is for you, ask yourself these questions.

1. Is your product special, and of high quality? It's tough to try to sell cheap merchandise abroad.

2. Are you flexible? Moving into an international market means catering to the tastes and needs of people whose cultures and tastes are different from those of Americans, and you have to evaluate the differences carefully.

3. Do you have the capabilities to translate brochures and product manuals into foreign languages? You not only have to be exacting in providing instructions, but could be liable if you make errors in providing operating data.

4. If you are selling electronic products, are they suitable for electrical current differences abroad?

5. Are product names acceptable? Some names may have unfavorable meanings or connotations in other countries.

6. Are you personally committed to exporting? Commitment must be more than a buzzword. You also have to have immeasurable patience, since preparations and clearances can take many months before you make a single initial shipment.

7. Are you willing to invest the money needed to expedite a foreign business? Getting organized can involve little cost, but once you get underway, costs—especially unexpected ones—can mount up.

8. Have you evaluated these cost potentials? You may, for example, have to make product modifications, pay extra production costs, provide translation services for your sales personnel, face greatly expanded telephone and other communication bills, and make plans to visit the countries in which you plan to market your product(s).

9. Can you sell at a competitive price abroad? Price differentials that are acceptable in the domestic market may not hold true in other countries.

10. Do you know what your competitors are doing? Foreign companies competing with you in the U.S. can often be a good sign that the same kinds of products are in demand globally.

Several model plans are presented, slightly condensed to eliminate material of little interest to the reader. The focus here is similar to that in the chapters on retailing. However, particular emphasis is placed on the problems and situations that arise when a business is involved with the regulations and cultures and customs of other countries besides the Untied States.

One section is devoted to elements of the small business plan that must be carefully researched and identified to incorporate the important factors regarding the conduct of business abroad.

A Proposal for

Birdsong Products

12A Potomac Mall
Arlington, VA 23109

submitted to

International Association of Investors

Fidelity Building
2206 East-West Highway
Silver Spring, MD 20910

subject

Request for Financing

Principals

THE PARTNERS

KAREN INOUE*

TINA MINOCCI

IONA MCGRADY

* Correspondence Address:
313–14 Lenox Hill Town Houses
Washington Square
Arlington, VA 23109

PROFILE OF THE COMPANY

Birdsong Products, formerly known as the Potomac Bird Sculpture Collection, is a growing business that started six years ago as a private collection of the three partners, who were curators at the Smithsonian Institution in Washington, D.C. Independently, they had each started collecting preeminent porcelain masterworks from all over the world, which they proudly exhibited to friends and families in their homes. They first met each other while attending an exhibit of garden bird and flower porcelain sculptures sponsored by the American Ceramic Association in Richmond, Virginia, and realized they had a great deal in common. Since all three lived in the Arlington, Virginia area, they began a joint program to attend ceramic sculpture exhibits up and down the east coast, and eventually pooled their collections in a vacant exhibit room loaned to them temporarily by the Virginia Museum of Art and Sculpture. They found that they could pay for the upkeep by charging a modest entrance fee for museum visitors who were particularly interested in ceramics, porcelain, and related media of the arts.

The next step was prompted when the museum needed the space back to accommodate its growing collection of art, and the three partners decided to rent an available gallery at the Potomac Mall in Arlington. Their initial plan was to continue their collective hobby as an art exhibit, but so many visitors asked where they could buy porcelains—particularly items from the growing collection of North American birds, which made up more than half of the exhibits—that a decision was made to buy and sell museum-quality aviary sculpture. At this point, the enterprise became officially registered as Birdsong Products.

During the past two years, Birdsong has thrived and increased its annual gross earnings from $120,000 to well over $2,000,000. At the same time, it has sharpened its merchandising focus so that *birds* are the only objects for sale, in what has become known as the "Winged Masterworks" collection. The only exceptions are occasional floral and arboreal porcelains, selected purely for their visual effect to enhance the color, the grace, and the varied beauty of the birds.

During the past two years, Birdsong has also started to develop a collection called "Birds of the World," with an eye on the international market. The company has already started to explore the export/import market and establish contacts and commercial connections that will build the business outside of North America.

FINANCIAL GOALS

The three partners in the gallery have conferred with representatives of the International Ceramic Association, the Virginia Museum of Art and Sculpture, and the Service Corps of Retired Executives (SCORE), and have made exhaustive studies of the markets, both at home and abroad. Based on favorable and encouraging reports from all of these sources, they have decided that this is a promising and appropriate time to establish an international mail-order division of the business, design and print an initial catalogue, and launch a postal campaign. Their accounting firm, Stouffer and Staley, has prepared a pricing and shipping prospectus and has helped them select a mailing list house, Dominion List Services, to prepare an initial, condensed roster of prospective customers. To this, they are adding the names of about 400 consumers who have bought figurines from Birdsong in the past.

Heartened by the prospects for this fresh adjunct to their business, the partners of Birdsong Products herewith petition the International Association of Investors (IAI) to solicit their members and organize a group interested in providing an equity investment to the company in the amount of $17,500. The assurance of success is high and the risk is low, and Birdsong is offering the backers a 20 percent share of the net income of its mail-order business during the first year.

MARKETING PROJECTION

At this stage in the company's development, the partners have evaluated the market many times over in the region it serves in northern Virginia and the District of Columbia. In brief, a profile of the most likely purchasers would indicate the following classifications:

Sex:	65 percent female
Age:	35–65
Marital status:	Married
Income level:	Middle to high
Interests:	The arts, decorating
Residence:	Single-family home
Home town:	Within a radius of fifty miles

Since the purchasing habits of consumers in other parts of the country have not yet been satisfactorily diagnosed in the minds of the partners, the mail-order market will initially be limited to this familiar region within a radius of fifty miles. Gradually, during the first year, it will be extended to cover all of Virginia, the District of Columbia, Maryland, and Delaware. During this period, preparations will be made for reaching prospective customers in foreign lands, initially in the United Kingdom. Lists will target addressees who fit the above consumer profile.

Small Business Plan for

The Spice Trade, Ltd.
*The Evolution of an Enterprise from a Domestic Shop
to an International Marketer*

submitted to

First National Bank of Trenton
*Barnegat Executive Park
Trenton, New Jersey*

submitted by

THE ST TRADE GROUP
*89 Ocean Boulevard
Tom's River, NJ 08753*

WHO WE ARE

The Spice Trade, Ltd. is a well-established retail store that specializes in spices, herbs, and exotic food derivatives used to add flavor and zest to wide varieties of dishes from the commonplace to the gourmet. It is owned and operated by three entrepreneurs who formed the ST Group six years ago to undertake a number of ventures in food retailing. Of four enterprises that were established during this time, one—The Spice Trade, Ltd.—proved to be far and away the most successful and is the only venture into which the ST Group is now putting its time, money, and effort.

The Spice Trade, Ltd. offers the best natural and fresh spices, herbs, condiments, and seasonings selected from daily rounds to farmers' markets, private farms, and other places where these products are cultivated or sold. During the last two years, the company has brought out a line of spices under its own label, marketed at the store and by mail in distinctive glass jars, each with a tag describing the contents and its best uses. The ST Group has also started publishing a line of mini-books, each describing one type or family of herbs and spices. These are also sold over-the-counter and by mail.

WHAT WE DO

We constantly evaluate the nature and categories of the products we acquire and place on the market to determine how they can best be displayed and presented and, more importantly, how we can educate purchasers about the most interesting and beneficial ways to use our products. We do this by word of mouth, printing brief descriptions on product labels, distributing our books, issuing press releases to food editors of local newspapers and consumer periodicals, and placing graphic posters and description cards in strategic locations in our store.

We have also investigated ways of improving the use of spices and seasonings through a consulting firm, Kitchen Researchers, Inc., which engages in product testing and will experiment with recipes to determine how they can be enhanced. As a result of this kind of research, our store features a "Recipe of the Week," in which we focus on ways that our products have added zest and gusto to rather commonplace dishes.

We are designing a mobile exhibit relating to all of our categories of natural products that come under the spice/herbs umbrella, for promotional and educational use. We have already contracted to take this exhibit to schools, state fairs, food trade exhibitions, and similar gatherings and presentations, and will be adding more locations and events as we go along. We have learned an interesting and pertinent fact: The more that people know about spices and herbs, the more they are likely to buy. So *education* is our most valuable sales tool.

WHAT WE NEED

The Spice Trade, Ltd. can move from its present situation as a community retail store to the position of an international trader with a relatively small financial boost. After consultation with our accounting firm, our attorney, and the marketing division of The National Spice Council, we are convinced that the conversion can take place if funded by no more than $25,000. This sum would be used for the following beneficial implementations and developments:

- Acquiring licenses to do business outside the United States
- Enlarging the store
- Engaging an international consulting service in the food field for marketing advice
- Making and sustaining contacts with food brokers abroad in the key countries of product origin

WHERE WE WILL GO

The Spice Trade, Ltd. will continue as a small-town retailer, but it will also establish an international mail-order service and broaden its resources. At the present time, and from the beginning, the company has purchased its products through local sources. While many of these products come from faraway places, our dealings have been strictly with suppliers in the United States. In the future, we will acquire some products directly from sources abroad, and eventually we will make business trips to other countries ourselves to seek out new and exciting kinds of spices, herbs, and other condiments and flavorings.

All in all, as an international export/import firm, The Spice Trade, Ltd. will be able to expand its operations enormously and build a bigger, more successful, and more profitable business.

Application for

International Traders
26B Asponaug Wharf
Warwick, Rhode Island

submitted for

Equity Financing for a New Business

submitted to

The Export/Import Bank of Rhode Island
Pawtucket Building
Providence, Rhode Island

BUSINESS BACKGROUND AND QUALIFICATIONS

International Traders is a privately managed consortium of four small businesses engaged respectively in importing merchandise in the following categories and from the specified foreign sources:

1. Crystal housewares and tableware from Ireland, Portugal, and the Scandinavian countries

2. Icons and other religious objects, both antique and reproductions, from the Baltic region, particularly Estonia and parts of Russia

3. Reproductions of antiquities from the Holy Land

4. Silver and gold jewelry from Sicily

Up to this time, the owners of the four businesses have imported and sold merchandise, individually and independently, to retailers in the area of eastern Rhode Island and southern Massachusetts. Their distribution has been limited and they have belonged to the consortium mainly for the purpose of obtaining data about the availability of supplies, current foreign exchange developments, and shipping and transportation problems and costs.

In this respect, International Traders has really served as a clearinghouse of information and has not been structured to assist its four member enterprises in advertising, marketing, distribution, or business growth.

DEVELOPMENT PLANS

International Traders is seeking venture capital or other financing in order to raise its status from that of a holding company to a full-scale, globally licensed, and certified import/export business on a worldwide scale. When thus established, the company will consist of four divisions, enlarged and developed from the existing partners:

1. Global Crystals, engaged in the procurement and sale of fine crystal housewares and tableware from countries recognized as the major producers of crystal, and expert in its design and fashioning

2. Icons of the World, a supplier of religious figures, sculptures, and ecclesiastical art, both registered antiques and fine reproductions, from the major countries of the world where Christianity has been dominant for 2,000 years

3. Holy Land Antiquities, specializing only in reproductions of fine art and artifacts from the ancient world now referred to as the Holy Land

4. Sicilian Silver, bringing to market fine jewelry and art, modern creations only, largely in silver, but with some offerings in gold and precious-metal combinations

The financial requirement for making this transition from a loosely organized consortium of dealers to an international export/import company of substantial size is in the nature of $90,000, in three equal installments over six months' time.

Small Business Plan for

The World of Rattan, Inc.

submitted to

The North Carolina National Bank
of Asheville, North Carolina

submitted by

CHARLES BENJI
P.O. Box 344
Asheville, NC 09923

WHO WE ARE

The World of Rattan, Inc. is owned by Charles Benji, a thirty-year resident and naturalized citizen of the United States. Mr. Benji's native home is Sri Lanka, where as a boy, he worked in the fields harvesting bamboo, jute, and cane, three essential materials needed in the creation of rattan and cane furniture. As he grew older, Mr. Benji later worked in the mills that produced furniture and finally worked in the retail sales and distribution of wicker and rattan furniture throughout his native home of Sri Lanka and throughout parts of Asia, Europe, and later the United States.

Although Mr. Benji has lived in the U.S. for the past thirty years, he has kept strong economic ties to his homeland and has been actively working in the importing and exporting of rattan furniture to other parts of the world.

OUR PLAN

It is Mr. Benji's wish to expand his own existing import/export furniture business using the contacts and economic alliances he has created in the past twenty years in the wicker and rattan furniture business. This business not only will be a wholesaler of furniture to other retailers throughout the world, but will also have retail stores handling rattan and wicker furniture in various outlet malls throughout the U.S., starting in the north and southeast. A catalog distribution business may be considered, but most of the retail sales will be managed through the outlet stores.

The primary source (main office) of the business is and will be located in Asheville, North Carolina, where Mr. Benji lives and where the first five stores will be located in and around the state of North Carolina. Mr. Benji will also be supplying some of his lines (on a wholesale basis) to other furniture retailers who have several existing stores in California and other parts of the west coast. It is hoped that these areas will become future valuable retail markets; however, at present the wholesale market will provide the necessary revenue for the creation and support of the retail outlet stores located in the southeast.

WHAT IS NEEDED

The World of Rattan, Inc. will need supporting expansion capital of $500,000 in order to create and purchase product for its retail stores, and to satisfy existing product supply commitments to retail clients in the southeast. This expansion capital will also be used for securing the necessary licensing for the retail stores (licensing for the wholesale business has already been secured), advertising, additional employees needed for the retail stores, and the necessary retail licensing needed for the North Carolina stores.

Small Business Plan for

South American Jewelers, Inc.
Providing Retail Jewelry at Wholesale Prices

Submitted to

L.H. Partnership, Ltd.
330 Peachtree Road
Atlanta, GA 30345

WHO WE ARE

L.H. Partnership, Ltd. is a limited partnership of two principals, Jacob Heinz and Marvin Steiner and their families. Both Steiner and Heinz are professional gemologists and own retail jewelry stores, "The Jeweler" and "Gems Unlimited."

The new business "South American Jewelers" will be used as a wholesaler for the two existing retail businesses, and as wholesale/retail stores in outlet-type malls in Florida, Georgia, South Carolina, and North Carolina.

South American Jewelers will provide unique gems of all qualities, primarily from South America and South Africa, in mall outlet settings. The initial number of new stores will be six, three in Florida (Orlando, Sarasota, and Key West), three in South Carolina (Myrtle Beach, Charleston, and Columbia), and three in Georgia (Atlanta, Savannah, and Athens). The North Carolina stores will open at a later date, based on the available revenue derived from the Florida, Georgia, and South Carolina stores.

INITIAL FUNDING

Start-up funding will be provided from L.H. Partnership, Ltd. for South American Jewelers in the amount of $750,000, which will be used for inventory purchases, retail rental, personnel, insurance, security system, and advertising. Both Steiner and Heinz plan to involve themselves initially in this venture; after a stable client base and market has been established, they will hire the necessary administrative and support personnel to manage all of the retail outlets.

Small Business Plan for

Animal Locators, Inc.

International Suppliers and Breeders of Exotic and Rare
Animals for Public and Private Animal Habitats
3535 Lakeshore Drive West • Key West, Florida 22341
(902) 534-6789

submitted to
Nationsbank of Key West and The Hope Foundation
for the Responsible Animal Preservation and Management
Palm Beach, FL

WHAT WE DO

The purpose of Animal Locators, Inc. is to *responsibly* breed and locate rare and exotic breeds of animals, fish, and reptiles with public and private institutions such as zoos, animal habitats, and aquaria throughout the world. Mission Statement: It is our hope that with the responsible, ethical and legal supply and management of creatures, that the need for the further exploitation of animals in the wild will cease, in favor of receiving animals from a legitimate breeder whose quality of stock and breeding capabilities will end the need for the capture of creatures from the wild.

The principals involved in Animal Locators, Inc. are: JoAnna Brimley, Ph.D., zoologist and animal behavioralist educated at Oxford's School of Veterinary Medicine; George Ditmar, Ph.D., DVM, The Ohio State University of Veterinary Medicine and The University of Pennsylvania School of Zoology and Veterinary College; Harold Zook, B.A., J.D., attorney, Cornell University and Harvard School of Law; and Belinda Howard, B.S., M.S., Ph.D., behavioral scientist and anthropologist, University of Tennessee, University of Georgia, and the University of Bristol. All of the principals plan to actively involve themselves in start-up and management of Animal Locators, Inc., having joint offices in Key West, Florida and in Bristol, England.

WHAT WE NEED

Animal Locators, Inc. requests a start-up sum of $2 million from Nationsbank of Key West, Florida and the Hope Foundation of Palm Beach, Florida. It is planned that both Nationsbank and the Hope Foundation will share a 50-50 contribution to the initial start-up funds, which will be repaid in the first ten years.

Since the principals are all seasoned professionals in their respective fields, business and academic contacts and their markets are already established and will be utilized by the firm.

Small Business Plan for

India Exports, Inc.
A Fine Importer/Exporter of India Silks and Other Fine Materials

submitted to

The Fleet Bank of Boston, MA
115 Federal Street
Boston, MA 10023

submitted by

THE NEW ENGLAND CLOTHING AND TRADING COMPANY
2230 Frederick Street
Boston, MA 11405

WHO WE ARE

The principal owner of The New England Trading and Clothing Company is Richard Harwick. Mr. Harwick is an established retailer in Boston and throughout Massachusetts, and has been in the retail business for twenty-five years. His plan for the new business, India Exports, Inc., is to expand his current retail sales market into an international clothing market in the New England area, with the intention of venturing abroad and into other major cities in the United States.

India Exports, Inc. will focus mainly on the fine silk products of India, with a variety of other materials as well. The company will use the existing connections and vendors of The New England Trading and Clothing Company along with a vendor connection in Bombay, India for its primary support and database in promoting the new retail venture. The New England Trading and Clothing Company already has an import/export license that will be used in its future marketing efforts with the India vendor.

FINANCING

This new business venture will be financially supported by a loan from the Fleet Bank of Boston and will be secured by existing collateral or stock in The New England Trading and Clothing Company. The total capital needed for this new venture will be $725,000, which will be repaid over a period of six years.

Chapter 11

The Wide, Wide World of the Internet

Small business searchers who use the Internet, either through their own familiarity with it or with the help of friends and researchers, are finding a sizeable, and increasing, variety of media to assist them, including on-line forums, home pages, newsletters, and library archives. Many such media can be invaluable to you generally in helping to plan your business, and particularly in composing and preparing a business plan. Of great significance is the fact that many of the people out there in Cyberspace are interested in small business and are dedicated researchers, or volunteers, who expect no recompense for their help other than the very excitement of assisting in a search that, in the end, can be rewarding.

There are literally hundreds of commercial firms that are listed as providers, for-profit online services that users subscribe to in order to be able to surf or roam the Internet. Among the most familiar names in this field are America On Line (AOL), AT&T Interchange, Compuserve, and Prodigy. With most of these, you pay an installation fee, telephone charges for the number used to access the online service (whether local or long-distance), and hourly rates for the time actually connected to the provider. These rates are based on your choice of three options: a minimum rate if you don't expect to use more than, say, ten hours a month; a middle-range rate for forty or fifty hours of use; and an unlimited time rate. For the first two, you pay by the hour if you exceed the maximum.

Through these online providers, you can reach a wide range of search tools, with names like Alta Vista, Infoseek, Lycos, Netscape, and Yahoo. They contain what are known as "home pages," which are introductions to the kinds of information and materials the user is likely to find. Once you have arrived in one of these search domains, you have the option of searching in two basic ways:

1. By entering the name of the subject for which you are seeking information, such as *business plans* or *financing resources.*

2. By entering the site address, which you may have found during the subject search in articles and other references, or from contacts you make in person or over the Internet (perhaps in e-mail). These are called Uniform Resource Locators (URLs), and have been likened to "post office addresses for the Internet." They generally begin with http://www. Some of them may seem a bit overpowering at first, since they may contain thirty or more letters, numbers, and symbols. But they penetrate the darkness and lead you to the light. They will also provide clues so that you can follow electronic stepping stones closer and closer to what you are seeking. You activate the search by typing the site address into the browser's location entry box; once this has appeared on your screen a vertical bar is displayed at the left-hand end of the long, horizontal box.

A Case of Mistaken Identity

There is a degree of confusion, not only among computer users but in the press, about two terms, *Internet* and *World Wide Web*, which are often used as synonyms. The Internet is the vast assemblage of thousands of networks, large and small in more than sixty countries around the globe, which are linked together to provide information. The World Wide Web (commonly referred to as just "the Web") is an Internet connection or bridge. Because it is visual as well as textual, and can also provide sound, it is the most appealing part of the Internet.

Although the Web can link computer users with almost all facets of the Internet, it is only one entity of the latter. It shares billing with other major elements of the Internet, most familiarly the following:

- *E-mail*, which makes it possible for users to send and receive personal messages.

- *Usenet*, public forums for news and discussion groups, some of which are specifically in subject areas like adoption.

- *File Transfer Protocol* (*FTP*), through which users can transfer excerpts from a gargantuan collection of subject files on the Internet to their home computers.

- *Gopher*, which is used to automate searches for information on specific subjects on the Internet. With this facility, for example, you could browse a card catalog in the Library of Congress.

- *Telnet*, which preceded the Web, is a primary text-based, not graphic, means of roaming the Internet.

Electronic Voices

Electronic mail, or e-mail as it is popularly called, is one of the common applications running on the Internet, most especially for entrepreneurs who need assistance. Its format and method of dialogue make it possible for users—no matter how many thousands of miles may separate them—to communicate with each other on a one-to-one basis. This quick and inexpensive form of communication can help you immensely in gathering facts and advice for the preparation, say, of a business plan.

While an e-mail letter can contain the same kinds of data you would place in a letter between post offices ("snail mail"), it can be transmitted instantly. Addressing an e-mail message is the most demanding function, since the address must be exact, right down to each letter of the alphabet, symbol, or punctuation mark. The address consists of two parts: (1) a local part, which is the mailbox name, log-in name, or user ID of the recipient, and (2) a host part, which identifies the computer itself and is familiar to the sender. These are customarily separated by an @ symbol, with no spaces. One way to envision this is that the local part is to whom the message is going, and the host part is where the person "lives" on the Internet.

"One way of getting your feet wet in a friendly, information-packed environment," says Jake Cargon, a small businessman in Topeka who has used the Internet more and more, "is to join an e-mail list. E-mail allows groups of people who share a common interest to form a group and send e-mail to everyone else within the group." In addition to being an excellent worldwide networking tool for small business managers, he adds, e-mail lists are a gateway to learn about other topical business online resources, such as Web sites, news groups, live chats, and even other e-mail lists. You will find a great deal of information in this manner for all kinds of business planning and written plans.

Bear in mind, though, that you have to be selective. On the one hand, you may solicit e-mail and be flooded with mail every single day. On the other hand, if you propose a subject that is of interest only to a handful of people out there in cyberspace, you may have to wait a week to get two or three electronic letters. You can also get on lists that use a digest format, so recipients can read through their mail quickly and then follow up only on the incoming arrivals that hit close to home.

RANGING THE INTERNET

Giving advice about using online services for computers and using the Internet, or World Wide Web, can be confusing and sometimes misleading. The reason? Online services like CompuServe and America Online (AOL) are constantly changing in the nature and extent of what they offer from month to month, and even day to day. And the sites that can be reached are equally volatile, as well as variable and sometimes erratic.

Computer users should start with generic terms that can lead to sites (positions) that are applicable, such as "small business," "entrepreneurs," and "business plans." This kind of exploration and survey will lead to programs that are relevant and valuable.

Help From Compact Disks

More easily used by those who are not computer-proficient are compact disks, known as CD-ROMs. These are thin, round disks that can be inserted into computers equipped for their usage, and which contain detailed information on just about any subject conceivable. There are many such selections on the topic of business plans. Some are programmed with fixed texts and graphics and can be used, like a printed encyclopedia to scroll to whatever subject area is of interest. In the case of business plans, for example, such a compact disk might contain not only information but samples of forms and plans. However, there are state-of-the-art versions of CD-ROMs that can interact with the computer, can store new information, and can be revised by users as they compile and edit texts or graphics for their own particular reference use. The prices of these disks, which once were very high but have gradually declined, vary with the nature and extent of the information and counsel they provide.

An Exercise in Getting From Here to There

One Internet site that has long been of value to small businesses is *Yahoo*, which is reached on the Internet address http://www.Yahoo.com. When the authors of this book spelled out "Business Plans" while doing research on this chapter, the response was that *Yahoo* had "Found 1 Category and 53 Site Matches for this subject." (That number, of course, would change from week to week, and even from day to day.) One of the fifty-three was captioned "Especially for Business Plan Writers." When this site was tapped, it produced—among many other topics—fifteen thumbnail descriptions of current books on small business (see Appendix, page 265), questions on writing plans answered by an expert, and a useful example of a business plan work sheet. It required less than one hour on a computer with only moderate capabilities and speed to assemble and print out this information—twenty-five pages in all—by a computer user with meager experience in searching the World Wide Web. Several Web sites were also quickly and easily located that provided instructions for writing business plans. Among the other common and most useful search engines are the following:

Lycos

Lycos offers a combination of more than fifteen classifications of subjects that include, among others, business, careers, culture, education, family, finance, government, health, home, lifestyle, news, science, social science, technology, and transportation.

If you enter any of these categories, you are likely to be able to surf further areas to find information about small business functions. If you do not get into categories, but simply search for entries under the general term *business*, you will enter a realm with more than 600 links to the subject.

Within the *Lycos* domain you will also find practical advice about many small business subjects. The *Lycos* search engine is valuable in that it also has book reviews of business directories and guidebooks, which contain lists of local, national, and regional agencies and support groups to contact.

InfoSeek

This universal service for searching the Web offers what has been described as "one of the most extensive databases of Web pages on the Internet." *InfoSeek* was originally available only by subscription, but has since received enough financial support from advertisers so that it is now available to users free of charge. Through a directory called *Topics*, you can browse through words and phrases that will help you to zero in on materials for your search, such as small business resources, grants and loans, and others that have been mentioned previously in this book. You can also limit your search to different media and types of documentation. As one searcher explained, "This can sometimes be very helpful and speed up certain areas of searching. If you have scoured the news media and general magazines, for example, and would now like to turn the spotlight on government publications, you can do just that."

A minute, but useful, refinement is a code that limits examples to your exact specifications. In most cases, when you type a phrase like "creating small business plans," you will trigger a threefold response. You will be given references to creative functions, small businesses, and planning. But if you enclose your keyword phrase in quotes, or join the words with hyphens, you will be given references *only* to resources relating to all three segments at the same time. Also, if you select as your subject a broad word like "business," you are likely to be told that there are hundreds—perhaps thousands—of pages of entries on the subject. But if you type in narrow subject categories, you will be much closer to the target.

A request for entries on "Start a Business," for example, turned up seven current topic coverages, such as "Small Business Help Center," "Starting a Business—Helpful Links," and "Cyperpreneurs Guide to the Internet," which is a guide for entrepreneurs to Internet-accessible resources. A request for entries on "Business Plan" also turned up seven appropriate texts, such as Preparing Your Business Plan, Outline for a Business Plan, and Business Plan Store, where you can order model business plans for your kind of business.

Not all of the Web pages you reach will necessarily be short, however. For instance, in the case of one *InfoSeek* Web site, the user was warned that this was "an extensive index of help," which was not an exaggeration when a view of it scrolled through more than 600 entries.

Alta Vista

Perfected by Digital Equipment Corporation, *Alta Vista* is one of the newer search engines and contains a massive offering of millions of Web pages. Don't be intimidated by this enormous scope, however. Once you have reached responsive sectors through the use of your key words, you can turn to an "Advanced Query" faculty that provides you with the ability to control the direction in which you want to proceed. "It's like a fishing expedition," explained one user. "You don't have to start out from shore and keep paddling around aimlessly, hoping to find some fish. It transports you instantly out to the fishing grounds where there are all kinds of finny creatures milling around. Then it hands you the right rod, reel, and bait so you can catch only the exact species of fish you have in mind."

INTERNET RELAY CHAT

You may say, "Well and good, I can generate hundreds of downloaded (printed) messages and texts through these search facilities, but I really want to talk to people out there, to ask detailed questions about preparing business plans, and get useful replies." The answer to this comment is that you can do just that—and without running up hundreds of dollars in phone bills. One increasingly popular facility on the Internet is the aforementioned IRC, which permits you to communicate directly with other human beings instead of having to read files, messages, reprints, quotes, and the like. Using an IRC access, you can connect to hundreds of "chat servers" around the globe, as well as converse with other computer users interactively.

As a Web page entitled *Info Avenue* describes IRC, "Imagine walking down the hallway of a huge building with doors on either side of you. Behind each door lies a room. The room may be empty or it may have one or more people inside. Over each door is a sign designating the topic of conversation taking place within that room at the time. As you roam through the building, you are free to open any door, see who is inside, and even enter the room and join the conversation."

This is what IRC can accomplish for you. After you have connected to a relay server, you examine the dozens of "chat" groups actually taking place on that server, and join the one of greatest interest. How do you "talk" to the others in that "room"? Once you have joined, all conversation takes the form of typewritten text. Whatever message you type on your keyboard is displayed on the screens of all the users in the chat group selected. And whatever these other participants type on their keyboards will also be displayed on every participant's screen, as well as yours. If you want to know how other entrepreneurs devised and submitted their business plans, and the degree of success or failure they experienced, IRCs are a good medium to use.

GLOBAL BULLETIN BOARDS

Described as "bulletin boards posted all over space," a newsgroup function termed *Usenet* is one of a growing number of sites that provide give-and-take dialogues on the Internet. These are similar to the chat groups described above in that they are organized by topics and attract participants who are specifically interested in those subject areas. However, instead of being interactive, they display bulletins that are posted at the site and which you can peruse and respond to at your leisure. In other words, you cannot "chat" back and forth on the spot, but you can send and receive information or ask questions. In some cases, you will get quick reactions, while in others a question you ask in a bulletin may not get a response for many hours or several days.

Since there are currently tens of thousands of newsgroups on the Internet, you can count on a few that will target almost any small business subject for which you want to compile information or suggestions. To participate in a newsgroup, you need a newsreader application so you can subscribe to the one of your choice. This step is important because joining makes it possible for you to limit the subject area of your interest and make sure that the results are worthwhile. It's like looking through a publisher's listing of 200 periodicals and then subscribing only to two or three that are likely to carry articles pertinent to your fields of activity and pursuit.

ENTREPRENEURS ON THE INTERNET

As in the case of many activities and functions in our lives, you don't have to sit back and wait for someone else to take the lead. You can drop in to do it yourself. You can, for example, devise your own page for the World Wide Web—an action considered too daring and iffy a few years ago, but increasingly commonplace today. Standard search engines on the Internet provide users with the site and instructions for creating and installing their personal pages. Some will even help you design the heading, logo, and format for a modest fee—if you feel a professional artistic touch is necessary to attract the audience you want to reach.

Users have full access to their own Web directories and sites twenty-four hours a day, seven days a week. If you decide you want to create a Web page, one way is to visit several Web sites like those above. Select ones that invite suggestions and discussion and ask how the creator of the page in question went about devising it and putting it on the Internet. You will also find instructions and tutorials offered by the search engine of your choice, such as Yahoo, Infoseek, or Lycos. These walk you through the information you need to create a Web page format. They will be identified by titles like "Web Basics," "Web Wizard Home Page," "WebForms," or simply "How to Construct Your Own Web." You will also find step-by-step instructions in practical books for beginners on computer programming.

Once you have developed your own Web site and contents, the next step is to enhance it with additional tools, graphics, and other additions that will attract more and better responses by making it attractive and meaningful for users visiting your site. After all, your goal is to achieve your business objectives, and if you seem to be professional and dedicated in your approach, you will upgrade the quality and value of the responses.

BUILD YOUR OWN WEB

If you are currently developing a Web page of your own to help you in your business planning or other operations, or are just considering doing so, visit the Info Avenue Web Development Tools Page. This is reached through Netscape on the Internet:

http://www.InfoAve.Netlsbnlweb-tools.html

Another excellent instruction program is "1179 Ways to Build a Better Web," created by the editors of *Windows Sources* magazine. The magazine can be contacted at:

Windows Sources Magazine
Ziff-Davis Publishing Company
5903 Christie Avenue
Emeryville, CA 94608
(800) 688-0448

Chapter 12

Business Schools as a Small Business Resource

"One major resource often overlooked by small business owners looking for information and guidance in the preparation of business plans," says the American Management Association, "is the American business school." You may not find one right at your back door, but you can always contact these schools by phone or mail. You should:

1. State the nature of the business plan you want to prepare.

2. Describe any problems you have or circumstances which have compelled you to seek information.

3. Ask whether graduate students and/or faculty members have undertaken any workshops in business plans that might be available to you.

4. Ask for suggestions about other sources of the kinds of information you seek.

Students at the Fuqua School of Business at Duke University, for example, recently undertook a major study of business plans that was actually used as reference for the chapter on business planning in this book (pages 1–21). The study was printed by the business school as a report, with typical forms and guidance, and has already been of great value to numerous entrepreneurs seeking to learn how to submit such a plan for a new business, and eager to know the most effective way to go about it.

MAJOR SCHOOLS OF BUSINESS

Following is a list of some of the colleges and universities with major business schools or Centers for Entrepreneurship in the United States:

Babson

Carnegie Mellon

Charleston (SC)

Columbia

Cornell

Dartmouth

Duke

Harvard

Indiana

Massachusetts Institute of Technology

New York University

Northwestern

Purdue

Stamford

University of California

Chicago

Michigan

North Carolina

Pennsylvania

Pittsburgh

Rochester

Southern California

Texas

Virginia

Vanderbilt

Wichita State

Yale

You will find others in a directory that is available in most public libraries: Peterson's Guide to Graduate and Professional Programs: An Overview (Peterson Publishing Company, Princeton, NJ, 1996). You will also find that the reference librarian in your public library can help you zero in on colleges and universities in your state, or even county, that have business departments engaged in managerial studies of particular interest to small business owners.

HOW TO MAKE AN EFFECTIVE CONTACT

Use the listings that follow or in the Peterson Directory to find the phone number of the office of the dean of the business school. (This office may not necessarily supply the published or printed materials you want, but will have information about studies that are pertinent.) State the kind of information you are looking for and ask to whom you should speak in order to obtain it. If you are not satisfied with the response (some dean's offices are deluged with phone calls and do not have the staff or facilities to answer these questions), you will almost certainly obtain help by phoning the business school library. Ask for the reference librarian and state your reason for calling.

If you prefer to write, or if the telephone response has been unsatisfactory, mail a letter on your business stationery. Include a stamped, self-addressed #10 envelope. The following letter is typical of ones that have proven to be useful in locating materials from business schools that cover small business operations, functions, and problems:

Reference Librarian
Business Library
ABC School of Business Management

Dear Sir:

By way of introduction, I am the owner of the Thrifty Department Store in Greenpoint, Georgia, a small business with 17 full-time employees, and annual sales of about three million dollars. There is a large influx of tourists in our area during the spring and summer and we would like to add a workshop to our business so that we can personalize "T" shirts and other garments and imprint some of the products we sell with local symbols. In order to accomplish this, I am told that my best course of action is to prepare a business plan and submit it to an appropriate lending institution to obtain the funds we need to construct and equip the proposed workshop.

Has the business school undertaken any seminars and reports on business plans that could be helpful to us in preparing our own proposal and plan? If so, I would very much like to obtain copies of typical plans and documents that might serve as models.

Enclosed is a stamped, self-addressed envelope for response. Or, if you prefer, feel free to call me collect at the phone number on the above letterhead.

Sincerely,

Alvin Brown
President, Thrifty

ADDRESSES OF THE MAJOR GRADUATE SCHOOLS OF BUSINESS

Babson College
Graduate School of Business
Babson Park, MA 02157-0310
(617) 239-4542 FAX: (617) 239-4194
Contact: Office of Dr. Robert E. Holmes, Dean

Carnegie Mellon University
Graduate School of Industrial Administration
Schenley Park, Pittsburgh, PA 15213
(412) 268-2265
Contact: Office of Dr. Robert S. Sullivan, Dean

Columbia University
Graduate School of Business
New York, NY 10027
(212) 854-6083 FAX: (212) 932-0545
Contact: Office of Dr. Meyer Feldberg, Dean

Cornell University
Johnson Graduate School of Management
Ithaca, NY 14853
(607) 255-6418
Contact: Office of Dr. Alan G. Merten, Dean

Dartmouth College
Amos Tuck School of Business Administration
Hanover, NH 03755
(603) 646-2460 FAX: (603) 646-1308
Contact: Office of Dr. Colin C. Blaydon, Interim Dean

Duke University
Fuqua School of Business
Durham, NC 27706
(919) 660-7703 FAX: (919) 613-7000
Contact: Office of Dr. Wesley A. Magat, Senior Associate Dean

Harvard University
Graduate School of Business Administration
Boston, MA 02163
(617) 495-6000
Contact: Office of Dr. Kim B. Clark, Dean

Indiana State University
Graduate School of Business
Terre Haute, IN 47809-1401
(812) 237-2000
Contact: Office of Dr. Herbert Ross, Dean

Massachusetts Institute of Technology
Sloan School of Management
Cambridge, MA 02139
(617) 253-6615 FAX: (617) 258-6617
Contact: Office of Dr. Glenn L. Urban, Dean

New York University
Leonard N. Stern School of Business
New York, NY
(212) 998-0900 (914) 323-5333
Contact: Office of Dr. George D. Daly, Dean

Northwestern University
J. L. Kellogg Graduate School of Management
Evanston, IL 60208
(708) 491-3300
Contact: Office of Dr. Donald P. Jacobs, Dean

Purdue University
Krannert Graduate School of Management
Evanston, IL 60208
(317) 494-4366
Contact: Office of Dr. Dennis J. Weidenaar, Dean

Stanford University
Graduate School of Business
Stanford, CA 94305-9991
(415) 723-2766 FAX: (415) 723-1322
Contact: Office of Dr. A. Michael Spence, Dean

University of California at Berkeley
Haas School of Business
Berkeley, CA 94720
(510) 642-1425
Contact: Office of Dr. William A. Hasler, Dean

University of California at Los Angeles
John E. Anderson Graduate School of Management
Los Angeles, CA 90024
(310) 825-6121
Contact: Office of Dr. William P. Pierskalla, Dean

University of Chicago
Graduate School of Business
Chicago, IL 60637
(312) 702-7121 FAX: (312) 702-9085
Contact: Office of Dr. Robert S. Hamada, Dean

University of Michigan
School of Business Administration
Ann Arbor, MI 48109
(313) 764-2343
Contact: Office of Dr. B. Joseph White, Dean

University of North Carolina
Joseph M. Bryan School of Business and Economics
Greensboro, NC 27400
(910) 334-5338
Contact: Office of Dr. James K. Weeks, Dean

University of Pennsylvania
The Wharton School
Philadelphia, PA 19104
(215) 898-7601
Contact: Office of Dr. Thomas P. Gerrity, Dean

University of Pittsburgh
Joseph M. Katz Graduate School of Business
Pittsburgh, PA 15261
(412) 648-1556 FAX: (412) 648-1552
Contact: Office of Dr. H. J. Zoffer, Dean

University of Rochester
William E. Simon Graduate School of Business
Rochester, NY 14627
(716) 275-3533 FAX: (716) 473-9604
Contact: Office of Dr. Charles Plosser, Dean

University of Southern California
Graduate School of Business Administration
Los Angeles, CA 90089
(213) 740-7846
Contact: Office of Dr. Randolph Westerfield, Dean

University of Texas
College of Business Administration
Austin, TX 78712
(512) 471-5921
Contact: Dr. Robert G. May, Acting Dean

University of Virginia
Darden Graduate School of Business Administration
Charlottesville, VA 22903
(804) 924-7481
Contact: Office of Dr. Leo I. Higdon, Jr., Dean

Vanderbilt University
Owen Graduate School of Management
Nashville, TN 37203
(615) 322-2534 FAX: (615) 343-1499
Contact: Office of Dr. Martin S. Geisel, Dean

Yale University
School of Management
New Haven, CT 06520
(203) 432-6035
Contact: Office of Dr. Stanley J. Garska, Acting Dean

ENTREPRENEURSHIP CENTERS

Babson College
Graduate School of Business
Babson Park, MA 02157-0310
Entrepreneurial Division
(617) 239-4567
Contact: Office of Dr. William Bygrave, Director

University of Charleston
Center for Entrepreneurship
Charleston, SC 29424-0001
(803) 953-6596

Wichita State University
Center for Entrepreneurship
1845 North Fairmount Street
Wichita, KA 67260-0147
(316) 689-3000 FAX: (316) 689-3687

Appendix

BIBLIOGRAPHY

When it comes to books and other reading materials, you will find no scarcity of information about subjects relating to small business planning, formal plans, presentations, and related topics. Quite the opposite, the problem is often to determine which ones are likely to be the most constructive and reliable for your purpose. In addition, you have the Internet resources discussed in Chapter 11, a sample of which is included in *Data from the Internet,* pages 267–300, with lists of business plan books.

Immediately following is a list of general reference works that are useful in business planning, as well as other topics of interest to business owners and managers.

BIBLIOGRAPHY: MAJOR REFERENCES

The following works are highly recommended as important sources of information and as resource guides for entrepreneurs and the owners and managers of small- and home-based businesses. Since some of these volumes carry high price tags, readers would do well to use them as references in libraries, or at least examine them before investing in their purchase.

Associations Yellow Book. 1998. Leadership Directories.

Published semiannually, this reference work profiles some 1,200 of the leading trade and professional associations in the United States that are vocational in nature, operate on a national level, and have annual operating budgets of $1 million or more. Included also are the names of some 14,000 officers and staff members of these organizations.

AT&T Toll-Free 800 Directory, Business Edition. 1998. AT&T Information Services.

Published semiannually, in the fall and spring, this edition contains over 160,000 toll-free numbers operating in the United States. Canadian, consumer, and specialized editions are also available. For those without directories, "800" toll-free numbers can be tracked through AT&T Directory Assistance: 1-800-555-1212.

Business Almanac & Desk Reference. Seth Godin, editor. 1998. Houghton Mifflin.

Referred to as "the first work to assemble and distill the most useful facts, rankings, contacts, and counsel specifically for the business community," this reference guide covers more than 700 topics, including thousands of addresses and phone and fax numbers, and advice on where to find more in-depth details. Essential information is easy for the reader to locate in ten extensive divisions: business law & government, communications, corporate management, finance, human resources, international, manufacturing, marketing, office management, and personal computers. More statistical than other general and small-business reference works, it contains hundreds of charts, maps, tables, graphs, and tabulations.

Business Organizations, Agencies, and Publications Directory. 1998. Gale Research.

Published biannually, the directory covers more than 34,000 organizations and publications that are helpful, including trade, business, commercial, labor, and nonprofit associations; government agencies; consultants; commodity and stock exchanges; diplomatic offices; franchise organizations; banks and savings and loan institutions; newspaper, periodical, and book publishers; information centers; schools of business; Internet contacts and sources; research centers; hotel and motel systems; special libraries; and a great deal of affiliated data. Entries list names, addresses, phone and fax numbers, titles, and persons to contact. Some entries include brief commentaries and other useful data. The directory classifies entries by type of organization, service, or publication, with a keyword index.

Directory of Corporate Affiliations. 1998. National Register Publishing Company.

Published annually, with quarterly supplements, this reference work is a set of six volumes that lists public and private companies worldwide: more than 15,000 parent companies and 60,000 subsidiaries and affiliates in the U.S. sections alone. The entries list names, locations, communications numbers for all media vehicles, names and titles of key officers, financial data, categories and lines of business operations, and outside service firms such as accountants, consultants, and legal counsels. The six volumes are divided according to national, public, and private groupings, while the format is alphabetical within each volume. A separate master index lists all entries, brand names, Standard Industrial Classification (SIC) codes, and geographical locations alphabetically.

Encyclopedia of Associations. 1999. Gale Research.

This directory is an invaluable tool for obtaining information on the associations connected with American businesses and industries. Gale also publishes directories of international, regional, and local associations.

Form Buyers' Guide. 1998. National Business Forms Association (NBFA).

An annual, this guide lists some 600 suppliers of commercial forms and other business printing, such as ad specialties, carbonless paper, labels, calendars, tags, cards, and printed stationery. The format is alphabetical, and cross-indexed by products and types of service.

Portable MBA Desk Reference. Paul A. Argenti. 1996. Wiley & Sons.

This 688-page guide, promoted as "An Essential Business Companion," is composed of two sections: *Part One,* an A-to-Z encyclopedia of key business topics on all major terms in accounting, economics, finance, international business, management, manufacturing, marketing, small business, and strategy; Part Two, a comprehensive directory of sources of vital professional information in dozens of categories, including small business, demographics, advertising, exporting, and importing. Each section pinpoints the most useful books, journals, on-line services, directories, trade associations, and other sources.

Sibbald Guides. 1999. Acorn Press.

Published annually with quarterly updates, these guides focus on groups of related states, such as Georgia, Florida, and the Carolinas in one volume. They cover several hundred private and public business corporations within each geographical segment, and list names, addresses, communications numbers, and names and titles of key personnel. They also provide brief histories and descriptions of each company, as well as financial data, including return on equity, sales revenues, balance sheets, and income statements.

The Small Business Encyclopedia. Charles Fuller, editor. 1999. Entrepreneur Magazine Group.

Conveniently arranged in three looseleaf volumes, this set was developed to provide information successively on Starting Your Business, Managing Your Business, and Growing Your Business. Each volume contains some 20 pertinent categories, covering such subjects as marketing, research, location, recordkeeping, ethics, business plans, franchises, start-up financing, insurance, legal matters, inventory control, communications, and security. Each topical section includes lists of associations, government agencies, on-line services, periodicals, books, and other sources on the subject area in question. Although the price of the triple-volume set is high—$149—purchasers have the advantage of obtaining updated pages from time to time and the privilege of contacting the publisher for specific information on almost any small business subject. They will also receive a copy of *Small Business Advisor,* a 664-page trade paperback, published by John Wiley & Sons, which is a condensation of the encyclopedia.

Small Business Sourcebook, eighth edition. Kathleen E. Maki, editor. 1997. Gale Research.

Priced at $190, this two-volume set contains more than 4,000 pages of annotated listings for 17,770 sources of information designed to facilitate the start-up, development, and growth of specific small businesses, as well as 3,815 listings for general small business topics. An additional 4,091 entries are provided on a state-by-state basis, along with references to 890 pertinent government agencies and branch offices. The format is such that readers who want to focus on specific business categories without having to roam throughout the two volumes, such as "Advertising Services," "Bookstores," or "Electrical Contracting," will find alphabetical sections that condense pertinent data in one place.

A Selection of Periodicals Devoted to Business Coverage

The following magazines and trade journals regularly provide articles, advertising, and other materials of interest to owners, managers, and other business executives (the circulation of each publication is in parentheses):

American Business (200,000)
Covers all phases of business, including those relating specifically to small- and medium-sized businesses

Entrepreneur (200,000)
Information and counsel for starting and maintaining small businesses

Home Business News (5,000)
For home-based business owners

In Business (50,000)
Information of value to small business owners

Inc. Magazine (600,000)
Read mainly by owners and managers of small- to mid-sized companies

Income Opportunities (325,000)
A wide-ranging guide to business opportunities, methods, and management

Marketing News (28,000)
Covers current developments and procedures in marketing and related subjects

Nation's Business (860,000)
Provides management assistance, primarily to owners and managers of small- and medium-sized businesses

Glossary
of
General
Business
Terms

account payable A liability to a creditor, usually for goods and services.

account receivable A claim against a debtor, usually for products delivered or services rendered.

acquisition In business terminology, usually a company or other substantial entity acquired.

advertising The action of attracting public attention and potential customers through various paid media.

assets The entries on an organization's balance sheet showing financial and tangible properties that are owned or that can be readily converted to ownership.

bar chart A business chart that uses vertical or horizontal bars proportionately to give a quick, visual impression of related or comparable data and statistics.

break-even point The point at which profits and losses are in balance.

business climate The attitudes and outlooks, as well as economic conditions, that prevail in any given locale.

capital Any form of material wealth, such as money or property, used or accumulated by an individual or organization.

capitalization As traditionally used in finance, the sum of the par value of a company's stocks and bonds outstanding.

capitation A set dollar limit that an employer pays to a health maintenance organization (HMO), regardless of how often employees use the services offered by the provider.

cash flow The movement of money into and out of a business.

certificate of incorporation A legal document certifying that an organization has been established as a corporation.

certified public accountant (CPA) An accountant who meets various prescribed requirements, including the passing of a uniform examination prepared by the American Institute of Certified Public Accountants.

circulation As applied to advertising, particularly magazines and newspapers, the number of copies of a publication sent to a standard list of readers, whether free or by subscription, and sold at newsstands and other retail outlets.

co-insurance Money an individual is required to pay for health plan services, after a deductible has been paid. Most commonly, the employee is responsible for 20 percent while the employer or the insurance company picks up 80 percent of the medical cost.

collaboration Working jointly with one or more individuals or organizations in a mutual venture.

collateral Security pledged against an obligation, such as stocks used to cover a loan.

common stock Ordinary capital shares of a corporation that have claim on the net assets of the organization after other obligations have been paid.

compatible A business system or operation that functions harmoniously with a complementary one.

compensation Money or other valuables given or received for service or contribution.

consultant A professional expert or specialist who advises clients and is paid a one-time fee or a continuing retainer.

copyright The exclusive right, granted by law to any individual or group, to sell or reproduce original works, usually extending for the life of the author plus 50 years after his or her death, if the work was created in or after 1978.

corporation A body of persons legally granted the right to be a separate entity distinct from those of its members.

cost control A business system devised to supervise, monitor, and control certain costs, whether specific or general.

decentralization The distribution of administrative powers or functions among individuals or groups other than those in central headquarters.

demographics Data researched and computed statistically to present specific information about the makeup of population segments. Such information might categorize people by sex, age, education, background, and income.

depreciation Recognized decrease in value because of wear and tear, damage, or decline in price.

direct mail Mail addressed directly by an organization to prospective customers or clients during advertising, promotion, or merchandising campaigns.

distribution In commerce, the process of moving goods from the manufacturer to the consumer or point of sale.

diversification The act of extending a business into other fields, related or unrelated, in order to increase profits or otherwise improve the value of the organization.

electronic data processing Popularly referred to as EDP, a process whereby electronic computers are used to organize the compilation of information.

employee assistance program (EAP) Counseling for alcoholism, drug abuse, or mental health.

employee turnover The nature and degree to which employees are joined to, or released from, an organization.

entrepreneur A person who creates, organizes, and operates a business venture (derived from the French *entreprendre,* to undertake).

equity The basic value of a business or property beyond any liabilities connected with it.

equity capital That portion of a business's capital that is furnished by stockholders.

excise An indirect tax levied on the production, sale, or consumption of certain commodities, such as tobacco or alcohol, within a country.

expenses, fixed Expenses that change very little or not at all during any specific period.

expenses, variable Expenses that commonly change from one period to the next and seldom remain fixed for any length of time.

facilities In business, a term used to designate structures or equipment on hand to facilitate an action or process.

forecasting In business or commercial operations, the action undertaken to determine what future events will be significant to an organization's status.

franchise Authorization granted by a manufacturer or other key business to a dealer, distributor, or independent operator to sell his products or services, generally in a retail outlet or commercial facility.

fringe benefits Benefits or things of value given to employees other than their wages or salaries.

graphics Illustrations, charts, or other visualizations used in advertising and promotion, for commercial presentations, and for training.

gross income The overall income received by a company prior to deductions such as expenses, taxes, and interest.

growth, controlled The monetary or physical growth of an organization that is controlled so it does not exceed certain limits during any given period of time or in any designated area.

growth, explosive Uncontrolled, and generally undesirable, expansion of a company or other organization.

guaranty loan A commercial loan that is guaranteed (or assumed) by a person or organization other than the one receiving the loan.

hardware In connection with computers, the physical equipment such as the keyboard and printer and monitor used in the process of compiling and storing information.

health maintenance organization (HMO) The provider of a health and medical insurance plan in which employees and/or their employer pay a fixed monthly fee for services, instead of a separate charge for each visit or service.

human resources The personnel used directly or indirectly to perform the necessary functions and operations, as contrasted to the physical and mechanical resources.

incorporation The act of establishing a business legally as a corporation.

inventory The total quantity of goods and materials held by a company or organization.

job description A formalized statement used by a company to define the nature, responsibilities, and duties of a specific job or assignment, and usually the remuneration promised.

joint venture A venture or enterprise in which two or more individuals or organizations agree to join forces for their mutual strength and benefit.

limited partnership A business partnership of two or more people, organized legally in such a way that individual responsibilities and liabilities regarding the business are limited and not necessarily shared equally.

logo, logotype A trademark or symbol to identify a company.

managed care A medical/health system that manages the quality and cost of health and medical services that individuals receive.

management The person or persons who manage a business or institution and who determine the nature of the operation, its objectives, and the personnel needed for the overall performance.

market Commercially, the size, location, and nature of the area in which a company can logically and realistically conduct its business.

marketing That function in a company that is directly concerned with the sale and distribution of products and materials or the activity of providing services to the public.

markup The amount added to the cost of materials or products, usually calculated to take into account the expense of overhead and the desired profit.

media In advertising and marketing, the plural of *medium* is commonly used to refer to all means of mass communication, such as newspapers, radio, TV, and magazines, that are used as vehicles for conveying information to consumers.

merchandising The promotion of goods and services, whether by advertising, publicity, sales programs, word of mouth, or combinations thereof, to help move goods from manufacturers to consumers.

net income Income retained by a company after the gross income has been cut by costs, taxes, fees, losses, and other deductions.

operations Those functions of a company that are designated by a combination of machines, manpower, equipment, and energy to accomplish specified objectives.

organizational chart A graphic chart, table, or diagram depicting the positions and relationships of people in an organization, or the layout of different departments.

orientation Introductory instructions covering a new situation or procedure.

owner's equity The basic value in a company, or share of its stock, assigned to the owner.

partnership A business contract entered into by two or more persons in which each agrees to share the expenses, labor, and responsibilities in a joint enterprise.

personnel The employees of an organization.

point of purchase The location at which the customers select goods they are going to buy in a retail establishment.

policy An overall plan or course of action in a business organization designed to guide managers and employees in making long-range actions and decisions for the common good.

presentation In advertising or business planning, a proposal made by one party to another in the form of verbal and/or graphic communications.

press release An announcement or account of circumstances or actions or other news in letter form, distributed by an organization to members of the press.

print media Newspapers, magazines, and other periodicals that are printed on paper and read by recipients, in contrast to other media, such as radio, that reach audiences over the air.

profit A gain or return, whether in cash or other valuables beneficial to the organization.

profit-and-loss (P&L) statement An account showing net and gross profit or loss over a given period of time.

promotion In marketing, an individual effort or a long-range campaign that is designed to help sell a company's products or services to prospective customers.

proposal A formal presentation of data designed to encourage the recipient or audience to view the creator's suggestions favorably.

prospect A person who is a likely purchaser of products or services, or seems favorably inclined to join an organization or agree to a point of view.

public relations The actions and methods employed by an individual or organization to promote public goodwill in regard to the person(s) engaged in the promotion.

publicity The act of distributing information or sponsoring an activity to generate favorable public interest.

quality control Systems and procedures designed to maintain quality in manufacturing, production, or processing.

readership The total number of people who read a periodical, such as a newspaper or magazine; it is determined by multiplying the circulation by the average number of people who read the periodical in question.

real property Buildings, structures, land, and in many cases inherent natural resources.

retail The sales of products, goods, and related services directly to consumers in limited quantities.

risk management The administration of plans, methods, and arrangements to reduce loss through various methods, such as security systems, insurance, and personnel training.

S Corporation A company incorporated specifically as a small business, with a limited number of stockholders and liability, and a lower tax burden than a regular (corporation.

sales tax A tax levied as a percentage of the price of products and services dispensed most commonly by a retailer or wholesaler.

saturation point In marketing and merchandising, the point that has been reached in sales beyond which there can be no increase in the number of buyers of products or services.

self-employment A situation whereby individuals earn their incomes through their own business, rather than as employees of someone else.

self-employment tax A tax assessment for people classified as "self-employed," in their own business.

service business An enterprise engaged largely in providing services rather than goods, products, or materials.

short-term money Money borrowed for a brief period of time at a specified rate of interest. It is usually dissolved with one or, at most, two to three payments.

software Programs that are prepared specifically to activate computers to provide and/or store data as instructed.

sole proprietorship A small business that is wholly owned and controlled by one person.

specialization The act of engaging in business operations that are limited in nature or concentrated in a particular area.

specialty goods Merchandise for sale that is limited in scope, application, and usefulness, such as health foods, garden tools, sewing materials, or craft supplies.

state of the art Systems, products, or equipment that represent the latest in technological advancement.

term money Money borrowed for a long period of time and repaid in installments. Interest may be fixed or variable. Collateral is usually required.

trademark A distinguishing symbol, legally registered for the exclusive use of the organization that intends to use it as a sign of recognition.

traffic pattern The arrangement of space in a commercial building or manufacturing plant that facilitates the flow of personnel, goods, or equipment in the course of operations or the conduct of business.

vendor A seller of goods and supplies to a business.

venture capital Funds made available for investment in an unproven enterprise; sometimes referred to as "risk capital."

warranty A stipulation, explicit or implied, in assurance of some particular in regard to a contract or business dealing that the quality of goods is what has been stated and that reparation will be made if this is not true.

wholesale The sale of goods in large quantities, most commonly to a retailer, but not infrequently to consumers directly.

withholding The portion of an employee's pay placed in reserve and not paid, in order to meet anticipated financial obligations, most commonly the payment of income taxes.

Data
from the
Internet

The following pages are examples of the kind of information and facts you can get from the Internet and World Wide Web. This example is from a global book-seller called Amazon. The site is listed as: **www.amazon.com**

Your Search Results

for: the title words include "Business Plans"

59 items are shown below.

Action Plans for the Small Business: Growth Strategies for Businesses Wondering Where to Go Next

> Shailendra Vyakarna / Hardcover / Published 1994
> Our Price: $25.00

All-In-One Business Planner: How to Create the Plans You Need to Build Your Business ~ Ships in 2–3 days

> Christopher R. Malburg / Paperback / Published 1997
> Our Price: $7.96 ~ You Save: $1.99 (20%)

Business Plans for Dummies (Serial) ~ Ships in 2–3 days

> Paul Tiffany, Steven Peterson / Paperback / Published 1997
> Our Price: $15.99 ~ You Save: $4.00 (20%)
> *Read more about this title . . .*

Business Plans That Win $$$: Lessons from the Mit Enterprise Forum ~ Ships in 2–3 days

> Stanley R. Rich, David E. Gumpert / Paperback / Published 1987
> Our Price: $10.40 ~ You Save: $2.60 (20%)
> *Read more about this title . . .*

Business Plans to Game Plans: A Practical System for Turning Strategies into Action (Taking Control Series)
~ Ships in 2–3 days

> Jan B. King, James Walsh (Editor) / Paperback / Published 1994
> Our Price: $23.96 ~ You Save: $5.99 (20%)
> *Read more about this title . . .*

Business Plans to Manage Day-To-Day Operations: Real Life Results for Small Business Owners and Operators/Book and Disk (Wiley Small Business Edition)

> Christopher R. Malburg / Paperback / Published 1995
> Our Price: $31.96 ~ You Save: $7.99 (20%)

Business Plans to Manage Day-To-Day Operations; Real-Life Results for Small Business Owners and Oper

> Christopher R. Malburg / Hardcover/ Published 1993
> Our Price: $95.00

The Complete Book of Business Plans: Simple Steps to Writing a Powerful Business Plan (Small Business Sourcebooks)
~ Ships in 2–3 days

> Joseph A. Covello, Brian J. Hazelgren / Hardcover / Published 1994
> Our Price: $20.97 ~ You Save: $8.98 (30%)

The Complete Book of Business Plans: Simple Steps to Writing a Powerful Business Plan (Small Business Sourcebooks)
~ Ships in 2–3 days

> Joseph A. Covello, Brian J. Hazelgren / Paperback / Published 1994
> Our Price: $15.96 ~ You Save: $3.99 (20%)

The Essential Business Buyer's Guide: From Cellular Service and Overnight Mail to Internet Access Providers, 401(K) Plans and Desktop Computers, the ~ Ships in 2–3 days

> Business Consumer Guide Staff, the Staff of Business Consumer gu /
> Paperback / Published 1997
> Our Price: $15.16 - You Save: $3.79 (20%)
> *Read more about this title . . .*

Filmmakers and Financing: Business Plans for Independents
~ Ships in 2–3 days

Louise Levinson, Louise Levison / Paperback / Published 1994
Our Price: $19.96 ~ You Save: $4.99 (20%)
Read more about this title . . .

Game Plans for Success: Winning Strategies for Business and Life from 10 Top NFL Head Coaches ~ Ships in 2–3 days

Ray Didinger (Editor), et al / Audio Cassette / Published 1995
Our Price: $11.90 ~ You Save: $5.10 (30%)
Read more about this title . . .

Game Plans for Success: Winning Strategies for Business and Life from 10 Top NFL Head Coaches ~ Ships in 2–3 days

Ray Didinger (Editor) / Paperback / Published 1996
Our Price: $11.96 ~ You Save: $2.99 (20%)
Read more about this title . . .

Game Plans for Success: Winning Strategies for Business and Life from Ten Top NFL Head Coaches ~ Ships in 2–3 days

Ray Didinger (Editor), National Football League / Hardcover / Published 1995
Our Price: $16.07 ~ You Save: $6.88 (30%)
Read more about this title . . .

How to Really Create a Successful Business Plan: Featuring the Business Plans of Pizza Hut, Software Publishing Corp., Celestial Seasonings, Ben & je ~ Ships in 2–3 days

David E. Gumpert / Paperback/ Published 1996
Our Price: $15.96 ~ You Save: $3.99 (20%)
Read more about this title . . .

Model Business Plans for Product Businesses ~ Ships in 2–3 days

William A. Cohen / Paperback / Published 1995
Our Price: $18.36 ~ You Save: $4.59 (20%)
Read more about this title . . .

Model Business Plans for Product Businesses ~ Ships in 2–3 days

> William A., Phd Cohen/ Hardcover/ Published 1995
> Our Price: $65.00
> *Read more about this title . . .*

Model Business Plans for Service Businesses ~ Ships in 2–3 days

> William A., Phd Cohen / Hardcover / Published 1995
> Our Price: $62.50
> *Read more about this title . . .*

Writing Business Plans That Get Results: A Step-By-Step Guide ~
Usually ships in 24 hours

> Michael O'Donnell/ Paperback/ Published 1991
> Our Price: $12.76 ~ You Save: $3.19 (20%)

Writing That Works: How to Improve Your Memos, Letters, Reports, Speeches, Resumes, Plans, and Other Business Papers ~
Ships in 2–3 days

> Kenneth Roman, Joel Raphaelson / Mass Market Paperback /
> Published 1995
> Our Price: $3.99 ~ You Save: $1.00 (20%)
> *Read more about this title . . .*

1995 Tax Facts on Life Insurance/Life & Health Insurance, Annuities Employee Plans, Estates & Trusts Business Continuation Vol 1

> Deborah A. Miner (Editor) / Paperback / Published 1995
> Our Price: $19.95 *(Special Order)*

Annual McGraw-Hill Survey : Business' Plans for New Plants and Equipment, 1986–89

> Economics Dept McGraw-Hill Publications Company / Paperback/
> Published 1986
> Our Price: $ 137.00 *(Special Order)*

Annual McGraw-Hill Survey 1987–90: Business' Plans for New Plants and Equipment

Paperback / Published 1987
Our Price: $150.00 *(Special Order)*

Business Insurance: Directory of Corporate Buyers of Insurance Benefit Plans and Risk Management

Paperback / Published 1984
Our Price: $55.00 *(Special Order)*

Business Plans Handbook: A Compilation For Actual Business Plans Developed by Small Business Throughout North America Vol 2

Kristin Kahrs / Hardcover / Published 1995
Our Price: $ 115.00 *(Back Ordered)*

Business Plans Handbook: A Compilation of Actual Business Plans Developed by Small Business Throughout North America

Kristin Kahrs, Karin E. Koek (Editor) / Hardcover / Published 1995
Our Price: $115.00 *(Back Ordered)*

Business Plans That Win Venture Capital

Terrence P. McGarty / Hardcover / Published 1990
Our Price: $ 140.00 (Back Ordered)
Read more about this title . . .

Business Plans to Game Plans: A Practical System for Turning Strategies into Action (Taking Control Series)

Jan B. King / Paperback / Published 1997
Our Price: $23.96 ~ You Save: $5.99 (20%) *(Not Yet Published—On Order)*
Read more about this title . . .

Developing Business Plans: McS Small Business Consulting Practice Aid 96-1

Paperback / Published 1995
Our Price: $ 16.50 *(Back Ordered)*

Employee Stock Ownership Plans: Business Planning Implementation, Law and Taxation

Robert W., Jr. Smiley, Ronald J. Gilbert (Editor) / Hardcover/
Published 1989
Our Price: $127.68 *(Special Order)*

Exporting: Strategic Plans for Business

Richard J. Pierce/ Hardcover/ Published 1997
Our Price: $27.97 ~ You Save: $11.98 (30%) *(Not Yet Published—On Order)*

Game Plans: Sports Strategies for Business/Audio Cassette

Robert Keidel / Audio Cassette / Published 1986
Our Price: $8.95 + $0.85 special surcharge *(Special Order)*

Grand Plans: Business Progressivism and Social Change in Ohio's Miami Valley, 1890–1929

Judith Sealander / Hardcover / Published 1988
Our Price: $30.00 *(Special Order)*

Insights into Excellence: Winning Game Plans from 21 Masters of Business Success

Speakers Roundtable Staff / Hardcover / Published 1993
Our Price: $ 19.95 *(Special Order)*

Model Business Plans for Service Businesses

William A. Cohen / Paperback / Published 1995
(Publisher Out Of Stock)
Read more about this title . . .

Opening Digital Markets: Battle Plans and Business Strategies for Internet Commerce

Walid Mougayar / Hardcover / Published 1997
Our Price: $17.47 ~ You Save: $7.48 (30%) *(Not Yet Published—On Order)*

Plan Ahead: Winning Real World Business Plans to Help You Succeed

Gina Ph.D. Vega / Paperback / Published 1998
Our Price: $18.36 ~ You Save: $4.59 (20%) *(Not Yet Published—On Order)*

The Prentice Hall Encyclopedia of Model Business Plans

Wilbur Cross / Paperback / Published 1998
Our Price: $19.96 ~ You Save: $4.99 (20%) *(Not Yet Published—On Order)*

Program for Writing Winning Business Plans

Richard H. Buskirk / Paperback / Published 1989
Our Price: $9.95 + $0.85 special surcharge *(Special Order)*

Retirement Benefit Plans: An Information Source book (Oryx Sourcebook Series in Business and Management, No 8)

Herbert A. Miller / Hardcover / Published 1988
Our Price: $43.50 *(Special Order)*

Successful Business Plans for Architects

R. A. McKenzie / Hardcover / Published 1992
Our Price: $42.00 *(Special Order)*
Read more about this title . . .

Survey of Advanced Sales: An Introduction to: Business Continuation, Executive Compensation, Retirement Plans, Estate Planning, Investments

Paperback / Published 1994
Our Price: $34.95 *(Special Order)*

Teacher's Manual and Lesson Plans for a Woman's Guide to Business and Social Success

Mpc Staff / Paperback / Published 1983
Our Price: $13.95 *(Special Order)*

Accelerated Growth Planning: Profit Improvement Strategies for Consumer, Industrial and Service Business Game Plans

MacK Hanan / Published 1978
(Hard to Find)

All-In-One Business Planning Guide: How to Create Cohesive Plans for Marketing, Sales, Operations, Finance and Cash Flow (An Adams Business Advisor)

Christopher R. Malburg / Published 1994
(Hard to Find)

All-In-One Business Planning Guide: How to Create Cohesive Plans for Marketing, Sales, Operations, Finance, and Cash Flow

Christopher R. Malburg/ Published 1994
(Hard to Find)

The Bureau of Land Management reforestation and stand enhancement programs, plans, and proposals for attacking backlogs and bookkeeping problems: hearing before the Subcommittee on Regulation, Business Opportunities, and Technology of the Committee on Small Business, House of Representatives, One Hundred Third Congress, second session, Portland, OR, May 9, 1994

(Hard to Find)

The Bureau of Land Management reforestation programs: plans and proposals for attacking backlogs and bookkeeping problems: hearing before the Subcommittee on Regulation, Business Opportunities, and Technology of the Committee on Small Business, House of Representatives, One Hundred Third Congress, Second session, Portland, OR, May 9, 1994

(Hard to Find)

Business plans: 25 ways to get yours taken seriously

Brian Finch
(Hard to Find)

Business Plans and Loan Applications That Work: A Book of Models Based on Real Documents

John R. Taylor / Published 1993
(Hard to Find)

Business Plans and Loans Applications That Work: A Book of Models Based on Real Documents

John R. Taylor / Published 1993
(Hard to Find)

Computer-Assisted Business Plans

Matt Oppenheimer, Gerry A. Young / Published 1986
(Hard to Find)
Read more about this title . . .

Game Plans: Sports Strategies for Business

Robert Keidel / Published 1986
(Hard to Find)

Game Plans: Sports Strategies for Business

Robert Keidel / Published 1985
(Hard to Find)

The Mother Earth News Handbook of Home Business Ideas and Plans

New York: / Published 1976
(Hard to Find)

Partners in profit: Partnerships business plans

John M. Townsend
(Hard to Find)

Small Business Pension Plans

Thomas Martin / Published 1982
(Hard to Find)

Strategy Management: How to Execute and Control Strategic Plans for Your Business

Kevin W. Tourangeau / Published 1980
(Hard to Find)

Teaching Business Writing: Approaches, Plans, Pedagogy, Research

Jeanne W. Halpern (Editor) / Published 1983
(Hard to Find)

WHAT IS AN SBDC?

An SBDC counsels, conducts research, and trains business people in a wide variety of business topics and provides comprehensive information services and access to experts in many fields. Each SBDC encourages unique local efforts, region to region, state to state, and community to community, to meet small business needs in its area. SBDCs develop and maintain partnerships among community organizations and local, state, and federal agencies, providing a focal point for broad networks of public and private resources at the community level. SBDC partnership programs and activities serving small businesses have contributed significantly to economic growth in each state.

Alabama
Alabama SBDC Consortium
Univ. of Alabama at Birmingham
Medical Towers Building
1717 11th Avenue, Suite 419
Birmingham, AL 35294-4410
PHONE: (205) 934-7260

Alaska
Alaska Small Business Dev. Center
University of Alaska Anchorage
430 W. Seventh Avenue, Suite 110
Anchorage, AK 99501
PHONE: (907) 274-7232

Arizona
Arizona SBDC Network
2411 West 14th Street, Suite 132
Tempe, AZ 85281
PHONE. (602) 731-8720

Arkansas
Arkansas Small Business Dev. Center
University of Arkansas at Little Rock
100 South Main, Suite 401
Little Rock, AR 72201
PHONE: (501) 324-9043

California
California SBDC Program
Department of Commerce
801 K St., Suite 1700
Sacramento, CA 95814
PHONE: (916) 322-3502

Colorado
Colorado Small Business Dev. Center
Colorado Office of Business Development
1625 Broadway, Suite 1710
Denver, CO 80202
PHONE: (303) 892-3809

Connecticut
Connecticut Small Business Dev. Center
University of Connecticut
2 Bourn Place, U-94
Storrs, CT 06269-5094
PHONE: (860) 486-4135

Delaware
Delaware Small Business Dev. Center
University of Delaware
Purnell Hall, Suite 005
Newark, DE 19716-2711
PHONE: (302) 831-2747

District of Columbia
District of Columbia SBDC
Howard University
6th and Fairmont St. N.W., Room 128
Washington, DC 20059
PHONE: (202) 806-1550

Florida
Florida Small Business Dev. Center Network
University of West Florida
19 West Garden Street, Suite 300
Pensacola, FL 32501
PHONE: (904) 444-2060

Georgia
Georgia Small Business Dev. Center
University of Georgia
Chicopee Complex, 1180 East Broad St.
Athens, GA 30602-5412
PHONE: (706) 542-5760

Guam
Univ. of Guam Small Business Dev. Center
Box 5061-U. O. G. Station
Mangilao, GU 96923
PHONE: 011 (671) 735-2590

Hawaii
Hawaii Small Business Dev. Center Network
University of Hawaii at Hilo
200 West Kiwili
Hilo, HI 96720
PHONE: (808) 933-3515

Idaho
Idaho Small Business Development Center
Boise State University
1910 University Drive
Boise, ID 83725
PHONE: (208) 385-1640

Illinois
Illinois Small Business Dev. Center
Dept. of Commerce & Community Affairs
620 East Adams St., 3rd Floor
Springfield, IL 62701
PHONE: (217) 524-5856

Indiana
Indiana Small Business Dev. Centers
Economic Development Council
One North Capitol, Suite 420
Indianapolis, IN 46204
PHONE: (317) 264-6871

Iowa
Iowa Small Business Development Center
Iowa State University
137 Lynn Avenue
Ames, IA 50014
PHONE: (515) 292-6351

Kansas
Kansas Small Business Dev. Center
Wichita State University
1845 Fairmount
Wichita, KS 67260-0148
PHONE: (316) 689-3878 Ext. 5371

Kentucky
Kentucky Small Business Dev. Center
U of KY, Center for Business Development
225 Business & Economics Building
Lexington, KY 40506-0034
PHONE: (606) 257-7668

Louisiana
Louisiana Small Business Dev. Center
Northeast Louisiana University, CBA
700 University Ave.
Monroe, LA 71209-6435
PHONE: (318) 342-5506

Maine
Maine Small Business Development Center
University of Southern Maine
96 Falmouth St.
Portland, ME 04103
PHONE: (207) 780-4420

Maryland
Maryland Small Business Dev. Center
Dept. of Economic & Employment Dev.
217 East Redwood St., 10th Floor
Baltimore, MD 21202
PHONE: (410) 767-6552

Massachusetts
Massachusetts Small Business Dev. Center
University of Massachusetts-Amherst
Room 205, School of Management
Amherst, MA 01003
PHONE: (413) 545-6301

Michigan
Wayne State Univ. Small Business Dev. Center
2727 Second Avenue
Detroit, MI 48201
PHONE: (313) 964-1798

Mississippi
Mississippi Small Business Dev. Center
University of Mississippi
Old Chemistry Building, Suite 216
University, MS 38677
PHONE: (601) 232-5001

Missouri
Missouri Small Business Dev. Center
University of Missouri
300 University Place
Columbia, MO 65211
PHONE: (573) 882-0344

Montana
Montana Small Business Dev. Center
Montana Department of Commerce
1424 9th Avenue
Helena, MT 59620
PHONE: (406) 444-4780

Nebraska
Nebraska Business Development Center
University of Nebraska at Omaha
60th & Dodge Sts., CBA Room 407
Omaha, NE 68182
PHONE: (402) 554-2521

Nevada
Nevada Small Business Dev. Center
University of Nevada, Reno
College of Business Adm-032, Room 411
Reno, NV 89557-0100
PHONE: (702) 784-1717

New Hampshire
New Hampshire Small Business Dev. Ctr.
University of New Hampshire
108 McConnell Hall
Durham, NH 03824
PHONE: (603) 862-2200

New Jersey
New Jersey Small Business Dev. Center
Rutgers Univ. Graduate School of Mgmt.
180 University Ave.
Newark, NJ 07102
PHONE: (201) 648-5950

New Mexico
New Mexico Small Business Dev. Center
Santa Fe Community College
P.O. Box 4187
Santa Fe, NM 87502-4187
PHONE: (505) 438-1362

New York
New York State Small Business Dev. Ctr.
State University of New York
State University Plaza, S-523
Albany, NY 12246
PHONE: (518) 443-5398

North Carolina
North Carolina SBTDC
University of North Carolina
4509 Creedmoor Road, Suite 201
Raleigh, NC 27612
PHONE: (919) 571-4154

North Dakota
North Dakota Small Business Dev. Center
University of North Dakota
118 Gamble Hall, UND, Box 7308
Grand Forks, ND 58202
PHONE: (701) 777-3700

Ohio
Ohio Small Business Development Center
77 South High Street
P.O. Box 1001
Columbus, OH 43266-0101
PHONE: (614) 466-2711

Oklahoma
Oklahoma Small Business Dev. Center
Southeastern Oklahoma State University
P.O. Box 2584, Station A
Durant, OK 74701
PHONE: (405) 924-0277

Oregon
Oregon Small Business Dev. Center
Lane Community College
44 W. Broadway, Suite 501
Eugene, OR 97401-3021
PHONE: (503) 726-2250

Pennsylvania
Pennsylvania Small Business Dev. Center
The Wharton School, Univ. of Penn.
4th Floor Vance Hall, 3733 Spruce St.
Philadelphia, PA 19104-6374
PHONE: (215) 898-1219

Puerto Rico
Puerto Rico Small Business Dev. Center
Central Administration, Univ of Puerto Rico
P.O. Box 364984
San Juan, PR 00936-4984
PHONE: (787) 250-0000 Ext. 2072

Rhode Island
Rhode Island Small Business Dev. Center
Bryant College
1150 Douglas Pike
Smithfield, RI 02917
PHONE: (401) 232-6111

South Carolina
The Frank L. Roddey SBDC
Univ. of S. Carolina, College of Bus. Adm.
Columbia, SC 29201-9980
PHONE: (803) 777-4907

South Dakota
South Dakota Small Business Dev. Center
University of South Dakota
414 E. Clark
Vermillion, SD 57069
PHONE: (605) 677-5279

Tennessee
Tennessee Small Business Dev. Center
Memphis State University
Bldg. 1, South Campus
Memphis, TN 38152
PHONE: (901) 678-2500

Texas-Dallas
North Texas-Dallas SBDC
Bill J. Priest Institute for Economic Dev.
1402 Corinth St
Dallas, TX 75215
PHONE: (214) 565-5831

Texas-Houston
Univ. of Houston SBDC
University of Houston
1100 Louisiana, Suite 500
Houston, TX 77002
PHONE: (713) 752-8444

Texas-Lubbock
N.W. Texas Small Business Dev. Center
Texas Tech University
2579 S. Loop 289, Suite 114
Lubbock, TX 79423
PHONE: (806) 745-3973

Texas-San Antonio
UTSA South Texas Border SBDC
UTSA Downtown Center
1222 North Main Street, Suite 450
San Antonio, TX 78212
PHONE: (210) 558-2450

Utah
Utah Small Business Development Ctr
Salt Lake Community College
8811 South 700 East
Sandy, UT 84070
PHONE: (801) 255-5991

Vermont
Vermont Small Business Dev. Center
Vermont Technical College
P.0. Box 422
Randolph, VT 05060
PHONE: (802) 728-9101

Virgin Islands
UVI Small Business Development Ctr.
Sunshine Mall, Suite 104
Frederiksted, St. Croix USVI 00840
PHONE: (809) 776-3206

Virginia
Virginia Small Business Dev. Center
901 East Byrd Street, Suite 1800
Richmond, VA 23219
PHONE: (804) 371-8253

Washington
Washington Small Business Dev. Ctr.
Washington State University
501 Johnson Tower
Pullman, WA 99164-4851
PHONE: (509) 335-1576

West Virginia
West Virginia Small Business Dev. Ctr.
950 Kanawha Blvd., East
Charleston, WV 25301
PHONE: (304) 558-2960

Wisconsin
Wisconsin Small Business Dev. Center
University of Wisconsin
432 North Lake St, Room 423
Madison, WI 53706
PHONE: (608) 263-7794

Wyoming
WSBDC/State Network Office
P.O. Box 3275
Laramie, WY 82071-3275
PHONE: (307) 766-3505

ASBDC

"Serving Small Businesses Across America"

Interstate Highways ······

SBDCs ★

Worksheets and Forms

This section contains examples of worksheets prepared by the SBA to help you evaluate projected annual sales and expenses, cash forecasts, balance sheets, and the management chain of command.

Projected Statement of Sales and Expenses for One Year

Total Jan Feb Mar Apr May Jun Jul Aug Sep Oct Nov Dec

A. Net Sales _____

B. Cost of Goods Sold _____

   1. Raw Materials _____

   2. Direct Labor _____

   3. Manufacturing Overhead _____

     Indirect Labor _____

     Factory Heat, Light, and Power _____

     Insurance and Taxes _____

     Depreciation _____

C. Gross Margin (Subtract B from A) _____

D. Selling and Administrative Expenses _____

   4. Salaries and Commissions _____

   5. Advertising Expenses _____

   6. Miscellaneous Expenses _____

E. Net Operating Profit
(Subtract D from C) _____

F. Interest Expense _____

G. Net Profit before Taxes
(Subtract F from E) _____

H. Estimated Income Tax _____

I. Net Profit after Income Tax
(Subtract H from G) _____

Estimated Cash Forecast

	Jan	Feb	Mar	Apr	May	Jun	Jul	Aug	Sep	Oct	Nov	Dec
(1) Cash in Bank (Start of Month)												
(2) Petty Cash (Start of Month)												
(3) Total Cash (add (1) and (2))												
(4) Expected Accounts Receivable												
(5) Other Money Expected												
(6) Total Receipts (add (4) and (5))												
(7) Total Cash and Receipts (add (3) and (6))												
(8) All Disbursements (for month)												
(9) Cash Balance at End of Month in Bank Account and Petty Cash (subtract (8) from (7)*)												

•This balance is your starting cash balance for the next month.

Current Balance Sheet Figures. A balance sheet shows the financial conditions of a business as of a certain date. It lists what a business has, what it owes, and the investment of the owner. A balance sheet enables you to see at a glance your assets and liabilities.

Use the blanks below to draw up a current balance sheet for your company.

Cash Flow

All businesses, no matter how large or small, function on cash and the orderly flow, or use of, that cash. A *cash-flow projection*, also referred to as a *cash forecast*, is a necessary tool for you to use in your financial planning and management. Since a projection shows all of the money entering and exiting your business, its most constructive function is the pinpointing of potential danger spots. The projection is quite simple—all you have to do is follow these steps from month to month:

- List cash balance at the beginning of the month
- Add: receipts
- Subtract: Disbursements
- Ending balance
- Surplus (+) or shortage (–)

The degree of detail you come up with will depend on several components, including the size of your company, the amount of financial activity during the period in question, and the kinds of items that you decide qualify as "disbursements" and "receipts." Sales figures alone, as an example, can be misleading if your company extends credit, since the payments for sales may not be received within the time frame being calculated. You can reduce errors by checking earlier cash-flow records to determine what the right calculations are for your type of operations. If your business is seasonal, or if receipts and disbursements vary considerably from month to month, you need to adjust your projections accordingly. Seasonal fluctuations tend to show up well in advance of seasonal peaks and valleys, and it is essential for you to ascertain the time lags between income you receive and disbursements you have to make to maintain your operations. The timing of purchases, for example, depends on such matters as the delivery schedules of suppliers, the availability of supplies, production time, and the proportions of inventories essential to your business.

Another crucial factor in projecting your cash flow is the kind of payment arrangements you make with vendors. The figures that are entered into the books from month to month should accurately reflect such agreements: whether vendors, for example, require full or partial payment before orders are processed, require little or no advance payment, or sell on credit.

Primary cash flow projections should cover major items like salaries, distribution, marketing, and utilities, but also less routine expenditures such as payroll taxes, sales taxes, income taxes, and emergency commitments. Disbursements that occur infrequently can be too easily overlooked in a monthly calculation of cash flow. Examples of some of the "strays" that result in cash-flow pitfalls are: insurance premiums, business gifts, entertainment, dues, and professional fees.

Monthly Cash Flow Projection

Name of business		Address		Owner		Type of business		Prepared by		Date	

Year	Month	Pre-start-up position		1		2		3		4		5		6		Total Columns 1–6	
		Estimate	Actual	Estimate	Actual	Estimate	Actual	Estimate	Actual	Estimate	Actual	Estimate	Actual	Estimate	Actual	Estimate	Actual
1. Cash on hand (beginning of month)																	
2. Cash receipts																	
(a) Cash sales																	
(b) Collections from credit accounts																	
(c) Loan or other cash injection (specify)																	
3. Total cash receipts (2a + 2b + 2c = 3)																	
4. Total cash available (before cash out) (1+3)																	
5. Cash paid out																	
(a) Purchases (merchandise)																	
(b) Gross wages (excludes withdrawals)																	
(c) Payroll expenses (taxes, etc.)																	
(d) Outside services																	
(e) Supplies (office and operating)																	
(f) Repairs and maintenance																	
(g) Advertising																	
(h) Car, delivery and travel																	
(i) Accounting and legal																	
(j) Rent																	
(k) Telephone																	
(l) Utilities																	
(m) Insurance																	
(n) Taxes (real estate, etc.)																	
(o) Interest																	
(p) Other expenses (specify each)																	
(q) Miscellaneous (unspecified)																	
(r) Subtotal																	
(s) Loan principal payment																	
(t) Capital purchases (specify)																	
(u) Other start-up costs																	
(v) Reserve and/or escrow (specify)																	
(w) Owner's withdrawal																	
6. Total cash paid out (5a through 5w)																	
7. Cash position (end of month) (4 minus 6)																	
Essential operating data (non-cash flow information)																	
A. Sales volume (dollars)																	
B. Accounts receivable (end of month)																	
C. Bad debt (end of month)																	
D. Inventory on hand (end of month)																	
E. Accounts payable (end of month)																	

Instructions for Monthly Cash Flow Projection

1. Cash on hand (beginning of month)	Cash on hand same as (7). Cash position, previous month
2. Cash receipts	
(a) Cash sales	All cash sales. Omit credit sales unless cash is actually received.
(b) Collections from credit accounts	Amount to be expected from all credit accounts.
(c) Loan or other cash injection	Indicate here all cash injections not shown in 2(a) or 2(b) above.
3. Total cash receipts (2a + 2b + 2c = 3)	
4. Total cash available (before cash out) (1+3)	
5. Cash paid out	
(a) Purchases (merchandise)	Merchandise for resale or for use in product (paid for in current month)
(b) Gross wages (excludes withdrawals)	Base pay plus overtime (if any)
(c) Payroll expenses (taxes, etc.)	Include paid vacations, paid sick leave, health insurance, unemployment insurance, etc. (this might be 10 to 45% of 5(b))
(d) Outside services	This could include outside labor and/or material for specialized or overflow work, including subcontracting
(e) Supplies (office and operating)	Items purchased for use in the business (not for resale)
(f) Repairs and maintenance	Include periodic large expenditures such as painting or decorating
(g) Advertising	This amount should be adequate to maintain sales volume
(h) Car, delivery and travel	If personal car is used, charge in this column, include parking
(i) Accounting and legal	Outside services, including, for example, bookkeeping
(j) Rent	Real estate only (See 5(p) for other rentals)
(k) Telephone	
(l) Utilities	Water, heat, light and/or power
(m) Insurance	Coverages on business property and products (fire, liability); also worker's compensation, fidelity, etc. Exclude executive life (include in 5(w))
(n) Taxes (real estate, etc.)	Plus inventory tax, sales tax, excise tax, if applicable
(o) Interest	Remember to add interest on loan as it is injected (See 2(c) above)
(p) Other expenses (specify each)	Unexpected expenditures may be included here as a safety factor
	Equipment expensed during the month should be included here (non-capital equipment)
	When equipment is rented or leased, record payments here
(q) Miscellaneous (unspecified)	Small expenditures for which separate accounts would not be practical
(r) Subtotal	This subtotal indicates cash out for operating costs
(s) Loan principal payment	Include payment on all loans, including vehicle and equipment purchases on time payment
(t) Capital purchases (specify)	Nonexpensed (depreciable) expenditures such as equipment, building, vehicle purchases and leasehold improvements
(u) Other start-up costs	Expenses incurred prior to first month projection and paid for after start-up
(v) Reserve and/or escrow (specify)	Example: insurance, tax or equipment escrow to reduce impact of large periodic payments
(w) Owner's withdrawal	Should include payment for such things as owner's income tax, social security, health insurance, executive life insurance premiums, etc.
6. Total cash paid out (5a through 5w)	
7. Cash position (end of month) (4 minus 6)	Enter this amount in (1) Cash on hand following month.
Essential operating data (non-cash flow information)	This is basic information necessary for proper planning and for proper cash flow projection. In conjunction with this data, the cash flow can be evolved and shown in the above form.
A. Sales volume (dollars)	This is a very important figure and should be estimated carefully, taking into account size of facility and employee output as well as realistic anticipated sales (actual sales, not orders received).
B. Accounts receivable (end of month)	Previous unpaid credit sales plus current month's credit sales, less amounts received current month (deduct "C" below)
C. Bad debt (end of month)	Bad debts should be subtracted from (B) in the month anticipated.
D. Inventory on hand (end of month)	Last month's inventory plus merchandise received and/or manufactured current month minus amount sold current month
E. Accounts payable (end of month)	Previous month's payable plus current month's payable minus amount paid during month
F. Depreciation	Established by your accountant, or value of all your equipment divided by useful life (in months) as allowed by Internal Revenue Service

Projected Cash Flow Statement

	1st qtr	2nd qtr	3rd qtr	4th qtr	TOTAL
BEGINNING CASH	22,116	12,741	18,928	399	
Add:					
Cash sales	28,500	41,500	27,000	83,000	180,000
Collection on receivables	0	0	0	0	0
Loan or other cash injection	0	0	0	0	0
TOTAL CASH AVAILABLE	50,616	54,241	45,928	83,399	
Deduct:					
Advertising	900	350	750	1,400	3,400
Bad debts	22	43	28	87	180
Credit card service charge	171	249	162	498	1,080
Dues and subscriptions	270	0	270	0	540
Insurance	300	300	300	300	1,200
Interest	987	947	905	863	3,702
Maintenance and repairs	114	166	108	332	720
Postage and supplies	399	581	378	1,162	2,520
Professional services	125	200	125	125	575
Rent	2,250	2,250	2,250	2,250	9000
Salaries: Employees	1,170	2,730	1,990	6,710	12,600
Salaries: Officers	2,600	2,600	2,600	2,600	10,400
Taxes	630	630	630	630	2,520
Telephone	270	260	270	280	1,080
Travel/entertainment	85	125	81	249	540
Utilities	450	450	450	450	1,800
Other operating expenses	675	675	675	675	2,700
Capital expenditures	0	0	0	0	0
Loan principal payment	1,557	1,557	1,557	1,557	6,228
Purchases (merchandise)	24,900	21,200	32,000	38,500	116,600
TOTAL CASH PAID OUT	37,875	35,313	45,529	58,668	177,385
NET CASH AVAILABLE	12,741	18,928	399	24,731	
Net cash increase or decrease	–9,375	6,187	–18,529	24,332	2,216

Income Projection Statement

	Industry %	J	F	M	A	M	J	J	A	S	O	N	D	Annual Total	Annual %
Total net sales (revenues)															
Cost of sales															
Gross profit															
Gross profit margin															
Controllable expenses															
Salaries/wages															
Payroll expenses															
Legal/accounting															
Advertising															
Automobile															
Office supplies															
Dues/subscriptions															
Utilities															
Miscellaneous															
Total controllable expenses															
Fixed expenses															
Rent															
Depreciation															
Utilities															
Insurance															
Licenses/permits															
Loan payments															
Miscellaneous															
Total fixed expenses															
Total expenses															
Net profit (loss) before taxes															
Taxes															
Net profit (loss) after taxes															

INSTRUCTIONS FOR INCOME PROJECTION STATEMENT

The income projection (profit and loss) statement is valuable as both a planning tool and a key management tool to help control business operations. It enables the owner-manager to develop a preview of the amount or income generated each month and for the business year, based on reasonable predictions of monthly levels or sales, costs and expenses.

As monthly projections are developed and entered into the income projection statement, they can serve as definite goals for controlling the business operation. As actual operating results become known each month, they should be recorded for comparison with the monthly projections. A completed income statement allows the owner-manager to compare actual figures with monthly projections and to take steps to correct any problems.

Industry Percentage

In the industry percentage column, enter the percentages of total sales (revenues) that are standard for your industry, which are derived by dividing

$$\frac{\text{cost/expense items}}{\text{total net sales}} \times 100\%$$

These percentages can be obtained from various sources, such as trade associations, accountants or banks. The reference librarian in your nearest public library can refer you to documents that contain the percentage figures, for example, Robert Morris Associates' *Annual Statement Studies* (One Liberty Place, Philadelphia, PA 19103).

Industry figures serve as a useful benchmark against which to compare cost and expense estimates that you develop for your firm. Compare the figures in the industry percentage column to those in the annual percentage column.

Total Net Sales (Revenues)

Determine the total number of units of products or services you realistically expect to sell each month in each department at the prices you expect to get. Use this step to create the projection to review your pricing practices.

- What returns, allowances and markdowns can be expected?
- Exclude any revenue that is not strictly related to the business.

Cost of Sales

The key to calculating your cost of sales is that you do not overlook any costs that you have incurred. Calculate cost of sales for all products and services used to determine total net sales. Where inventory is involved, do not overlook transportation costs. Also include any direct labor.

Gross Profit

Subtract the total cost of sales from the total net sales to obtain gross profit.

Gross Profit Margin

The gross profit is expressed as a percentage of total sales (revenues). It is calculated by dividing

$$\frac{\text{gross profits}}{\text{total net sales}}$$

Controllable Expenses

- *Salary expenses*—Base pay plus overtime.

- *Payroll expenses*—Include paid vacations, sick leave, health insurance, unemployment insurance and social security taxes.

- *Outside services*—Include costs of subcontracts, overflow work and special or one-time services.

- *Supplies*—Services and items purchased for use in the business.

- *Repairs and maintenance*—Regular maintenance and repair, including periodic large expenditures such as painting.

- *Advertising*—Include desired sales volume and classified directory advertising expenses.

- *Car, delivery and travel*—Include charges if personal car is used in business, including parking, tolls, buying tips, etc.

- *Accounting and legal*—Outside professional services.

Fixed Expenses

- *Rent*—List only real estate used in the business.

- *Depreciation*—Amortization of capital assets.

- *Utilities*—Water, heat, light, etc.
- *Insurance*—Fire or liability on property or products. Include workers' compensation.
- *Loan repayments*—Interest on outstanding loans.
- *Miscellaneous*—Unspecified; small expenditures without separate accounts.

Net Profit (loss) (before taxes)

- Subtract total expenses from gross profit.

Taxes

- Include inventory and sales taxes, excise tax, real estate tax, etc.

Net Profit (loss) (after taxes)

- Subtract taxes from net profit (before taxes).

Annual Total

- For each of the sales and expense items in your income projection statement, add all the monthly figures across the table and put the result in the annual total column.

Annual Percentage

- Calculate the annual percentage by dividing

$$\frac{\text{annual total}}{\text{total net sales}} \times 100\%$$

- Compare this figure to the industry percentage in the rust column.

BALANCE SHEETS

Balance sheets are statements of the assets, liabilities, and capital of a business organization, usually computed over a predetermined period of time or on a specific date. Think of them simply as all of the elements on your company books that have to be "balanced" in order for you to know where your business stands financially. By comparing today's balance sheets with those of last month's, or six months ago, you can more readily see how you are doing. A typical balance sheet contains four sections:

1. *Current assets*, which include cash, accounts receivable, inventory, notes receivable, and marketable securities.

2. *Fixed assets*, which include real estate, equipment, long-term investments, and miscellaneous assets.

3. *Current liabilities*, which include taxes, notes payable, accounts payable, and accrued liabilities.

4. *Long-term liabilities*, which include mortgage payable, bonds payable, and notes payable.

The fundamental structure of a balance sheet is:

$$\text{Assets} = \text{Liabilities} + \text{Capital}$$

INSTRUCTIONS FOR BALANCE SHEET

Figures used to compile the balance sheet are taken from the previous and current balance sheet as well as the current income statement. The income statement is usually attached to the balance sheet. The following text covers the essential elements of the balance sheet.

At the top of the page fill in the legal name of the business, the type of statement and the day, month and year.

Assets

List anything of value that is owned or legally due the business. Total assets include all net values. These are the amounts derived when you subtract depreciation and amortization from the original costs of acquiring the assets.

Current Assets

- *Cash*—List cash and resources that can be converted into cash within 12 months of the date of the balance sheet (or during one established cycle of operations). Include money on hand and demand deposits in the bank. e.g., checking accounts and regular savings accounts.

- *Petty cash*—If your business has a fund for small miscellaneous expenditures, include the total here.

- *Accounts receivable*—The amounts due from customers in payment for merchandise or services.

- *Inventory*—Includes raw materials on hand, work in progress and all finished goods, either manufactured or purchased for resale.

- *Short-term investments*—Also called temporary investments or marketable securities, these include interest-or dividend-yielding holdings expected to be converted into cash within a year. List stocks and bonds, certificates of deposit and time-deposit savings accounts at either their cost or market value, whichever is less.

- *Prepaid expenses*—Goods, benefits or services a business buys or rents in advance. Examples are office supplies, insurance protection and floor space.

Long-term Investments

Also called long-term assets, these are holdings the business intends to keep for at least a year and that typically yield interest or dividends. Included are stocks, bonds and savings accounts earmarked for special purposes.

Fixed Assets

Also called plant and equipment. Includes all resources a business owns or acquires for use in operations and not intended for resale. Fixed assets, except for land, are listed at cost less depreciation. Fixed assets may be leased. Depending on the leasing arrangement, both the value and the liability of the leased property may need to be listed on the balance sheet.

- *Land*—List original purchase price without allowances for market value.
- *Buildings*
- *Improvements*
- *Equipment*

- *Furniture*
- *Automobiles/vehicles*

Liabilities

CURRENT LIABILITIES

List all debts, monetary obligations and claims payable within 12 months or within one cycle of operations. Typically they include the following:

- *Accounts payable*—Amounts owed to suppliers for goods and services purchased in connection with business operations.
- *Notes payable*—The balance of principal due to pay off short-term debt for borrowed funds. Also include the current amount due of total balance on notes whose terms exceed 12 months.
- *Interest payable*—Any accrued fees due for use of both short- and long-term borrowed capital and credit extended to the business.
- *Taxes payable*—Amounts estimated by an accountant to have been incurred during the accounting period.
- *Payroll accrual*—Salaries and wages currently owed.

LONG-TERM LIABILITIES

Notes payable—List notes, contract payments or mortgage payments due over a period exceeding 12 months or one cycle of operations. They are listed by outstanding balance less the current portion due.

Net Worth

Also called owner's equity, net worth is the claim of the owner(s) on the assets of the business. In a proprietorship or partnership, equity is each owner's original investment plus any earnings after withdrawals.

Total Liabilities and Net Worth

The sum of these two amounts must always match that for total assets.

Balance Sheet

COMPANY NAME

As of_____, 19 __

Assets		Liabilities	
		Current liabilities	
Current assets		Accounts payable	$_____
Cash	$_____	Notes payable	$_____
Petty cash	$_____	Interest payable	$_____
Accounts receivable	$_____	Taxes payable	
Inventory	$_____	Federal income tax	$_____
Short-term investments	$_____	State income tax	$_____
Prepaid expenses	$_____	Self-employment tax	$_____
		Sales tax (SBE)	$_____
		Property tax	$_____
Long-term investments	$_____	Payroll accrual	$_____
		Long-term liabilities	
Fixed assets		Notes payable	$_____
Land	$_____	Total liabilities	$_____
Buildings	$_____		
Improvements	$_____	Net worth (owner equity)	
Equipment	$_____	Proprietorship	$_____
Furniture	$_____	or	
Automobiles/vehicles	$_____	Partnership	
		(name's) equity	$_____
		(name's) equity	$_____
Other assets		or	
1.	$_____	Corporation	
2.	$_____	Capital stock	$_____
3.	$_____	Surplus paid in	$_____
		Retained earnings	$_____
4.	$_____	Total net worth	$_____
Total Assets	$_____	Total liabilities and total net worth	$_____

(Total assets will always equal total liabilities and total net worth.)

Current Balance Sheet

For

_____

(name of your company)

as of

_____

(date)

Assets
Current Assets

Cash $_____
Accounts Receivable $_____
Inventory   _____

Fixed Assets
Land $_____
Building $_____
Equipment   _____
  Total   _____
Less
Depreciation   _____ $_____

Total   _____

Liabilities
Current Liabilities

Accounts Payable $_____
Accrued Expenses   _____
Short Term Loans   _____

Fixed Liabilities
Long Term Loan $_____
Mortgage   _____

Net Worth $_____

Total $_____

Getting the Work Done

Your manufacturing business is only part way home when you have planned your marketing and production. Organization is needed if your plant is to produce what you expect it to produce.

Organization is essential because you as the owner-manager probably cannot do all the work.

You'll have to delegate work, responsibility, and authority. A helpful tool in getting this done is the organization chart. It shows at a glance who is responsible for the major activities of a business. However, no matter how your operation is organized, keep control of the financial management. Examples are given here to help you in preparing an organization chart for your business.

In the beginning, the president of the small manufacturing company probably does everything.

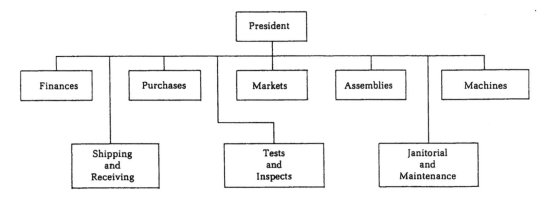

As the company grows to perhaps 50–100 employees, the organization may begin to look something like the chart below.

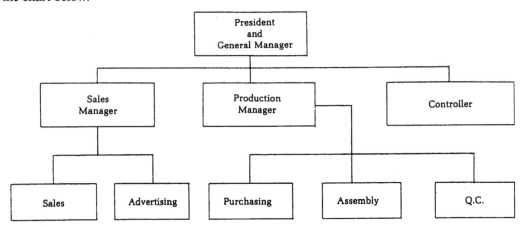

In the space that follows or on a separate piece of paper, draw an organization chart for your business.

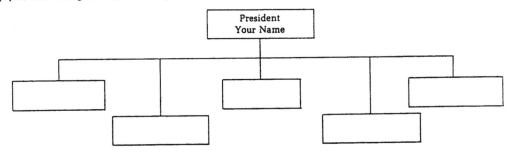

It is important that you recognize your weaknesses early in the game and plan to get assistance wherever you need it. This may be done by using consultants on an as-needed basis, by hiring the needed personnel, or by retaining a lawyer and accountant.

The workblock below lists some of the areas you may want to consider. Adapt it to your needs and indicate who will take care of the various functions. (One name may appear more than once.)

Manufacturing   _____

Marketing   _____

Research and
Technical Backup   _____

Accounting   _____

Legal   _____

Insurance   _____

Other: _____

_____   _____

_____   _____

_____   _____

_____   _____

_____   _____

Projected Balance Sheets

	Start-Up	End Yr 1	End Yr 2
ASSETS:			
Current Assets:			
Cash..........................	$ 20,000	22,116	24,731
Inventory.....................	$ 22,000	25,000	30,000
Total Current Assets...............	$ 42,000	47,116	54,731
Fixed Assets:			
Equipment......................	$ 6,000	6,000	6,000
Less accumulated depreciation.......	$ 0	−1,200	−2,400
Net Fixed Assets..................	$ 6,000	4,800	3,600
TOTAL ASSETS	$ 48,000	51,916	58,331

Projected Balance Sheets

	Start-Up	End Yr 1	End Yr 2
LIABILITIES:			
Current Liabilities:			
Current portion long-term debt......	$ 4,671	6,228	6,228
Total Current Liabilities.............	$ 4,671	6,228	6,228
Long-term Debt.....................	$ 37,329	31,101	24,873
TOTAL LIABILITIES	$ 42,000	37,329	31,101
TOTAL EQUITY	$ 6,000	14,587	27,230
TOTAL LIABILITIES .... **AND EQUITY (Net Worth)**	$ 48,000	51,916	58,331

THE BREAK-EVEN RATIO

You are already familiar with the term "to break even," which simply means the point at which profits and losses are in balance. The *break-even ratio*, which is useful for any owner or manager of a business, can inform you before you even undertake your first sale or service contract, how much income you need to pay your bills and otherwise meet your expenses. Here is how you can quickly and easily determine your break-even ratio:

1. Calculate the average amount it *costs* you to produce (or buy) what you plan to sell, or to deliver your services.

2. List the amount you are going to *charge* for your product(s) and/or service(s).

3. Add up all of the *fixed costs* you have in your business, such as utilities, mortgage or rent, advertising, wages, and other expenses you incur from month to month, regardless of what amounts you sell to customers and clients.

4. Now put that data into this formula:

$$\text{BREAK EVEN} = \frac{\text{FIXED COSTS}}{1 - \dfrac{\text{AVERAGE COST OF PRODUCT}}{\text{AVERAGE PRICE YOU CHARGE FOR PRODUCT}}}$$

The following are examples of work sheets prepared by the SBA to help you evaluate your personal skills as a manager, the allocation of space, laws and regulations affecting your business, financial needs, preparing a planning document, and a rating sheet on sites.

Implementing a Management Plan

Personal Skills Survey

After achieving success, many small-business owners find that their enterprise levels off and they cannot maintain the same pace. It is never too early to take stock of your personal attributes and capabilities and relate them to what is needed to continue the pattern of growth.

The essentials to consider are:

EDUCATIONAL ELEMENTS

Reading habits that contribute to business and professional knowledge _____

_____

Meetings and conferences that broaden my views or provide data of value _____

_____

Available courses that could improve my present capabilities _____

_____

Subject areas in which I am strong _____

_____

Subject areas in which I am weak_____

_____

People inside the company who could help to orient me on certain topics _____

_____

People (contacts) outside the company to whom I could turn for orientation, either free or at cost _____

LEADERSHIP CHARACTERISTICS

Ability to communicate _____

_____

First-hand knowledge of jobs and assignments of people who work for me _____

_____

Ability to judge people _____

_____

Facility at establishing priorities _____

_____

Grasp of situations and circumstances, both commonplace and unusual _____

_____

Rapport with people, both inside and outside the company _____

_____

Effectiveness at motivating people to work on behalf of our objectives_____

_____

Decision-making qualities _____

_____

Willingness to seize the initiative _____

_____

Sympathy for others, especially in sensitive situations _____

_____

Sound judgment _____

_____

Powers of persuasion _____

_____

Self-control in trying situations_____

_____

Readiness to listen to others, at all levels _____

_____

Genuine interest in people and what motivates them _____

_____

IMAGINATION AND CREATIVITY

Conviction that creative efforts are fun, as well as productive _____

_____

Powers of imagination _____

_____

Ability to conceptualize in terms understandable to other people _____

_____

Sense of humor _____

_____

Rating creativity high when reviewing candidates for jobs or assignments _____

_____

Originality _____

_____

Resourcefulness _____

_____

Power to concentrate _____

_____

Fascination with approaches and procedures that are different _____

_____

Innovative skills _____

_____

Ability to visualize and make rough, if not finished, sketches of subjects _____

_____

Preference for people who are not afraid to express ideas, even though controversial __

_____

No-Nonsense Quiz: Overall Qualifications

It is relatively easy for most entrepreneurs to ask themselves whether they have the technical skill to operate a manufacturing business, the grasp of monetary matters to deal with financial challenges, or the experience and training to develop effective marketing plans.

But ask yourself, in all honesty, whether you qualify in areas that are more personal and intangible. Like these, for example:

How do I really feel about managing people, as well as business operations? _____

_____

_____

Do I assume responsibility willingly? _____

_____

_____

Can I make decisions without agonizing over the pros and cons? _____

_____

_____

Am I really glad to see my business grow, or would I prefer to cut back a little? _____

_____

_____

When I propose ideas that may be somewhat off the usual course, do people trust my instincts? _____

_____

_____

Am I likely to be stubborn when I have an idea that my colleagues try to shoot down? ____

_____

_____

Do I hold grudges? _____

_____

_____

Can I forgive my employees and others who make serious, but honest, mistakes?_____

_____

_____

Am I able to work long hours sometimes, as needed, without becoming a workaholic?

_____

_____

Am I able to delegate responsibilities well, particularly as the business grows? _____

_____

_____

Do I approach projects with vigor and enthusiasm, even if I may be feeling temporarily under the weather? _____

_____

_____

WORKSHEET FOR THE ALLOCATION OF SPACE

This form will help you outline alternatives for improving the use of space for employees, operations, production, and other essentials.

Space Used For	Current Space	Amount Needed	Future Plans
Headquarters			
Office Management			
Accounting			
Meetings			
Departments:			
(1)			
(2)			
(3)			
(4)			
Production			
Personnel			
Storage			
Advertising			
Marketing			
Transportation			
Security			
Training			
Cafeteria			
Test Room			
Recreation			

Laws and Regulations that Affect Your Business

The growth of your business has implications not only in terms of taxes but also in regard to certain government laws and regulations. Familiarize yourself with the following regulations. Mark the ones that are applicable to your business and note the reasons why. These are federal regulations for the most part but can tie in with local legislation as well. (They are listed alphabetically, not by priority.)

Age Discrimination in Employment Act _____

Civil Rights Act_____

Clayton Act _____

Consumer Credit Protection Act _____

Consumer Products Safety Act_____

Employee Retirement Income Security Act _____

Equal Credit Opportunity Act _____

Equal Employment Opportunity Act _____

Equal Pay Regulations _____

Fair Credit Billing Act _____

Fair Credit Reporting Regulations _____

Fair Debt Collection Regulations_____

Fair Labor Standards Act _____

Fair Packaging and Labeling Act_____

Federal Trade Commission Act _____

Federal Wages and Hours Regulations _____

Federal Warranty Regulations _____

Fibrous Materials Regulations _____ .

Flammable Fabrics Regulations _____

Food, Drug and Cosmetic Act _____

Hazardous Substances Regulations _____

National Labor Relations Regulations _____

Natural Materials Regulations _____

Occupational Safety and Health Act _____

Pure Food and Drug Act _____

Robinson-Patman Act_____

Sherman Antitrust Act _____

Social Security Regulations _____

Wheeler-Lea Act _____

What Further Financial Needs Do You Have?

As you continue to grow, are you staying financially stable and meeting your obligations, as well as improving your profit-and-loss picture? Some points to check and keep in mind are:

Cash on hand _____

Cash elsewhere _____

Accounts receivable _____

Possible bad debts _____

Accounts payable _____

Possible discounts _____

Other liabilities _____

Value of inventory _____

Fixed assets:

    Land _____

    Structures _____

Variable assets:

    Equipment _____

    Vehicles _____

    Supplies _____

    Furniture and furnishings _____

Operational expenses:

    Salaries _____

    Commissions _____

    Other personnel costs _____

    Office _____

    Plant _____

    Utilities _____

    Advertising and promotion _____

    Communications _____

    Insurance _____

    Security _____

    Depreciation _____

Taxes and duties:

    Personnel _____

    Real Property _____

    Commercial and business _____

    Carrying _____

    Other _____

Gross profits _____

Net profits _____

Losses _____

PREPARING A PLANNING DOCUMENT

I. Title page

    A.   Name of firm

    B.   Time period covered by plan

    C.   Date of preparation

II. Table of contents

III. Executive summary

    A.   The firm and its environment

    B.   Current position and outlook

    C.   Goals

        1. Financial

        2. Nonfinancial

    D.   Strategies

        1. Marketing and sales

        2. Production

        3. Research and development

        4. Organization and management

        5. Finance

IV. Sales and revenue plan

    A.   Sales and revenue objectives

    B.   Product/service line strategies

        1. Target customers

        2. Sales objectives

        3. Pricing policies

        4. Advertising, promotion

        5. Distribution

    C.   Marketing and sales organization

V. Production plan

    A.   Production schedule

    B.   Production costs and standards

        1. Materials

        2. Labor

    C.   Operating policies

        1. Inventory management

    2. Maintenance

    3. Purchasing

    4. Subcontracting

  D. Facilities

  E. Capital expenditures

VI. Research and development plan

  A. Assignment of responsibilities

  B. Management plan

    1. Objectives

    2. Expenses

VII. Organization and management plan

  A. Organizational structure

  B. Management policies and objectives

    1. General philosophy

    2. Recruitment and selection

    3. Training and development

    4. Compensation

  C. Position descriptions (if appropriate and needed)

  D. Résumés

VIII. Financial plan

  A. Schedules

    1. Income statements

    2. Balance sheets

    3. Cash-flow summary

    4. Financial performance summary

    5. Departmental budgets

      a. Marketing and sales

      b. Production

      c. Research and development

      d. Administration

  B. Policies

    1. Debt management

    2. Investments

    3. Use of earnings

    4. Profit sharing

TITLE PAGE AND TABLE OF CONTENTS

The document should have a title page that states the name of the firm, the time period covered or addressed by the plan, and the date of final preparation of the document. If the plan is to be used to raise funds, the time frame should be defined in terms of periods—that is, year 1, first quarter, and so forth, rather than by specific dates. A table of contents follows the title page. The table of contents identifies each major section of the plan and the page number on which that section begins. If appropriate, a list of exhibits should also be included in the table of contents.

Executive Summary

In general, the executive summary presents an overview of the firm and the highlights of the completed business plan. Specifically, the executive summary should include the following subsections:

1. The firm and its environment: A brief description of the firm, its purpose in the marketplace (what it is trying to do for whom in terms of providing products or services), its general product/service lines, and the factors that affect its operation and success.

2. Current position and outlook: An assessment of the firms current market position and of its potential for growth and improvement. This section should be a condensed description of the results of the situational analysis, as described in Chapters 3 and 4. The description should address the firm's strengths and weaknesses and the perceived outlook in terms of threats and opportunities.

3. Goals: A list and brief explanation of the improvement goals and objectives that the firm has established for the period covered by the plan.

4. Strategies: Brief descriptions of the major thrusts and improvement actions to be taken in each of the components of the plan—for example, marketing and sales, production, and finance.

The purpose of the executive summary is to present highlights and a brief, but informative, overview of what the firm is and where it is going. In general, the executive summary should not exceed five pages in length.

Sales and Revenue Plan

The sales and revenue plan identifies planned sales in terms of both units and revenue and outlines the basic marketing and sales strategy for achieving the planned sales levels. To be a useful management tool, the sales and revenue plan should describe the assumptions that underlie the marketing and sales objectives and decisions.

The sales and revenue plan should include the following information:

1. A schedule of quarterly or monthly and annual sales and revenue objectives differentiated, as appropriate, by product/service lines.

2. A description of marketing strategy for each product/service line in terms of target customers, pricing strategy and discount policies, advertising and promotion efforts, and distribution networks.

3. A budget for marketing and sales expenses differentiated, as appropriate, by product/service lines.

4. An organization of marketing and sales responsibilities.

The description should also identify any plans for new product introduction during the period covered by the plan.

Production Plan

The production plan identifies planned production levels and outlines the basic production or operations strategy for achieving these levels. Similar to the sales and revenue plan, the production plan should describe the assumptions that underlie the production objectives and decisions. The main assumptions are the cost of raw materials and production supplies, labor costs, and productivity standards.

The description of the production plan should include the following information:

1. A schedule of quarterly or monthly and annual production objectives differentiated, as appropriate, by product/service lines.

2. Productivity and production cost standards for each product/service line.

3. Inventory policies for both raw materials and finished goods.

4. Equipment utilization and maintenance policies.

5. Production facilities.

The description should also identify any plans or requirements for capital expenditures related to plant and equipment.

Research and Development Plan

If it is appropriate and applicable, the research and development plan identifies the assignment of responsibilities for R&D activities and the specific R&D objectives and budget for the period covered by the plan.

Organization and Management Plan

The organization and management plan identifies the organizational structure of the firm and describes the firm's policies and standards for managing its human resources.

The organization and management plan should include the following information:

1. A statement of the firm's general management philosophy.

2. An organizational chart.

3. A description of authority and responsibilities among, or position descriptions for, the various positions within the firm.

4. Productivity measures and standards for the various positions within the firm.

5. Policies and procedures for recruitment and selection of personnel, training and development, and compensation.

6. Labor relations policies.

Rating Sheet on Sites

Grade each factor: 1 (lowest) to 10 (highest)
Weigh each factor: 1 (least important) to 5 (most important)

Factors	*Grade*	*Weight*
1. Centrally located to reach my market.	_____	_____
2. Raw materials readily available.	_____	_____
3. Quantity of available labor.	_____	_____
4. Transportation availability and rates.	_____	_____
5. Labor rates of pay/estimated productivity.	_____	_____
6. Adequacy of utilities (sewer, water, power, gas).	_____	_____
7. Local business climate.	_____	_____
8. Provision for future expansion.	_____	_____
9. Tax burden.	_____	_____
10. Topography of the site (slope and foundation).	_____	_____
11. Quality of police and fire protection.	_____	_____
12. Housing availability for workers and managers.	_____	_____
13. Environmental factors (schools, cultural, community atmosphere).	_____	_____
14. Estimate of quality of this site in years.	_____	_____
15. Estimate of this site in relation to my major competitor.	_____	_____

HOME-BASED BUSINESS PLAN WORKSHEETS

This section contains tips and examples of worksheets prepared by the SBA to help you evaluate information for developing or improving a home-based business.

Time Management

For both the novice and the experienced business person planning a small home based enterprise, an early concern requiring self-evaluation is time management.

It is very difficult for some people to make and keep work schedules even in a disciplined office setting.

At home, as your own boss, the problem can be much greater To determine how much time you can devote to your business, begin by drafting a weekly task timetable listing all current and potential responsibilities and the blocks of time required for each. When and how can business responsibilities be added without undue physical or mental stress on you and your family? Potential conflicts must be faced and resolved at the outset and as they occur, otherwise your business can become a nightmare. During the first year of operation, continue to chart, post and checkoff tasks on a daily, weekly and monthly basis.

Distractions and excuses for procrastination abound. It is important to keep both a planning and an operating log These tools will help avoid oversights and provide vital information when memory fails.

To improve the quality of home work time, consider installation of a separate telephone line for the business and attach an answering machine to take messages when you do not wish to be distracted or are away from home. A business line has the added advantage of allowing you to have a business listing in the phone book and, if you wish to buy it, an ad in the classified directory.

Is A Home Based Business Site Workable

- Where in the home will the business be located?

- What adjustments to living arrangements will be required?

- What will be the cost of changes?

- How will your family react?

- What will the neighbors think?

It will be important to set aside a specific work area. For example, more than one fledgling business ledger has gone up in smoke, been chewed by the family dog, or thrown out with the trash when business records were not kept separate from family papers. Ready access to business records during work hours is essential, but they must be protected.

Check the reasons below for and against working at home that apply to you. List any additional drawbacks or obstacles to operating this business at home.

Pros	Cons
Lower startup costs	Isolation
Lower fixed costs	Space limitations
Tax benefits	Zoning
Lifestyle flexibility	Security concerns
No commuting	Household
	interference

Note that changes in personal habits will be required. Examples:

- Self discipline to keep TV off while working.
- Limiting personal telephone calls in length and number
- Diligence in meeting work deadlines when no one is checking.

Ask family members to comment on pros and cons. Their concerns may require reconsideration of some specifics.

Is A Home Based Business Site Allowable?

Now you will want to investigate potential legal and community problems associated with operating the business from home. You should gather, read and digest specialized information concerning federal, state, county and municipal laws and regulations concerning home based business operations.

Check first! Get the facts in writing. Keep a topical file for future reference. Some facts and forms will be needed for your business plan. There may be limitations enforced that can make your planned business impossible or require expensive modifications to your property.

	My Level of Interest	Personal Strength	Market Strength	Total Points
Personal services				
—house cleaning				
—babysitting	_____	_____	_____	_____
—tutoring	_____	_____	_____	_____
—secretarial	_____	_____	_____	_____
—catering	_____	_____	_____	_____
—direct mail	_____	_____	_____	_____
Handicrafts				
—needle work	_____	_____	_____	_____
—ceramics	_____	_____	_____	_____
—jewelry design	_____	_____	_____	_____
—upholstering	_____	_____	_____	_____
Artistic work				
—painting	_____	_____	_____	_____
—photography	_____	_____	_____	_____
—prints	_____	_____	_____	_____
—wire sculpture	_____	_____	_____	_____
—engraving	_____	_____	_____	_____
Repair services				
—small appliances	_____	_____	_____	_____
—furniture	_____	_____	_____	_____
—clothing	_____	_____	_____	_____
—TV and radio	_____	_____	_____	_____
—automotive	_____	_____	_____	_____
Instruction skills				
—languages	_____	_____	_____	_____
—math	_____	_____	_____	_____
—gourmet cooking	_____	_____	_____	_____
—music	_____	_____	_____	_____
—home repairs	_____	_____	_____	_____

	My Level of Interest	Personal Strength	Market Strength	Total Points
Mail order ideas				
—product sales	_____	_____	_____	_____
—repairs	_____	_____	_____	_____
—business service	_____	_____	_____	_____
Seasonal products				
—foodstuffs	_____	_____	_____	_____
—clothing	_____	_____	_____	_____
—gift items	_____	_____	_____	_____
Party sales				
—cookware	_____	_____	_____	_____
—plants	_____	_____	_____	_____
—plastic goods	_____	_____	_____	_____
—cosmetics	_____	_____	_____	_____
Your own ideas				
_____	_____	_____	_____	_____
_____	_____	_____	_____	_____
_____	_____	_____	_____	_____

For other ideas, check your local public library for one or more of the publications listed in the Resource section of this publication.

SCORING

0 to 10	Almost a sure loser.
11 to 15	Reconsider but proceed with caution.
16 to 20	Some potential here, worth further study
21 to 25	Probably a winner, if you answered correctly.
26 to 30	How can you lose?

This checklist should give you a good idea of the kind of business that would suit you best and why.

prostat1	PROJECTION OF FINANCIAL STATEMENTS	
	THREE RUNNING YEARS PROFIT AND LOSS	
	($000's omitted)	
	PROFIT AND LOSS	
	Direct Sales	19.45
	Contract Sales	58.50
	NET SALES	77.90
	Less: Materials Used	2.85
	Direct Labor	16.30
	Other Oper. Expense	0.30
	COST OF GOODS SOLD	19.45
	GROSS PROFIT	58.50
	Less: Sales Expense (8% sales)	6.25
	Warranty (.1% sales)	0.08
	Gen. and Admin. Exp.	9.00
	Burden (50% labor)	8.15
	OPERATING PROFIT	34.95
	Less: Other Exp. or Inc. (Net)	
	Income Tax Provision (28%)	9.70
	NET PROFIT	25.10
	P & L RATIO ANALYSIS	
	Sales	1.00
	Cost of Goods Sold	0.25
	Gross Margin	0.75

Index